Northwest Historical Series
IX

THE KOOTENAI RIVER FROM THE SOUTHWEST CORNER OF TOBACCO PLAINS

An up-stream view. Just below the highway cut in the middle distance is the mouth of the tributary Tobacco River; just above it is the faintly visible field in which the old tobacco gardens were located. So too, the Black Water, Wa-na-...

Flathead and Kootenay

The Rivers, the Tribes
and the Region's Traders

by

OLGA WEYDEMEYER JOHNSON

THE ARTHUR H. CLARK COMPANY
Glendale, California
1969

Contents

Illustrations

Appreciation

For help with the early chapters of *Flathead and Kootenay,* the writer owes a great deal to Dr. Carling I. Malouf, who spent many hours checking the manuscript and supplying information. The published sources relied upon most heavily for the early chapters are Prof. Harry Holbert Turney-High's two classic studies of the Flatheads and the Kutenais; these have been supplemented by as many additional sources as possible, including interviews with living elders of the tribes.

Lorena Burgess of Perma, Montana, was helpful in establishing contacts with informants on the Salish-Kootenai Reservation. The writer is also grateful for her encouragement, her hospitality and the use of her library. Other persons who assisted in various ways are too numerous to list here; these include librarians of some five states and British Columbia; the writer repeats her thanks to them all.

NOTE ABOUT WORKS CITED IN THE FOOTNOTES

All works listed in the Bibliography at the end of this volume are cited in the footnotes in brief form only: author's surname and title. Works not in the Bibliography are cited in full in the footnotes.

Theme

The Flathead Indians and the Kutenai Indians[1] knew the smell of sagebrush as keenly as they knew the smell of pine and alpine fir. Their range in the mountain heartland of the now international West, where they lived hidden until after 1800, included the foothills section of the Plateau country to the west of the Continental Divide, and the fringes of the Great Plains to the east. Even today these tribes, who never opposed the White men in dramatic violence, are little known outside the region where they have been corralled.

Included with the natives first called by White men "Flatheads" are their neighbors and language relatives the Pend d'Oreilles, the Kalispels and more incidentally the Spokans. By the time the White men were writing about them, all these people were mingling in much the same territory, and since there was very little difference in the way they spoke, they were confused in the accounts; "Flathead" was the name often applied to them all.

This is also the story of the White men for whom the Kutenais and Flatheads trapped a few fortunes in furs, among them some of the most renowned traders of the North West and Hudson's Bay companies; and of the

[1] Ethnologists prefer the term "Kutenai" for the tribe (see p. 50). Canadians spell the name of the river "Kootenay;" in the United States the same river is "Kootenai."

Indian women who bore many of these traders their children. The account is carried into the time when full-bloods and mixed-bloods became involved with White miners and settlers who came upon them like high water, quoting the authority of their governments far east across the continent.

After the American traders reached the mountains, the Kutenais and Flatheads were in the thick of the competitive international scramble for the beaver of Old Oregon. Of all the natives the early American and British traders dealt with in the region, these were perhaps the most welcoming and the most trustworthy. Though they were friendly, yet like other North American natives when overcome by the Whites, they were constitutionally unable to cower, kowtow or servilely conform.

The Kutenais and Flatheads lived in what is now northern Idaho, eastern Washington, western Montana east and west of the Rocky Mountains, southeastern British Columbia, and southwestern Alberta. They thought no more of crossing the Continental Divide on foot than we do of crossing it in railway or motor cars. They knew the way as no wheel-borne travelers can – stick and stone, berry patch and bear den, swamp, cliff, burn, skyline and cloud sign, river crossing, elk track, battle site, burial mound, tree-shelter of a trail-side birth, cave of a guardian spirit quest.

In the Tobacco Plains country west of the Divide, now crossed by the Canadian-United States boundary line, the Kutenais sowed and harvested sacred plants for ceremonial smoking before they ever heard of White men. The western-most bands of the Kutenais were more devoted to fishing and to village life than were their relatives farther up the Kootenai or east of the mountains. They seldom used skins to cover their dwellings; they seldom "went to buffalo;" yet they joined the rest of the tribe for the Sun Dance – considered by White students to be a Plains ceremonial.

The Flathead groups, whose winter camps were south of the Kutenai range, didn't raise even tobacco. Like their Columbia Plateau neighbors on the west and northwest, and like the Kutenais of historic years, they were fishermen and hunters and harvesters of roots and berries; like other Indians all the way to the Pacific, they told their children legends of how Coyote brought the salmon up the streams from the sea for their people. Yet by the time the White men found the people whom they first called Flatheads – the upriver or Southern Flatheads – they were in the habit of procuring most of their salmon already dried, from Columbia River Indians, in exchange for buffalo products taken east of the Rockies.

The long-ago natives of the Great Plains and the long-ago natives of the Columbia Plateau, with the Continental Divide between them, lived quite differently – a difference that held true from economics to religion. Did the Flathead and the Kutenai people belong to the Plains or to the Plateau, and where was their original range in the Northwest, and how did they get there?

Tackling these questions is an expedition into a rough and splendid country that left its mark upon the people who walked and worked here with stone-age tools in their hands, and plentiful riches in their heads and hearts. Then soon after 1800 came the White men, who had left their own stone age behind them some five thousand years before, and now brought to the Pacific Northwest their astounding possessions, and their strange and arbitrary rules for commerce, conduct and religion – rules which so many of them broke at will.

But the intruders brought along also their personal needs. Aside from the celibacy and self-denial of the Black Robes, and the tenacious devotedness of the traders to accumulating more property than they could use, the needs of these bearded, pale-skinned, comically wrapped creatures turned out to be familiar after all: they had to have food, fire, water and shelter; they had to have companionship and fun; they had to have women; they had to feel proud.

Flathead and Kootenay

Home

THE BIG TRENCH

Where the riotous land plunges from the sheer peaks of Banff Park northeastward toward the easeful prairies of Alberta, to the noise of quick waters destined for Hudson's Bay via the Saskatchewan, Kutenai Indians used to brave the rigors of trail and climate for the meat they could take; the locality was famed in early times for the large quantity of game to be found here. Perhaps the Kutenais never lived so far north all winter long, at least not in historic times, but they remained here enough to build substantial shelters. A little to the south, "Along the Clearwater, and near the foot of the mountains, are still to be seen [around 1800] the remains of dwellings of Kootenays. . . The same are observed along Rivière de la jolie Prairie and Ram river . . . and even as far down as our present establishment," Rocky Mountain House, on the North Saskatchewan midway between today's Edmonton and Calgary, Alberta.[1]

A contemporary informant believes that the prairie Kutenais would go as far east as Cree country around Battleford, Saskatchewan, and that their real headquarters used to be just south of Coleman, Alberta, which is not far east of Crow's Nest Pass; and that "just

---

[1] Coues, *New Light on the Early History of the Greater Northwest,* 703; see also 687.

after horse times" they wintered around Natelle, B.C.[2]
This is getting into territory known later as Blackfeet
range; but in earlier times the Blackfeet lived farther
east and north, while Kutenaian groups occupied the
plains and foothills all through the country around
Browning, Montana, and even as far south as Sun River
west of Great Falls, Montana.

West of the Divide, Kutenais camped regularly at
the source of the Columbia, and the Kootenay River
was their own for all its westward circling distance. On
the upper Columbia and the upper Kootenay, the native
inhabitants were in a deep valley, not very wide,
scooped north-south out of the mountains for an epic
distance – the Rocky Mountain Trench, by its length
and uniformity one of the greatest of such features on
the earth's alluring surface. From Tobacco Plains bor-
dering the Kootenai just before it turns westward, these
hardy hikers sometimes ranged another hundred miles
or more farther south along the Trench, into the country of the Pend d'Oreille Flatheads around Flathead
Lake, and evidently up every stream that leads to the
lake. All the waters and peaks in western Glacier Park,
along the North Fork of the Flathead River, bore ancient Kutenai names,[3] and one of the tobacco garden
sites was on the upper South Fork. On the lower Kootenai River, further west, Kutenais inhabited the Purcell Trench that runs north-south for three hundred
miles between the Purcell and Selkirk ranges and extending ranges to the south. Some of the Kutenais once
used to travel even farther west, encountering the
Okanogans at the Arrow Lakes of the Columbia.

People moving about in the timbered area of the

---

[2] Gravelle, interview.   [3] See Schultz, *Signposts of Adventure.*

BUFFALO ON THE FRINGE OF THE MONTANA PLAINS, EAST OF THE DIVIDE
An 1880 photo by L. A. Huffman. Courtesy of Montana Historical Society.

In the Whitefish Range, East of the Tobacco Plains Country

Looking north into the Canadian Rockies, the view lies west of the Divide, and west of the valley of the North Fork of the Flathead River.

Photo by Winton Weydemeyer.

THE KOOTENAI RIVER IN ONE OF ITS MORE PEACEFUL STRETCHES

A summer view, up-river, between Rexford and Libby, Montana.

Photo by Winton Weydemeyer

FLATHEAD LAKE LOOKING TO THE SOUTHEAST

Photo by Guest, Kalispell.

Rocky Mountain Trench – bottoms, benches and several very rough little mountain ranges intruded among the plains – are not much aware of the valley's grand general contours. But when they come out onto the open flats or rolling hills, the measured majesty of that eastern wall announces itself like thunder, and will not be ignored. "This stupendous chain," noted the Jesuit Father De Smet, "appears like some impregnable barrier of colossal firmness." [4]

South of the Lower Flathead Valley (the valley below the lake) is the smaller tributary valley of the Jocko, where the Southern Flatheads were to be settled by the United States government, the last of them bitterly against the will of their chief. South of the Jocko, a detached spur of the east Trench wall nudges westward the south-flowing Flathead River and the north-flowing Missoula River until they meet to continue northwest-by-north as the Clark Fork (the name now applied to the whole Deerlodge-Missoula-Lower Flathead water course), whose waters eventually emerge from Pend d'Oreille Lake as the Pend d'Oreille River. The trail along the Clark Fork northwestward out of the Trench toward the Columbia, through the old range of the Kalispels, was an inter-tribal thoroughfare that became even more deeply worn after the White men built trading posts along the way.

South of the Jocko Valley, the Trench loses its decisive form in the irregular ridges that bound and interrupt the Missoula Valley. One of David Thompson's maps, drawn from his experience in the region during the early years of the nineteenth century, names the

---

[4] De Smet, *Oregon Missions and Travels,* 205.

Missoula Valley *Nemisoolatakoo.* Mixed-blood Duncan McDonald in later years said the Missoula River was known to the Flatheads as *In-ma-soo-latkhu,* meaning sparkling water. Others spelled it *Im-i-sul-itiku,* and said it meant chilling water, or waters that chill or frighten: where these waters left the Missoula Valley, through the *Port d'Enfern* or Hell Gate Canyon, defending Flathead allies and Plains Piegan raiders met bloodily in horse and gun days. A great shifting of tribes had by then taken place; in earlier times this windy canyon was known more peaceably as a marker on the approximate boundary between the ranges of the Pend d'Oreilles and their friendly relatives, the Southern Flatheads.

Upstream south of Hell Gate lie the fanned-out valleys of three rivers: to the east the Blackfoot, "the river of the great road to buffalo;" in the center the upper Clark Fork, earlier known as the Deerlodge; and to the west the upper Bitterroot, originally the "Flathead River" or "Clark's River" of Meriwether Lewis. All this was the western land of the Flathead group first so named. From the head of the Blackfoot due east of Hell Gate, they crossed the Divide by Rogers Pass to the immediate headwaters of the Missouri, or branched north to Lewis and Clark Pass looking down on Dearborn River, from where it was a short and easy crossing to Sun River – the "Medicine River" of Lewis.

Or from the head of the Clark Fork, near Butte of today, the Flatheads topped the east-west jog of the Divide range to the southern Missouri tributaries, and ranged even as far southeast as the upper Yellowstone River and the Crazy Mountains and Little Belts. In the spacious high valleys of the Jefferson, Madison,

Gallatin and Yellowstone there was less timber and more grass than west of the divide – and a view opening more and more widely toward the illimitable Plains, out of whose mysterious horizons came the bison, and eventually enemy tribes, and at last the White Men.

But it was in the western-most valley of the Clark Fork system, the Bitterroot, that Lewis and Clark found the Flatheads in 1804. This hundred-mile-long valley is walled on either side by mountains nearly as lofty as the ranges of the Divide itself, including on the west a scarp section of the Bitterroot Range that extends almost due north-south for seventy miles. The scarp faces west; down its precipitate timbered surface cascade scores of creeks whose waters empty eventually into the Columbia by way of the Salmon and the Snake. The drainage systems of these two wild rivers were the scene of the last desperate rivalry of British and American fur men; their gorges appalled but did not halt early White wagon trains bound for western Oregon.

Even as geese fly, the distance south from the old Kutenai hunting ground northeast of Banff to the Flathead hunting grounds on the upper Yellowstone is five hundred miles.

AS THE LAND WAS LAID

The resurgent mountains that are now with us in the Flathead-Kootenay country once reached a mile or more nearer to the sun than they do today; their tops have worn off that much since they were slowly upthrust from the last of a series of ancient sea beds. The debris of pre-glacial age swamps or lake beds forms parts of the high valley floors among the headwater streams of the Missouri. Then came the glaciers. Be-

sides the great Cordillerian ice sheet that lay at times
five thousand feet deep at the present Canadian-United
States boundary line, locally-formed glaciers up to
many miles in extent formed in the higher mountains,
leaving a thousand lakes or more at all altitudes in the
Kootenay-Flathead country.

The residential range of the prehistoric Kutenais and
Flatheads west of the Continental Divide drains to the
Columbia River. The last ice age was a time of incred-
ible drama in the Upper Columbia drainage area,
where lay the lower tongue of the main Cordillerian
glacier. Ice masses equal to the lumped dream-dams of
several generations of army engineers blocked the Kootenai and Clark Fork rivers to create Glacial Lake
Kootenai and Glacial Lake Missoula, with the former
sometimes spilling over into the latter at either side of
the soaring Cabinet Mountains. Eventually the ice
front began to retreat northward, and the glacial lakes
disappeared. By this time the bottom of the Rocky
Mountain Trench had been scoured so nearly level that
its rivers could travel almost as easily south as north, or
north as south.

The young Kootenay River, born of ice and snow
where the east Trench wall merges with the Continental
Divide range in the north, comes down fast to the valley, then for more than fifty miles flows roughly south
not fifteen miles from the parallel northward course of
the Columbia. At the head of the Columbia's source
lake, only a mile of swampy flat separates the two
waters.

Here in the vicinity of Columbia Lake, the Kootenay,
like other rivers in similar predicament further north,
could hardly make up its mind whether to flow north

or south for the duration. Today its course continues southward, but a legend of the Kutenai people implies that once upon a time the upper Kootenay crossed that swamp to the lake and thus formed the actual headwaters of the Columbia.[5] Father De Smet when he visited this locality in 1845 observed how the two rivers were separated by a bottom land across which the Columbia received a portion of the waters of the Kootenay during the spring flood season. Forty years later an English dreamer was to dig a canal here in the hope of taming the Kootenay to behave as he chose.[6]

Tobacco Plains and the more northern bunch-grass flats up toward Columbia Lake are but cosy little prairies compared to the spacious Flathead Valley in the southern part of the Trench, with the greatest fresh-water lake in the West for its handsome centerpiece. (Lake Tahoe in California is sometimes claimed to be larger by a few acres.)

In the winter the natives, like the Whites who later joined them, fished profitably through the ice of the lake. On rock faces along the lake shore and in a number of similar locations in the lake region are ancient paintings of uncertain origin; some natives believed they were put there by spirits, other that they were news messages; most thought they were records of successful guardian spirit quests by young men who fasted and prayed there. Below the lake the outlet river cuts deeply through the Polson moraine and continues south and west to the Clark Fork.

The Rockies, in the time span of their present elevation, are young as mountains go. Even those valleys of

[5] See p. 255.

[6] See W. A. Baillie-Grohman, *Sport and Life in Western America*. London: Horace Cox, 1900.

the Kutenai and Flathead country that were not scoured by glaciers, nor covered by coarse glacial debris upon which the top soil is still thin, seldom have the deep organic deposit that encouraged other native Americans, as far north as the Dakotas, to raise food in gardens. The Mandans had, besides, warm nights for their corn, and more dependable summer rainfall. Just east of the Divide ranges, where the Kutenais and Flatheads once lived or camped, the gullies formed by early torrential outwash from the Rockies were subsequently filled and smoothed by fine soil during ages of light rainfall; but this high, rather deep-soiled plain continues comparatively arid; the farmers here today either irrigate, or they store and bank the production of rainy years to tide them over the drought years.

It could be said that the mountain tribes did not farm because conditions were unfavorable for cultivating crops, or because fish and game and native roots and berries were plentiful, or because these people came from northern hunting stock or coast fishing stock and had never heard of raising crops. It could be said they were disinclined to settle in villages not only because they must follow the game, but because unlike the peoples of more montonous desert or prairie, they were forever tempted to explore anew the fascinating ups and downs, and the intricate cover growth and water patterns, of their range.

At any rate, they fished in the lakes and streams; they dug bitterroot in the dry flats and camas in damper swales; they hunted among the shallow-rooted evergreens that were adapted to the thin soil of the mountains, or in the open country. The drought-resistant and high-protein buffalo grass that grows among the sagebrush of the eastern foothills and Plains was rich ration for thundering herds of bison and soundless herds of antelope, and in the days before settlement, for other animals now retreated to the mountains, including elk and bear. So did the taller bunchgrass support deer, elk, moose and caribou in the mountains. So were they both to nourish a fateful import from the old world – horses.

On the Move

For reasons dim to us, but doubtless as logical as all other natural reasons, the birthplace of human-like creatures seems to have been in the eastern hemisphere, and partly at least in Asia, some 600,000 years ago. The first men known by their bones to have looked very much like our nextdoor neighbors, however, roamed Europe only as recently as 55,000 B.C. Conceivably it was some relatives of theirs who reached North and South America from Asia as the ancestors of the native Indians we have known on these continents. They came either by sea, or by ice, or across a far-north land bridge that has since submerged. The first North Americans we know of, through archeological discoveries in the Southwest, apparently lived here 15,000 years ago or even earlier, and were Mongoloid in type. Recent excavations in eastern Washington, near Flathead-Kutenai country, seem to reveal that people lived in that region too in times almost as ancient.[1]

As the successive waves of various Asian people came across to present-day Alaska, some of these immigrants walked or boated directly south along the narrow

---

[1] Associated Press news story, *Grants Pass Courier* (Ore.), July 24, 1964. Archaeologists from the University of Washington were said to have unearthed a skull and artifacts along the Palouse River, indicating that the site had been inhabited 10,000 to 14,000 years ago.

coastal strip of what is now western Canada, and there some of their descendants still live. Earlier or later peoples, or both, hunted and fished their way farther inland and took the prairie way south, part of them fanning out toward the Pacific, part of them toward the Atlantic; the greatest number, however, kept on south by the easy Great Plains route, and eventually reached Mexico and South America. In telescoped bird's-eye view from today, the movements of these native Americans about the spaces of the continents are a spectacle more colossally dramatic than any puny picture epic by a Cecil de Mille. East or west, south or north, these men, women and children went on foot, often using their dogs as beasts of burden. The little horses once native in North America they did not domesticate, but hunted for food – which may explain the extinction of the animals as a species. All this moving about was not of course a grand scurrying. In some cases migrations were sudden or frequent, and the distances covered might be drastic; in other cases a whole stack of generations called a single spot home. An Arizona cave equipped with a precious spring of water is believed to have been inhabited for ten thousand years.

In Mexico some of these people of Asian ancestry settled down among their flourishing crops to build great cities, and a stratified social structure with slaves at the bottom and priests at the top. Their ritualistic religion involved human sacrifices to the sun or the sun god. War, sometimes necessary for defense against incoming peoples or because of clashing interests among established groups, became also "necessary" as a means of supplying captives for mass sacrifices. Among the Aztecs, warfare was regarded as a sport, with scheduled

appointments for engaging in battle; surprise attacks
were considered unethical.

Long before the Spanish conquest, influences and
sometimes tribal groups from these rich southern
sources had been bouncing back northward to affect the
lives of tribes-people all through the southern and eastern part of what is now the United States, far up the
Mississippi Valley, and evidently into the western
Great Basin between the Rockies and the coast ranges.
Mexican-born ways, traveling via peoples of our present south, eventually were seeded into almost every
tribe in North America.

Among the more or less primitive groups occupying
the mid-section of the continent in recent pre-historic
times were the Algonkian-speaking people, who fought
or mixed with the earlier comers in the east, and seem
to have been more often worsted than not. They were
originally a quite peaceable people; some of them now
learned the arts of torture from the Iroquois – inher-
itors of Mexican traditions – just as in time the Flatheads of Montana would learn the same retaliatory
practices from the Algonkian Blackfeet.

Where, all this time, had been the Flatheads and the
Kutenais? Had they come to their rugged mountain
valleys direct from the Asia-to-America crossing, and
unlike so many of the other immigrants, had they settled there to stay, without any explorations to the south?

The Salish-speaking Flatheads had language relatives throughout the Pacific Northwest, but the Kutenais spoke a tongue distinct and unique. The two
groups are here considered together not because of any
traceable kinship – unless it be a surmised very ancient
membership in the Algonkian group – but because

they shared their first White associates and are presently settled in the same area; because for at least two hundred years before reservation days they so often crossed the Rockies, separately or together, and had to deal with the same enemies; because both tribes were hybrid mountaineers and plainsmen.

Plateau people when they met the White men had no very enlightening legends about predecessors in their hunting grounds. The Flatheads, like their neighboring Salish relatives, used to tell how their land was once inhabited by a race of giants, a race of dwarfs, and by the Foolish Folk who only recently had disappeared. The dwarfs were supposed to have domesticated some animals like small horses, which they did not ride, but occasionally killed for food. The Foolish Folk were described as squat and very strong, and absolutely fearless because they knew no better. They lived in holes in the ground, went naked, and were repulsively callous, obscene and cruel.[2]

Turney-High identifies the Foolish Folk with the *Semte'use* of supposedly recent times, to whom Teit gave an actual range in the mountains between the Southern Flatheads and the Kutenais, and who are sometimes thought to have been Pend d'Oreille. He also points out that two ancient skeletons found in the Flathead country are those of individuals similar in build to these people or peoples. One and perhaps both skeletons lay in flexed position, knees to chin, a burial custom rarely attributed to present-day natives of the region. Dr. Malouf, however, does not see any likely connection between the legendary dwarfs or the Foolish Folk, and the *Semte'use* or the ancient skeletons.

---

[2] Turney-High, *The Flathead Indians*, 15.

MONTANA CLUES

The earliest people known in the range later occupied by Kutenais and Flatheads, hunted a now-extinct type of bison about 7,000 B.C., when the region to the north and northwest was still bleak with ice. These Folsom men, remains of whom have been found near Helena, Montana, lived widely throughout the North American plains; they all seemed to conform to the Mongoloid type. They left no traces in western Montana, where Glacial Lake Missoula may have occupied the valleys at this period. Gradually, as the edge of the ice sheets drew northward, the climate on the plains became drier, and the bison and other large game animals began to disappear. Now the native hunters worked more as individuals, searching out small animals, while the women scrounged for vegetable foods.

Farther south the drought was still more severe; hungry people from the Utah-Nevada region, who are known for this period as the Foragers, now moved hopefully up into southern Montana and Idaho, where they lived on roots, berries, insects and grass seeds, and what little fish and game they occasionally found. These were the first inhabitants of western Montana, so far as archeological investigation has yet revealed. In common with their contemporaries of the Montana plains, they still knew nothing of bows and arrows, but hunted with the atlatl, a javelin-like device for throwing stone points or stone-tipped darts.

These Foragers, like the more recent western Shoshones or other Uto-Aztecan peoples, and the Shahaptin tribes (Nez Perce, etc.), left shaped stones which they had used to crush vegetable foods, and traces of roasting pits, such as the Kutenais and Flatheads used in later times. But neither the Salish nor the Kutenai language seems to resemble any of the Ute or Shahaptin tongues.

During the worst dry periods, the population withdraw from eastern Montana. When the cyclic changes of climate brought more moisture and game back to the northern plains, sometime since the beginning of the Christian era, people moved into the Montana prairie from the east and south, and quite possibly from the northeast. It was these Late Hunters who introduced the bow and arrow here. They also brought a crude type of pottery. Some details of the artifacts from this period "point toward the western Great Lakes or the upper Mississippi Valley."[3] This reference would be to Algonkian people, who used some coarse pottery that may have come all the way from Asia, in spite of the fact that hunters don't usually pack pottery around. It is believed that none of the tribes presently living on the Montana plains was there before 1600 A.D. Pottery brought to southern Montana by the modern Shoshones dates from 1700 or later.

Both the Salish and the Kutenaian tongues have occasionally been likened to the Algonkian. Any possible relationship between the Rocky Mountain folk of this story, and the folk of the Great Lakes region, would almost surely date back to a time when both groups lived farther north. Their southward migration would have taken many generations, even many thousands of years, although some of the known life-ways of the Kutenais and the Flatheads suggest that possibly they

---

[3] Lowie, *Indians of the Plains,* 188. (Copyright, 1954, by McGraw-Hill Book Company; quoted by permission of McGraw-Hill Book Co.)

were more recent arrivals from Asia than most native Americans.

Neither the ancestral Flatheads nor the ancestral Kutenais seem to have ranged very far east nor very far south of the present homeland of the tribes. It appears that they have been in their present region at least since the beginning of the 17th century. They may have come south – separately – on the western borders of the Plains, or in the Rocky Mountain Trench (though this is thought to have held ice longer than the lands to either side), or through the wild and watery country of what is now western British Columbia.

THE SALISH

The Flatheads called themselves the Salish, variously rendered as Selish, Salees, *Selic, Silix, Selictcen,* etc. To those who originated the term, it probably meant simply "The people." The White men soon were applying it to all the Indians who spoke languages similar to Flathead; or they used it to designate the language itself.

Ancient people who lived in the Clark Fork valley some five thousand years ago and left traces recently discovered, were probably erstwhile Foragers from the Great Basin. But a prehistoric skeleton excavated near Flathead Lake, a locality settled somewhat later, had been buried with household implements of shell that must have come from the Coast.

At least twice in her long life of about sixty years, she had broken her leg, the left femur or thigh bone. Both fractures showed that the Indians had skill in setting broken leg bones. They could not prevent a serious bone disease from spreading, however, and the woman became a complete invalid. Allowing several years for the disease to spread through the pelvis and to the backbone, it is clearly evident that her relatives made every effort to prolong her life. Even though their economy required them to move from place to place, someone stayed behind to care for her; excellent evidence that these people took care of their aged and infirm.[4]

This woman, Dr. Malouf thinks, was probably Salish.

Of the artifacts found at various levels along Flathead Lake, it is reported:

> The articles from the oldest level are of basalt and are relatively long and broad. This seems to indicate a close cultural affinity with the Plateau to the west. In the second level the articles begin to show a slight Plains influence. Points are shorter and narrower and some flint is apparent. The latest cultural remains show a tremendous Plains and White influence.[5]

Residence sites along Swan Lake, a widening of Swan River in the mountains east of Flathead Lake, indicate that this area probably was inhabited continuously during the period of the Flathead Lake residence. There is no apparent western influence along the Swan. A definite trail of tools and weapons and ornaments from the Plains leads through the Swan Valley from Sun River and into the Flathead Valley. The earliest Flathead Valley residents known to the White men were the Pend d'Oreilles, but all the Flathead peoples testify that they are comparatively recent arrivals in the region. Whether the earliest Salish artifacts found here were left by their direct ancestors is still a question.

The Salish are one of the most widespread and numerous Indian peoples of North America. Yet the range of the Flatheads before about 1650 is still conjectural. Their nearest Salish-speaking neighbors were

---

[4] Malouf, "Montana's Original Inhabitants."

[5] Biggar, "Development of the Lower Flathead Valley." See also Griswold, "Archaeological Sites in the Flathead Lake Region."

the Colvilles, Coeur d'Alenes, Okanogans, Sanpoils and
Shuswaps. The fartherest were the Bella Coolas on the
west coast of what is now British Columbia, and the
Tillamooks of present-day Oregon. La Farge regarded
the Coast Salishan groups as "unquestionably immigrants from the Plateau." "It is generally assumed,"
writes another ethnologist, "that the Coast divisions [of
the Salish] were relatively late entrants into the area,
pushing down the Fraser River and spilling over the
Cascades into Western Washington. . . There was
a certain amount of intercourse between these coast
people and their interior relatives," but strong differences have developed between the speech and culture
of the two groupings.[6] Logically the Flatheads, fartherest from the Coast, and in particular the Southern
Flatheads as distinguished from the Pend d'Oreilles,
seem the most differentiated. Dr. Malouf says that the
Flathead dances and ceremonials showed more buffalo
complex than the Pend d'Oreille.

David Thompson's praise of the Flatheads in general,
whom he called "a fine race of moral Indians, the finest
I had seen," is but one of the earliest of a long list of
such eulogies by the explorers.[7]

It will be easier to picture these movements of the
natives about the great Pacific Northwest, after becoming better acquainted with the pre-settlement Flatheads and the influence exerted upon them by the composite excitement of Great Plains culture.

---

[6] Drucker, *Indians of the Northwest Coast,* 11, 14. (Copyright, 1955, by
McGraw-Hill Book Co.; quoted by permission of McGraw-Hill Book Co.)

[7] Thompson, *Narrative,* 422. See also herein page 139.

THE SINGULAR KUTENAI

The "sturgeon-nosed" Kutenai canoes (used occasionally also by neighboring Salish), designed with ends flaring at the bottom into underwater snouts which made the craft easier to handle in the turbulent waters of the region, have excited many a traveler and professor, who claim that they are duplicates of canoes traditionally built by Siberian natives in the Amur Valley.

The Kutenai spoke a tongue astonishingly distinct from that spoken by any other known native tribe of America. Early White men who met them often recognized the musical quality of their language, although one explorer at first reaction called it "guttural and unpronounceable by a European, every word appearing to be brought up from their lowest extremities with difficulty." [8] Fur trader Ross Cox, who was much more accustomed to hearing Indians talk, said that the Kutenai language "bears no affinity whatever to that of any of the western nations. It is infinitely softer and more free from those unpronounceable gutturals so common among the lower tribes." [9] The best that Boas could do after extensive study was to remark that "While Kootenay stands alone lexically, some of its peculiarities of morphology suggest comparison with Shoshonean (Nahuatl), Athapascan and Siouan stocks." [10] But at a later date Edward Sapier, author of an Encyclopedia Britannica article on Indian languages, after much hesitation included Kutenaian in the Algonkian-wakashan stock,

[8] Palliser, *Journals and Reports*, 1860, p. 73.

[9] Cox, *Adventures on the Columbia River*, 233. Father Wilfred P. Schoenberg, S.J., notes in his introduction to the *Kootenai Grammar* prepared by Philip Canestrelli, S.J: "This [Kutenai] language bore no more resemblance to Kalispel than English bears to Greek or Hebrew."

[10] Boas, "The Kootenay."

thus tentatively relating the Kutenai people to the Blackfeet who were so often their enemies in the years after the mountain tribes had horses. One of Turney-High's most reliable informants claimed that the Piegans, though not the other Blackfeet, were an offshoot of the original Kutenai stock.

Sometime, somewhere, these people must have lived for a long, long period unto themselves, and there learned to speak in their very own way about their actions and activities, their minute observations of nature, their feelings and imaginings. Or if they once had American neighbors with whom they exchanged language elements, these neighbors have disappeared. The unique Kutenai tongue, devoid of b, v, f and r consonant sounds, and rich in vowel variations, has a lilting sound from the rising inflection of the phrase endings. "The Kutenai are very proud of the phonetic difficulties of their language," Turney-High wrote. "They are quick to point out that almost all Kutenai can learn Salishan, but Kutenaian is too much for the Flathead, Kalispel, Coeur d'Alene, and others, even after they have been married to Kutenai mates for a lifetime." [11] This does not mean that no adult outsiders, Indian or White, ever learned to speak the Kutenai tongue; it only means that they seldom learned it expertly or fully.[12]

Chamberlain mentions particularly the large number of suffixes and prefixes of various types as "a notable feature of this interesting tongue." Subtleties of meaning were often conveyed by slight changes in vowel sound, inflection, tonal pitch or gesture. Boas' vocab-

---

[11] Turney-High, *Ethnography of the Kutenai,* 189.

[12] Father Lambeaux, a priest among the Canadian Kutenais, worked for twelve years among them but did not succeed in finishing his Kutenai dictionary (Iverson, *History of Wardner, B.C.,* 57). See, however, herein, p. 329.

ulary for the "Kutenai Tales" includes illuminating groups of words closely related by construction – given here in translation: nape of neck, foot of mountain; beaver dam, place with thick trees; he hated him, he likes it, he pities it; to travel by canoe, to dance, to catch fire, to talk or discuss.

In more than language the Kutenais seem to have been distinct. Curtis, speaking with regret of the state of some Kutenais under early reservation conditions, remarked: "Their degredation is the more regrettable since the Kutenai physiognomy seems to promise much. It is far less heavy and gross than the Plains type or the types of the surrounding Plateau area. It is such as one associates with intelligence and character."[13] The photographic portraits which accompany Curtis' article, taken around the turn of the century among Canadian groups, confirm his judgment.

Turney-High notes that "To this day the Kutenai are a silent, reserved people, disliking the noise and confusion in which the Flathead delight."[14] Although born out by some other observers who comment on the depressing effect of the constant fear of the Piegan in which the Kutenais lived, this seems to be a facile generalization. Chamberlain, for instance, wrote that "On the whole the Kootenay (especially the young men) gave evidence of a gay and lively temperament and a capacity for thoroughly enjoying themselves."[15] It does appear that the Kutenais were a conscientious

---

[13] Curtis, *The North American Indians,* VII, p. 120. "Less heavy of feature" does not mean that the over-all shape of the skull was not broad and strong in most individuals. A contemporary mission priest remarks on the handsome skull structure of many Kutenai heads – "almost suggesting the heads of buffaloes."

[14] Turney-High, *Ethnography of the Kutenai,* 117.

[15] Chamberlain, "The Kootenay."

people. Turney-High said that the concept of purity was strong in Kutenai religion. Teit's characterization, after talking to the Salish neighbors of the Kutenais, has the likely sound of moderation. The Kutenai, he wrote, were considered "easy-going, not very war-like, rather reserved and cautious, honest and sincere." [16]

Some observers have considered the Kutenais lighter-skinned and less Asiatic in appearance than other Northwestern natives, and have been led to believe by traces of Welsh in their language that they may be the long-sought White or Welsh Indians supposedly descended from a Welsh Prince. So stirs once more the persistent legend of Prince Modoc or Madog, and his colony of Welshmen, who according to a pamphlet published by the imaginative English adventurer, Francis Loves, in 1774, settled in Florida in the twelfth century. These settlers supposedly became the ancestors of the "Welsh Indians" or "White Indians" who later scattered over the continent. The Verenderyes from French Canada were hunting these phantom people in what is now Dakota and eastern Montana in the 1730s; the artist George Catlin believed he had found them when he came among the Mandans a century later. When the Lewis and Clark party first met the Flatheads in 1805, and found them "the likelyest and honestest savages we have ever yet seen," having "a brogue or a bur on their tongue," they supposed them to be "the Welch Indians if there be any such." [17]

Lewis and Clark soon discovered that the Flathead tongue was strictly native American. Although some

---

[16] Teit, *The Salishan Tribes of the Western Plateaus,* 325. David Thompson called the Kutenais "a mild, intelligent race of men." (*Narrative,* 409)

[17] Thwaites, *Journals of Lewis and Clark,* VII, p. 150.

contemporary students are still intrigued by the apparent Welsh elements in the speech of Upper Kutenai people, investigation shows no convincing evidence of relationship between these Rocky Mountain folk and the descendants of British Islanders usually referred to as the White Indians. Bancroft reported that Indians of Lower California once heard Welsh sailors talking, and took them to be their brothers![18]

Later-day Salish admitted to Turney-High that the Kutenai were the oldest people of the region. Little archeological exploration has been done in their range, either east or west of the divide. The Kutenais themselves have almost no tradition suggesting that ancient people lived in their land before them. At the northern bow of the Columbia River, the Kutenais in earliest horse times displaced the ineffectual Snare Indians, some of whom they drove northward, while others they enslaved or killed. These long-time inhabitants of an inhospitable region made their living largely by snaring small animals and sometimes larger ones; the Snaring River took its name from them. They were so wretched and defenseless that they were commonly hunted down by the surrounding tribes somewhat as a sport, but they were no more a separate race of people than the Shuswaps and Stonies who arrived in this locality later.[19]

Flathead Lake Kutenais have said that the stone-rimmed battle pits east of the lake were built by the

---

[18] David Thompson, first White trader among the Kutenais, was of Welsh family. It is quite possible that he taught his trappers the numeral names which became traditional with them, and which are now pointed out as Kutenai words so closely resembling the Welsh.

[19] Diamond Jenness, "The Snare Indians," *Royal Society of Canada,* 1939, includes quotations from various historical sources on these people. See also Moberly, *Rocks and Rivers of British Columbia,* 85.

"Koyokees," an "old-time people." They may have
been talking about the legendary *Kuyo'kwe* (connected
with Coyote, the spirit of mischief?); or about the
Iroquois trappers who were in this region by 1800 or
very soon afterwards, and so may have been the first
"traders" to anger the Blackfeet by taking arms into the
Flathead-Kutenai country.[20] Angus McDonald said
that the mountains west of the Mission Valley "contained many an old hidden Blackfoot fort, occupied in
the days of blood." [21]

When the Kutenais spoke of themselves, they almost
always used a term indicating the particular band to
which they belonged. Sometimes they used the general
term *sanka (Asanka, Ksanka, Coo-sunga),* occasionally
said to mean "standing up straight" like an arrow in
the ground. As the incoming White men encountered
these people, they wrote of them as Kootenayes, Kou-
ttainis, Cottonies, Cattanahowes, Koutaine, Kitinqu,
Eta-go'tinne ("who roam about the valleys in the
mountains" [22]) etc.

The word has been translated as "People of the
Waters or Lakes," from the Athabascan words *Coo,*
meaning water, and *tinneh,* meaning people, although
part at least of the Kutenais lived early on the Plains.
Frank Linderman popularized the interpretation
"Deer Robes," but he was referring to the designation
for the tribe (or perhaps for part of the tribe only) in
the sign language, which has nothing to do with the
word Kutenai itself. More persistent investigations

[20] T. White, "Battle Pits of the Koyokees." For the Koyokee legend, see
Boas and Chamberlain, *Kutenai Tales,* 312. Teit, *op. cit.,* 302, lists *Yilikwe* as
"a corruption of the word Iroquois."

[21] Angus McDonald, "A Few Items of the Old West," 192.

[22] Morice, "The Denes."

have revealed that the word Kutenai is derived from *Tunaha* or *Ktunaha (Kitunáqua, Kotounaha)*, the name of a group of Kutenaian people who once lived entirely east of the Rockies.[23]

Although the Flatheads were so accomplished as buffalo hunters and eventually as horsemen, the Kutenais seem to have associated more with Plains people, and probably earlier, than the Flatheads did. Turney-High says, for example, that the Kutenai method of butchering buffalo was identical with the Blackfeet method. The Mountain Crees and the Piegans were early the friends of the Kutenais, though just how early is not clear. The Kutenais may also have known the Kiowas who were in eastern Montana during the eighteenth century; certainly they knew some of the Shoshones or Snakes. Both the Shoshonean Comanches and the Northern Shoshones hunted to the east of the Flathead and Kutenai range, at times going north into Alberta. "The influence of the Plains can be readily discerned," Curtis wrote of the Kutenais. "Yet the foundations are distinctive . . . the Kutenai possess a culture in many respects peculiar to themselves." [24]

TRIBAL BANDS

There is a fairly general, though debatable, belief that all the modern Kutenai bands sprang from the Big Village on lower Tobacco Plains, where lived the *Aka-*

---

[23] *British Columbia Yearbook,* 1897; Jenness, *Indians of Canada;* Morice, *op. cit.,* etc. The ethnologists spell the word "Tunaxa" with the "x" dotted below, indicating in sound "a deep h, like an Arabic r, deeper than the Spanish jota (j) or the French uvular r" (Malouf correspondence). The word is accented on the first "a." A Kutenai informant told Paul Baker the word should be Kataggay. Paul Flinn says the Lower Kutenais pronounce it *Tanawkaw.*   [24] Curtis, *op. cit.,* VII, p. 120.

nekunik, or the People *(nik, nek, neek, nike)* of the
Flying Head, referring to the Lame Knee legend which
is known also to many other tribes, some as far east as
the Seven Nations of the Iroquois.[25] Other Upper Kutenai bands were the People of the Lakes (Columbia
Lakes), and the People of the Pines at present-day Fort
Steele or Cranbrook, B.C.[26] The Tobacco Plains and
other Upper Kutenai folk were also known to the Flatheads as the *Skalzi* or *Skalziulk,* the Up-river People.

It is thought that the first Lower Kutenai branch
settled at Bonners Ferry, well below the white water of
the canyons upriver. The Middle Kutenai Baptiste
Mathias said that "the earliest known Kutenai chief
was named Feather. He was said to have left the Upper
Kutenai country, and resided on an island in the Kootenai River, near Bonners Ferry, Idaho." [27] These people were called by the early White men the Canoe
Indians, or occasionally the Lake Indians, from Kootenay Lake; or most often the *Arcs-a-plat* or Flat Bows,
the name given them by the *voyageurs,* because they
sometimes made straight wooden bows of broad, flat
form. Salish tribes referred to them as the *Selkola',*
meaning unknown. A Kutenai designation was the
place-name *Akuklahlhu* or *Akloklako,* meaning swamp.

[25] Or *Aqk'anequonik* (Chamberlain, *op. cit.*) ; the place as *Yakelahnoklolak-
makanay* (Peeso, interview), *Akanuhnik* (Curtis), or *Akanoxan* (Wissler).
For a modern version of the legend see Bert Davis, *Legend of Lame Knee.*
This contains no mention that the severed head did any flying. The flying
heads are sometimes chronicled in a separate but related story: "The legends
of Seven Heads and Lame Knee approach in nature and content the European
folk tale." (Chamberlain, *op. cit.*)

[26] Columbia Lakes tribe: *Akesknuknik* (Curtis, *op. cit.*), *Akiskemikinik*
(Turney-High, *op. cit.*), *Aqkisknukinik* (Chamberlain, *op. cit.*) ; People of
the Pines: *Adamnek* (Curtis), *Aqkamnik* (Chamberlain).

[27] Malouf and White, "Early Kutenai History."

The Kootenay Lake or Creston people, who early separated from the group at Bonners Ferry, were called
Ac-Ko-Ko-Nuck-ers, or Men of the Lake, to distin-
guish them from the *Ac-Ken-Mit-To-Kers* or Men of
the River.

Turney-High's informants seemed to believe that the
Middle Kutenais, whose villages were up and down the
river above and below Libby, Montana, came there
from down river, breaking away from the Lower Kutenai groups. Yet Curtis believed them to be of Tunaha
blood. To the tribe these Kutenais were known as the
Akayenik (Ay-Kaye-Neck, Ac-Ke-Ye-Nick), or people of Arrow Village. Supposedly this name was associated with the Yaak River, thought of as the arrow
(ak) that fitted into the great southward bow of the
Kootenai River. The village site most often referred to
in remembered times as that of the *Akayenik,* however, was some distance upriver from the mouth of the
Yaak, nearer the mouth of the Fisher, on the north
bank of the Kootenai; and the people who lived here
were sometimes called the Thigh People.[28] A village at
the mouth of Pipe Creek, opposite today's Libby, was
known by the place name *Ok-sa-wak,* a term relating to
the pipe stone found along the creek. One of the first
settlers to arrive at the location of present-day Troy
reports that there were many tipi frames and drying
racks along the river here about 1890. Artifacts found
recently near the mouth of the Yaak suggest a one-time
village at this location also.

This generally accepted grouping of the bands into

---

28 See herein p. 147. There was also a village across the Kootenai and about
seven miles up the Fisher, mentioned by Thompson, which was probably at
the location known to later Kutenais as *Ya ka kis ka ki* (Davis, "Kutenai-
Blackfeet Campaign in Fisher River Country").

Upper, Middle and Lower Kutenais is of course arbitrary, and has not always been followed. Kutenai people also dwelt at Arrow Lakes, part of that confusing group known as the Lake Indians, of whom there were many villages on Arrow, Slocan and Kootenay Lakes, and along the Columbia River in the vicinity of the present international border. Most of the Arrow Lakes Indians were Salish: Okanogans of the Kettle Falls (Colville) group, and Shuswaps from farther north. Yet when fur trader Alexander Ross visited the Lakes in 1825, he was greeted by the son of a Kutenai chief who had emigrated to this vicinity from further east thirty years earlier; the son claimed to be the then-chief of some two hundred of the Lake Indians, who called themselves the *Sinatcheggs* (or *Sinajextee,* said to refer to a trout living in the local lakes). Arrow Lakes Kutenais intermarried with the Salish, but eventually quarelled with them, and agreed to keep thereafter to Kootenay Lake.[29] There were still a few people known as Kutenais at Arrow Lakes after the opening of the British Columbia Reserves, though they may have been of mixed blood. Most of the Lake Indian descendants are now on the Colville Reservation with other Salish people.

On the other side of the Rockies in early times, the Tunaha also were divided into different groups. Teit thought there were "Kutenai-Tunaha" whose home villages were east of Glacier and Waterton parks, and

---

[29] A bloody renewal of the old quarrel threatened at Kettle Falls in 1826, but peace was maintained by the intervention of a British trader (Douglas, *Journal,* 206). The fact that the Kutenais in this case were from Columbia Lake (or so Douglas wrote it) suggests that Upper Kutenais, as well as Lower, claimed territory at Arrow Lakes. (See also Kate Johnson, *Pioneer Days of Nakusp and the Arrow Lakes,* published by the author at Nakusp, B.C., 1952.)

"Salish-Tunaha" who ranged further south on Sun River and near Great Falls (modern place names). He reported that the Sun River Tunaha intermarried with both the northern Tunaha on the one side and the Flatheads on the other, and were intermediaries between them in trade. "Since the Kutenaian tongue is so difficult, probably Salish was much spoken among the Sun River mixed bloods, and even by Tunaha full-bloods when trading with the Flatheads. This circumstance may account for Teit's self-admitted confusion about these two groups." [30]

Old band divisions of the Flatheads and Pend d'Oreilles are not clearly known, as they were blurred by tribal movements before the coming of the White men and during the earliest fur trading days. From Teit's account, the Southern Flatheads sound like very good mixers; they intermarried not only with the Tunaha but also quite frequently with members of the Pend d'Oreille bands who hunted and camped north and south of Hell Gate, with the different Shoshonean people they met, and sometimes with the Nez Perces. One band of the Flatheads apparently spent a good share of each year near Three Forks, another further down the Yellowstone River system, one in the Big Hole Basin, another on the Upper Clark Fork. How early these people used the Bitterroot Valley is a question. The dearth of archeological material in the area, according to Dr. Malouf, indicates that it had not been long occupied.

Teit included the Flatheads, Pend d'Oreilles, Kalispels and Spokans in his "Flathead Group." Simon Francis, a present-day Kutenai leader at Bonner's

---

[30] Malouf, interview.

Ferry, calls the Pend d'Oreilles the "Lower Flatheads;" they lived down the Clark Fork stream system from the Upper Flatheads or Southern Flatheads (those first so-called by the Whites). These Pend d'Oreilles were early referred to by David Thompson as the Canoe Flatheads. Teit said they were sometimes known as the Lake Flatheads (from Flathead Lake); this applied to the Upper Pend d'Oreilles, as distinguished from the Kalispels, the River Flatheads, who had a tradition that they stopped for a time at Priest Lake on their way south to the Pend d'Oreille River. The French designation of these people as Pend d'Oreilles is said to have referred to the shell ear rings they wore, and exchanged with other tribes; Fred Peeso believes, however, that all the tribes of the region commonly wore ear rings. The terms Pend d'Oreille, Kalispel (Calispel, Kully-spell, Coospellar, Kullas-Pulas, Kahilspelm, Kali-spelum, etc.) and Spokan were hopelessly confused in the early accounts of the region's history. Either of the first two terms was sometimes used to refer to the whole group.

The common usage at present is to consider the Kalispels as Lower Pend d'Oreilles, and the Spokans as an indefinite group of roaming traders who early camped on the Spokane River, and may have been as much Colville (Kettle Falls) Okanogans as Kalispel Flatheads. "Spokan" is a Salish term said to mean "the sun;" the Spokans practiced a non-Plains sun worship. Their chief in 1812 was *"Illimspokanee or the Son of the Sun."*[31] Curtis listed three groups according to range: the *Sintutuúli* or Muddy Creek (Hangman Creek) people; the *Sinhomene* or Salmon-trout people,

[31] Cox, *op. cit.,* 104.

on Hangman Creek and the Little Spokane River; and
the *Tskaistsihlni* or the people of the Little Falls of the
Spokane.[32]

The Kalispels as now designated ranged from the
Thompson Lakes and Thompson Falls area down the
Clark Fork to Pend d'Oreille Lake and along the outlet river, sometimes hunting and fishing as far north as
the Salmon River in southern British Columbia. One
or more bands camped regularly near present-day Chewelah, Washington, close to the Okanogans. The word
Kalispel is usually said to refer to the camas grounds
near Cusik, Washington;[33] some have said the term
meant "flat place at the head of a lake," and thus was
applicable also to the site of Kalispell, Montana. The
large band of "Flat Heads" found by David Thompson
near Bonner's Ferry in the early years of the nineteenth
century was probably Kalispel.

There were in early times bands or winter camps of
Pend d'Oreilles in the Upper (northern) Flathead
Valley, possibly as far north as today's Columbia Falls
(mouth of Bad Rock Canyon); west of the lake on
Camas Prairie; and in the Lower Flathead Valley.
When the Kalispels and the Flathead Valley Pend
d'Oreilles went east to buffalo, they customarily trav-
eled by way of Bad Rock Canyon or Echo Lake to
Marias Pass; or up the canyons opening into the Lower
Flathead Valley or the valley of the Jocko, and thence
through Swan Valley to Lewis and Clark Pass which
gave easy access to Sun River. Whether the Pend d'Or-

---

[32] Curtis, *op. cit.,* VII, p. 54; see also Teit, *Salishan Tribes,* 378.

[33] When the Kalispels first entered the region from the north, and looked
down from a mountain onto the valley at the bend of Pend d'Oreille River,
they saw a "lake" that turned out to be a sea of blossoming camas, or so goes
tradition (Curtis, *op. cit.,* VII, p. 51).

eilles ever had home villages on Sun River, and how
early they lived in the Missoula Valley, we do not exactly know. Teit was told that after the extinction of
the *Semte'use*, who were supposed to have lived to the
south of the Swan Valley, the Pend d'Oreilles, "claim-
ing to be the tribe most related to them, occupied their
country for hunting and root digging, including the
large camas grounds near Missoula. The latter, however, were also used to some extent by the [Southern]
Flathead." [34]

An alert young Flathead of today, whose wife has a
strong strain of Pend d'Oreille blood, insists with feeling that the notion of definite boundaries separating the
peoples of the region was invented by the White men,
who can't conceive of a life without private real estate
protected by fences and laws. Just because the first
White men in here found some Pend d'Oreilles camped
in a certain locality, he says, they declared this to be
Pend d'Oreille land – and so forth – when actually all
the tribes were at peace and hunted and visited back and
forth, intermarried, and used the same land. This is an
extreme viewpoint, but enlightening. It may apply only
to the Flathead groups of the region. Simon Francis
writes that although a modern treaty between the Kutenais and the Flatheads allowed temporary encamp-
ments in each other's territory, before the treaty "No
Kootenai was ever any good to be seen along the Flathead River [referring to the lower Flathead-Clark
Fork-Pend d'Oreille] at any time, and no Flathead was
ever any good to be seen along the Kootenai river."
Such a state of affairs would have to antedate the fur-

---

[34] Teit, *Salishan Tribes,* 308.

trading era, during which the Kutenais often traded on the Clark Fork and occasionally at other posts far outside their more customary range. Certainly with the changing conditions that began even before the traders arrived, the different groups of the region shifted readily from supposedly traditional camping and hunting grounds, and peaceably intermingled.

Menus

TRANS-MOUNTAIN BOUNTY

To these people who were both "Prairies" and "Mountainaires,"[1] the Continental Divide was not so much a barrier as a point to stop for breath. The breathlessness was from the climb, the altitude, the view, and the anticipation of a land and life in many ways a rich contrast to whichever land they had just left behind and below them.

Ranging on both borders of the Rockies, the Flatheads and Kutenais seem to have lived on the whole pretty well. Bison were taken when they could be reached. The herds on the Plains were immense, but they drifted over vast distances; in pre-horse years it was often impossible to overtake them. Nor could the other prairie-ranging animals always be found. When the Plains failed them, the Kutenais and Flatheads turned westward into their mountains. Here they could almost always find some game animals, as well as fish, bulbs, roots and berries, and plenty of wood and water.

The composite range of these tribes was not, however, as purely a paradise as some writers about them have suggested. "Well-watered" the mountains certainly are as to streams and lakes; but during many years the annual moisture falls mostly as snow in the

---

[1] Olden terms used by informant Gravelle.

winter season. A late freeze or a dry spring could ruin the berry crop. In the drier summers, forest fires spread, game took to inaccessible canyons, or to heavy timber or high mountain back country. On the prairie too the summers were often without rain. If – as well it might – a long and bitter winter followed, stored food supplies gave out early, and many of the weakened game animals died, while the remainder were almost impossible to reach.

On the whole, however, the homelands of these people were comparatively productive for the support of non-agricultural people who were willing to move about. And move about the Kutenais and Flatheads did, traveling a good part of the year in bands or family groups; the whole country was home.

OUT OF THE WATERS

The food specialty of the Plateau peoples was salmon. The Southern Flatheads had to cross the Bitterroot Range into what is now Idaho to find salmon, and here in the high headwaters the runs were thin; they were often obliged to procure dried salmon in trade from the western or Lemhi Shoshones, and from the Nez Perces or other mid-Columbia people. The Pend d'Oreilles seldom had any Pacific salmon to eat. Kalispel and Spokan fishermen took salmon on the lower Pend d'Oreille River, and the Kalispels sometimes traveled to Salmon River in what is now British Columbia; Spokans might go to Kettle Falls on the Columbia, or they might trade for salmon with Columbia River tribes.

The Kutenais, however, had in season a profuse supply of salmon in the Columbia River at its head, where these fish came to spawn. The site of the little modern settlement of Athelmer was traditionally known as the Salmon Grounds. The Kutenais, always a canoe people, often took their salmon with spears, while the Southern Flatheads, who seldom traveled by water, took theirs in cone-shaped fish traps or weirs constructed usually of willow. Cleaning the salmon and other fish was women's work, and after everyone had had his fill of the fresh fish, it was the women who dried the remainder of the harvest for storage. They preferred to sun-dry the strips of flesh on pole racks, rather than to smoke them.

Members of the Kutenai bands who lived on the upper (eastern) stretches of the Kootenay River enjoyed the salmon, and took trout in streams or lakes at any season; but in remembered times they considered bison meat their staple menu item. The Kutenais whose home villages were on the lower reaches of the river, however, depended heavily upon fish all year around. Some of them often went to Arrow Lakes or the upper Columbia for the salmon harvest; the salmon could not ascend the cascades between Kootenay Lake and the river's outlet into the Columbia. At home they used river sturgeon, which sometimes weighed twenty pounds or more, bulltrout, and other kinds of native fish. In the wide riverbottom flats at what is now Bonner's Ferry, and north to Kootenay Lake, the receding of spring flood waters left fine quantities of fish stranded in pools and sloughs, or so nearly stranded that it was possible to cut off their escape, and to capture them in large nets manipulated dextrously from canoes.

Having plenty of fish in their home waters, and plenty of brush-browsing deer in the river flat, the Lower Kutenais wandered less often afield, cultivated

village life, lived communally, and were peaceably inclined. They seldom went to buffalo; they hunted deer
by concerted drives, though there was also individual
hunting for which each family head was assigned his
private territory in the surrounding mountains.

Indians on the Pacific Coast, to whom skill in fishing
was a virtue to be rewarded not only in this world but
in the next, noticed as they watched the annual passage
of the mature salmon from the sea up the river, that
no salmon returned; they did not recognize the parr
as young salmon. So they believed that the salmon were
immortal, and that "The fish swam into the rivers voluntarily to feed mankind (and bear), died, and were
reborn in the ocean. Here was something that called for
major ritual in order to keep it going, as well as for
great care in returning all salmon skeletons intact to
the water."[2] Yet the only description of fishing ceremonials found for the Plateau folk concerns the Lower
Kutenais, at the Bonner's Ferry site, where no salmon
occurs.

The Lower Kutenai fish festival has been nowhere
more vividly described than by the Jesuit missionary
Father De Smet, who observed it in 1845.

> I arrived among the Arcs-a-plats in time to witness the grand fish
> festival, which is yearly celebrated; the men only have the priv-
> ilege of assisting there at. Around a fire fifty feet long, partially
> overlaid with stones of the size of a turkey's egg, eighty men
> range themselves; each man is provided with an osier vessel,
> cemented with gum and filled with water and fish. The hall
> where this extraordinary feast is celebrated is constructed of rush
> mats, and has three apertures, one at either extremity for the
> entrance of guests; the middle one serves for transporting the fish.

[2] La Farge, *Pictorial History of the American Indians,* 209.

All preparations being complete, and each man at his post, the chief, after a short harangue of encouragement to his people, finishes by a prayer of supplication to the Great Spirit, of whom he demands an abundant draught. He gives the signal to commence, and each one, armed with two sticks flattened at the extremity, makes use of them instead of tongs, to draw the stones from the embers, and put them in his kettle. This process is twice renewed, and in the space of five minutes the fish are cooked. Finally, they squat around the fire in the most profound silence to enjoy the repast, each trembling lest a bone be disjointed or broken – an indispensible condition of a plentiful fishery. A single bone broken would be regarded as ominous, and the unlucky culprit banished from the society of his comrades, lest his presence should entail on them some dread evil.[3]

It seems more likely that the fish festival was an infiltration to the Plateau from the Coast, rather than to the Coast from the Plateau. When David Thompson met two old men from the Lower Kutenai band at the headwaters of the Columbia in 1807, they drew a chart of their country and from there to the sea, described the tribes along the river, and assured him that it was only "the voyage of a summer moon" from Kootenay House to the sea and back again. Archaeological evidence indicates that an important trading center once existed at Bonnington Falls, where the Kootenay meets the Columbia. There is also a strong possibility, to be considered later in this story, that the Kutenai people once lived somewhat further west than in known times. Although there is no published description of a fish festival among the Upper Kutenais, Iverson does report that the coming of the salmon to the sources of the Columbia used to be greeted with celebration.

---

[3] De Smet, *Oregon Missions,* 198.

BIG GAME

The Plateau-type double-curved bows of wood, or laminated mountain sheep horn, backed or bound with sinew and sometimes finished with rattlesnake skin, were admired and sought after by other tribes. Henry wrote that "These people [just west of the mountains] make the handsomest bows I have ever seen, always preferred by other Indians. I have known a Piegan to give a gun or a horse for one." [4] The compound bows were made only by tribes of the northwestern section of the continent; they were "new out of Asia, and got down as far as the Shoshones."

Indian bowmen up and down and across the continent got ready for a group hunt by going through a lot of devotional maneuvers. The more formidable the animal sought, the more elaborate the body painting, the more extended the dancing. In the Northwest, bear and bison were the most exciting fellow-antagonists. When the highly-organized village Hopis of the Southwest staged a pre-hunting dance, they wore identical costumes of dictated and awesome design, including horned masks, and performed in meticulous unison. Roving northern peoples such as the Blackfeet danced in less formalized movements; and the Plateau peoples, particularly those individualistic mountain men, the Flatheads and the Kutenais, didn't mind being even more spontaneous.

Among the Kutenai, if the hunting prospects looked poor, a shaman would sing during the night, and the next morning – supposedly – bison would be found near the camp. Flatheads sometimes danced under direction

---

4 Coues, *op. cit.,* 713.

of a special shaman or spiritual leader who asked for a blizzard to drive the buffalo toward the camp. A contemporary reservation woman says of a Pend d'Oreille forebear that he used to "make like a buffalo" and afterwards the animals would come near so that he and his people could kill them. The late Flathead leader Eneas Granjo related:

> Whenever the game was scarce the people have one Indian to sing a spiritual song to draw the game nearer. This Indian sings his song and the people that are in the Tipis put out all the fires; when the singer finishes, the people light the fires again and in the ashes they can see the tracks of buffalo and the medicine man tells the Indians where to hunt in the morning.

In Peter Ronan's account of Flathead hunts,[5] the medicine man seems more practical. He endured much fasting and dancing, but he also sent out runners to locate the bands of buffalo and signal their whereabouts. After he had heard from enough of his runners, he came to his inspired decision about when and where to start the drive toward the newly-constructed corral with its central charm pole. This buffalo drive was organized much like the deer drive of the Lower Kutenai.

The buffalo might be driven into corrals or canyons, or over bluffs or cliffs. Driving buffalo over cliffs in mass slaughter has generally been thought of as a drama enacted by the Blackfeet, because known sites are in present Blackfeet territory; "piskun" is the Blackfeet word for buffalo jump. But this area was previously occupied by Kutenaian people, and to some extent by Flathead and Shoshonean groups. The Kutenais and Flatheads, and Plateau peoples living even

---

[5] Ronan, *Historical Sketch of the Flathead Indian Nation,* 48-53.

farther west, had long used surrounds and jumps for elk and other big game. Alexander Henry reported Kutenai buffalo jumps in the Banff area around 1800. "Conceivably the Kutenais were the originators of the practice on the Plains," observes Dr. Malouf. Observes Bert Davis, "I don't believe any particular tribe ever had a monopoly on driving game over cliffs or into mud holes or other natural traps, where the lay of the land was right. Even the coyotes have that figured out."

When a camp planned a surround or drive, the hunters had to be restrained and organized in a severe discipline not often observed by the mountain people. The tribes that came into the central Plains from other directions used strong police forces to control the critical preparations for a bison hunt. Kutenai and Flathead hunts, however, were not always communally managed. In their hunting as in their dancing, these folks often attacked the problem as individuals or family groups, avoiding the possible terror of a stampede by seeking out small groups of the bison, or disorganized and preoccupied bands at salt licks, river crossings or mud holes. De Smet told of seven Flathead hunters who got 189 buffalo in a single skirmish. One of them killed three animals practically unarmed – the first with a stone, striking a cow between the horns, another with a knife; the third he downed with a spear thrust and then strangled.

Each bison downed was a lavish prize, comparable to a truckload order from a shopping center. Every part of the animal was put to some use. At the kill, the Flatheads often ate the liver, sometimes raw; the heart, kidneys and roasted guts were choice morsels first enjoyed. The Kutenais told Turney-High they never

GAME AND FISH TAKEN IN THE
BORDERS OF THE TOBACCO
PLAINS COUNTRY IN THE EARLY
YEARS OF WHITE SETTLEMENT
Photo by Andrew Campbell.

BITTERROOT IN BLOOM
Photo by Winton Weydemeyer.

SITE OF EARLY CAMPS OF THE LOWER KUTENAIS, DURING FLOOD IN JUNE 1961
Looking east, up-river, to Bonners Ferry. Ditches and dikes have now tamed the area
for farming; spring flooding such as this, typical in older times, is now infrequent.
The Libby Dam is intended to provide even more secure flood control for this area.

used the entrails, and were disgusted by the Blackfeet
habit of eating liver hot out of a newly-slain animal.
(Older Blackfeet men often ate the testicles with relish,
seeking virility.) An early resident of Bonner's Ferry,
however, saw Kutenais at the settlement slaughterhouse
seizing upon discarded entrails of cattle with vocal
delight, and even devouring intestines as fast as they
could squeeze the contents out of them.[6] Who can say
whether this was a traditional practice, or a desperate
compulsion forced upon the Kutenais by the economic
upsets of the White invasion?

In earlier years bison ranged on the west side of the
Divide in southern Idaho and southwestern Montana,
including the Bitterroot Valley, though it is believed
they had come here from further east in not very ancient times. Gravelle says that sometimes a few buffalo
were seen on Tobacco Plains, probably after they had
drifted over the lower passes. One Kutenai woman told
her part-White granddaughter how buffalo stampeded
through a winter camp in Crow's Nest Pass, knocking
down the lodges and scattering the campers, and how
some of the invaders were killed on the ice of the little
lake there, as they helplessly skidded and sprawled. A
part-Flathead oldster remembers from his childhood
a detailed story of the time when the Flatheads first
saw buffalo. The herd had worked into the valleys of
western Montana from the south, having been driven
earlier into the Great Basin by White hunters on the

---

[6] Corbeill, correspondence. Actually, on the frontier there was no fixed line
between White and Red blood when it came to a taste for animal guts. George
F. Ruxton in his *Adventures in Mexico and the Rocky Mountains,* (London:
John Murray, 1847) gave a greasily gruesome picture of two "Canadians"
devouring buffalo intestines as an exciting contest, one stationed at either end
of the snake-like mass coiled between them.

Plains. The Flatheads, according to this account, had to learn from the Shoshones how to kill and butcher the strange game, for there were no buffalo in the Yellowstone country until the descendants of this herd passed over the Divide eastward.[7]

Between buffalo hunts, other meats assumed their comparative importance. Father De Smet, after visiting the free trader Francois Morigeau and his wife and family at the head of the Columbia in 1845, gave

> . . . an honorable mention of his [Morigeau's] royal *couisine a la sauvage*. The first dish he presented contained two paws of bear. A roast porcupine next made its appearance, accompanied by a moose's muzzle; the latter I found delicious. Finally, a great kettle containing a sort of hotch-poch or "salamagundi" was placed in the midst of the guests, and each one helped himself according to his taste: buffalo, venison, beavers' tails, hare, partridges, etc., made an agreeable, substantial and [flavorous] soup.[8]

In the Upper Kutenai range, says Peter Andrew, "Caribou were thick in the old days. The people would save the caribou for hard times; buffalo were easier to hunt for they were in open country. There were hardly any whitetail deer here in early times, but some blacktail [mule deer]; there were goat, sheep and elk. My people used mountain goat skin for blankets, elk and buffalo hides for tipis and clothing."

David Thompson often spoke of "antelopes" in the Kootenai country in the early years of the 19th century, but in most cases at least he was referring to whitetail

---

[7] Vinson, interview. Below the southern loop of the Kootenai River, in the vicinity of Libby, a well-preserved buffalo skull was found by ditchers in the mid-twentieth century, beneath several feet of peat soil. Note Curtis, *op. cit.*, VII, p. 70 fn. 1; Cox, *op. cit.*, 202; Thompson, *op. cit.*, 396; Francis D. Haines, "Western Limits of the Buffalo Range," in *PNWQ* XXXI, Oct. 1940, p. 389.

[8] De Smet, *Oregon Missions*, 210-11.

deer. A Kutenai camp in the Fisher River country was
known as *Neltope,* said to mean antelope. Contemporary Indians claim that a terrible winter of deep
snow in the fur-trader years wiped out the last of the
buffalo and antelope in the interior valleys of the Koo-
tenai-Flathead country. According to some Kutenai
informants, nearly everyone in the village went out for
drive-hunting of deer, moose or elk.

> A place was found where the animals could be driven into a nar-
> row place such as between hills or mountains. Sometimes it was
> necessary to erect a barricade. The men who were more active
> would go out a distance and start the animals toward the barri-
> cade. The children, older men, and women would be stationed in
> such a way as to herd the animals into the proper enclosure. Men
> had been appointed to do the killing when the animals got to the
> barricade.[9]

After pleading with the animal spirits to put the
game within his reach, and triumphantly killing all he
could for his needs, the hunter came back to camp to
eat heartily – and to implore the forgiveness of the
animals for the necessity of taking their lives. The
animals were fellow beings to the Indians, who knew
them so intimately, and respected them often fearfully.
The hunters solved their dilemma by believing that the
spirits or souls of the animals were not destroyed, but
hovered about, watching to see that their flesh and bones
were treated with meticulous consideration. Even today,
Dr. Malouf says, Flathead hunters close the eyes of
slain animals before butchering. This, according to

---

[9] Baker, *The Forgotten Kutenai,* 33. John Mullan in his report on "A Military Road from Fort Benton to Walla Walla" noted that the Indians set fires
in the high country to burn the tree moss and thus force the deer to go into
the valleys.

Turney-High, is "in order to prevent the animal from seeing what is happening to its body."

Lorena Burgess listed among other indigenous foods of the regional Indians, frogs, birds and birds' eggs.

NATURAL GARDENS

The Flatheads got some root vegetables from the Nez Perces in trade, but they had lots of camas *(Camassia esculenta* and *C. quamash)* and bitterroot *(Lewisia rediviva)* in their own territory. The Pend d'Oreilles had both plants in the Little Bitterroot Valley, Camas Prairie west of Flathead Lake, in the Flathead Valley proper, and in the Missoula Valley. The Upper Kutenais had more bitterroot than camas, the Lower Kutenais more camas than bitterroot, for camas prefers damper ground. Sometime in May or early June the women, after simple ceremonials, went out into the gravel flats or the hotter slopes of open sandhills, to harvest the bitterroot,[10] using horn diggers or long willow sticks with fire-hardened tips and horn handles. The beauty of the large, silken-pink flowers was part of the bounty. The workers peeled away the reddish outer skin from the fat, fantastically-branched roots, and used the starchy inner roots fresh or dried as an addition to meat stews. The dried roots were sometimes ground to a powder for forming into cakes. The natives did not find the bitter favor unpleasant. Eaten alone, the root was an effective medicine for digestive upsets. Also collected early in summer for boiling were the little

---

[10] Kutenai *nakamchu* (Curtis); Flathead *spetlem* (Turney-High). Contemporary informants say that the roots were dug whenever the skin would peel off easily, about when the flowers were starting to bloom. The bitter part, one woman says, is in a little seed-like part in the top of the root – possibly the embryonic growth for the following year?

bulbs of Spring Beauty *(Claytonia lanceolata)* and Yellow-bells *(Fritillaria pudica)*.

In July or early August, the camas was ready.[11] The roundish bulbs, which had earlier borne fragile blue lily-flowers on slender scapes, sometimes got to be two or three inches in diameter, but were usually smaller. It required a great number of these bulbs, and long baking between layers of wet grass in a pit, to produce a meal's amount of black, gelatinous, sweetish substance which could also be dried for storing. David Thompson reported that camas bulbs collected and dried in 1811 were still good in 1847, though they had lost their "fine aromatic smell." Roots of bitterroot collected by Meriwether Lewis in 1806 lay for several years in an eastern museum before one of them was experimentally planted; it grew and blossomed – inspiring the specific name *rediviva*.

Another baked dish, but a sad substitute for camas, was prepared from the black or gray tree "moss," [12] used in times of food scarcity, or as a sort of condiment mixed with onion, or as a filler with other foods. Large trees were sometimes cut down to secure a supply. Moss would fill up stomachs, but that was about all. Pines, tamaracks and aspen trees supplied a special food delicacy. In May, at about the time the bitterroot was ready for digging, the sweet sap was running just right

[11] Flathead, *ithoe* (Turney-High) or *ethwa* (Teit) ; Kutenai, *há-pi* (Curtis). Camas provided "a source of complete vitamins, stored by Nature in a single bulb. It is said man can survive longer on camas alone than [on] any other one or two articles of food." (Gladys Sipes, *History of Camas Prairie; ms.* in Lorena Burgess library.)

[12] The lichen *Alectoria jubata,* evidently called by the Flatheads *skautemikan* (Ellen Nye, "Mary Ashley," Johns *Collection*), and by the Kutenais *a'sa* (Turney-High). Note pp. 4, 5 in Weisel's "Ten Animal Myths of the Flathead Indians."

in the cambium layer of the trees, and the Kutenais in particular used to cut great chunks of bark in order to scrape or peel the inner layer or *suk'naukk*. The scarred trees resulting from this harvest still mark the locations of old native camp grounds in the range. Present-day Kutenais who tasted *suk'naukk* when they were children remember that it "sure was good." [13] Other tasty treats included the young inner stem, and later the seeds, of the spring sunflower *(Balsamorrhiza sagitatta)*, toasted seeds of evergreen trees, and mushrooms.

Children scrambling over the rocks would report the first berries to ripen each season. Gooseberries were as sweet as plums when fully ripe. In good years there were plenty of Juneberries *(Amelanchier,* also called Serviceberries and Saskatoon berries),[14] strawberries (the Kutenai name for Bowman Lake in Glacier Park meant "big strawberries"), red and black raspberries, chokecherries, elderberries, and many less flavorsome fruits eaten when the people were hungry enough. The acrid buffalo berries were dried for a special winter dessert made by beating them to a froth with a little water.[15]

Then in late summer, camps were moved to the huckleberrying grounds on mountain slopes and high mountain benches. Bears, felt to be the nearest to fellow-creatures of all the animals, competed for the crop, providing fascination and danger, occasionally injury or death.[16] Harvesting huckleberries was a serious eco-

---

[13] T. White, "Scarred Trees in Western Montana."

[14] Saskatoon berries are said to contain three times as much iron and copper as prunes or raisins.

[15] Mose Mathias, interview. Mountain buffalo berry, *Shepherdia canadensis;* prairie form, *S. argentea.*

[16] For an account of the dreadful injury of a Kutenai man by a bear, see *Woodstock Letters,* II, pp. 159-60. See also Thompson, *Narrative,* 340-41.

nomic business, but it was also a time of visiting and adventure. Relatives and friends from different bands met in the huckleberry patches; at the least, it was an opportunity for young people of the camp or band to associate informally, though the men were supposed to be fishing, bird-hunting, practicing marksmanship or wrestling, while the women and children did most of the berry picking. Regional legends are full of the things that happened to women out after huckleberries.

Huckleberries, Juneberries and chokecherries formed the bulk of the dried fruit supply, which was stored separately or mixed in birch-bags, baskets and boxes with pulverized dried meat to form the typical pemmican. Most other fruits were enjoyed right off the bushes, or served fresh in camp on plates of bark, leaves or moose-horn, or serving dishes fashioned of roots, bark or clay.

COOKERY AND POTTERY

The natives ate bison and other meats boiled, roasted, broiled or dried. Among the Kutenais and Flatheads, meat was often roasted in small covered pits heated by hot stones from the campfire. The Kutenai taste seems, however, to have run to boiled dishes, often seasoned with herbs such as peppermint or with the small onions that grow freely in the range. The common boiling "kettle" was made by lining a hole in the ground with rawhide, filling it with water, and heating the water by dropping in hot stones. Utensils were also made of hollowed-out wood, sewed bark or woven roots. The Flatheads in historic times usually obtained their baskets from the Nez Perces or Coeur d'Alenes in trade for buffalo products. The Kutenais, or at least the

Lower Kutenais, made coiled baskets of simple form and design, using split cedar roots often so tightly put together that the resulting utensils were waterproof.

North of the Shoshones, the only potters of the Plateau were the Kutenais, and occasionally their neighbors, the Salishan Sanpoils. The Kutenai pottery described by Turney-High was extremely crude, commonly formed by punching a fist into a rounded mass of damp, sand-tempered clay, and smoothing the outside. But Schaeffer learned that these people used to make shallow, flared serving dishes, as well as flowerpot type cooking pots, by pressing a clay mixture inside molds usually formed of bark. According to what Wissler was told, Kutenai pottery was sundried, and their cooks never used it over the fire; instead, they dropped hot stones into the pot contents, just as they did with bark or basketry utensils or skin-lined boiling pits. Wissler though this logical, since the Kutenais "lived on the edge of the area occupied by the stone boilers of America" (who were the Assiniboines in particular.)[17] An informant on the upper Kootenay River, however, told Schaeffer that sometimes his people used to harden their pots in "kilns" similar to roasting pits for food; such utensils could be used directly over the fire.

The Kutenai potters mixed their clay with some suitable sand, or crushed rock, and sometimes added an adhesive obtained from fish. Both an effective clay, as well as sandstone for crushing, were found near Fairmont Hot Springs at the foot of Columbia Lake; this place was known as *yaki itkenitkyitski me,* "where pots are made." Cooking pots were commonly formed with

[17] Wissler, *Indians of the United States,* 36. See also Schaeffer, "Molded Pottery among the Kutenai Indians."

horizontal projections at the rim for hand-holds, or with pierced ears for inserting willow handles.

So far as is known, the Kutenais did not decorate their pottery, as they did not in prehistoric times superimpose decorations upon their clothing or their lodges. Yet inevitably some artisan would take special pride in the form and finish of his or her handiwork in clay, as Kutenai dressmakers took just pride in the skilled preparation of the skins and the luxuriant self-material fringe used to trim the garments.

The characteristics of the Kutenai ceramics indicate that it must have been learned from the Blackfeet, who learned it from the Sarsi, an Athabascan people to the north; or perhaps the Kutenais had direct contact with the Sarsi as well as with the Blackfeet. The Lower Kutenais were said never to have made pottery except occasionally when visiting their relatives upriver near Columbia Lakes, where the materials were handy. The very simple pots made by the Sanpoils, an Okanogan people who ranged north and west from the Upper Columbia, obviously were learned from the Upper Kutenais.

All of the simple prehistoric pottery of the northern Plains resembled pottery made long ago in Siberia.

HARVEST RITES

Turney-High believes that the pre-horse Flatheads, like typical Plateau folks, made more traditional to-do over the gathering of the vegetable crops than they did over hunting. "However," he wrote, "religious and magical observances centering on food were not particularly complicated." There was a First Roots dance to usher in the bitterroot and camas season, and thanks were given to the sun upon eating the first meal of these foods. This was followed by a thanksgiving festival which apparently "long antedates the preoccupation with the bison which later days were to know." [18] The women, who gathered and cared for the vegetable crop, took part in the dancing and praying; everyone dressed in his best for the occasion.

Each year when berrying season came around, the Kutenais rejoiced by staging the Grizzly Bear dance, a religious celebration with "strong economic connotations," and for the Kutenais second in importance to the Sun Dance. Inside a large dance tipi erected for the occasion, the adults of the village squatted in a circle surrounding the central fire and facing the altar at the back of the lodge, where a grizzly skull held the place of honor. Arranged about the skull and hanging above it were the medicine bags of the participants, who had also brought their ceremonial pipes ready for smoking. Before the altar knelt the Bear shaman, who talked and sang to the Bear Spirit, then passed his rattle to the next man or woman in line as a signal for him to sing his own song or recite his deeds. Meanwhile individuals rose and danced within the circle as they felt inspired, or offered their pipes toward the Bear, in thanksgiving for the berry crop which he shared with them, and in appeal for his continued intervention for them in time of trouble.[19]

FOOD, ECONOMICS AND SOCIAL STANDING

Although bison meat belonged to the man who had killed the animal, no well-supplied hunter was apt to be a pig with his carcasses just because he had been smart,

---

18 Turney-High, *Flatheads,* 34, 35.   19 Turney-High, *Kutenai,* 184.

energetic or lucky. To be able to give away meat – or any other property – made him feel a bigger and better man, and built up his prestige with the other members of his group. Sometimes after a hunt the chief, or one of the chiefs, would go about the camp, or send a crier, announcing the names of those who had no meat; then the women would rush to give to the less fortunate families, thus heaping credit upon their own. The chiefs themselves were often the most generous of all with their property, for they had to set a good example.

Of course each family could eat, dry and transport only a limited amount of meat. The very best investment when a man had extra bison meat "was to bank it in the stomachs of his friends," who later could usually return the favor.[20] Nevertheless, the fatherly attitude of chiefs and leading men in making themselves poor – at least comparatively, or periodically – for the sake of their needy, is in fine democratic contrast to the attitude of many aboriginal chiefs and kings in other parts of the world, who were often expected to confiscate the property of their subjects at whim.

The practice of giving away surplus food and property was sometimes elaborated among the Flatheads and Kutenais, by staging special feasts or parties; but the mountain tribes never entered into orgies of competitive giving such as the Pacific Coast pot-latches, or even such as the pot-latches of simpler form observed by some interior tribes, as the Okanogans and Thompsons. Nor did the practice mean that there were no grades of distinction among members of the bands and tribes, nor any respect for personal accumulation of

[20] Underhill, *Red Man's America,* 164. (Copyright, 1953, by University of Chicago Press; quoted by permission of Univ. of Chicago Press.)

property; the very power to give was a signal of such distinction. Words in the Flathead vocabulary, at least in modern times, meant "trashy people" and "the contemptible poor."[21] One of the critical duties of a Flathead chief in horse days was to determine village protocol by assigning the position of the family lodges in the semi-circular camp pattern, according to the rank of their owners; the center of the arc was the chief's position; flanking him were the sub-chiefs and his most honored friends. The Kutenai head chief, however, had his lodge in the exact center of the camp or village circle.

The rich were the more honored because the people knew they could only attain that state through industry, hardihood, bravery, integrity, keenmindedness, cleverness at gambling — and the favor of the spirits. "Wealth" included not only what we would call practical material possessions, but also medicine bundles and the power granted by a man's guardian spirit: highly useful power which supposedly enabled him to banish ill health, control the weather, locate game, ward off attack by animals, or defeat the enemy — if he were good, and faithfully performed his revealed rites.

21 Turney-High, *Flatheads,* 160.

Year after Year

BEGINNINGS

Before babies were born to these natives, their mothers, and among the Flatheads their fathers too, had to be very careful to observe a long list of taboos in order to protect the child from pre-natal and post-natal harm. When her time came, the mother was assisted by midwives as she squatted on a robe and grasped a mounted wooden bar. If the labor were prolonged or unusually difficult, a shaman might be called in; his treatment consisted largely of smoking rites, prayers, or the manipulation of charms.

When going away from the lodge, Kutenai and Flathead mothers took their babies along on their backs in birchbark cradle baskets, baby bags of skin, or cradleboards of wood (Kutenai, *Ackinko-matl;* Flathead, *Im-pol-aih*). The older wooden cradleboards were short, not coming above the baby's head; only after the women were mounted did these tribes make taller cradleboards to which the babies' heads could be harnessed for better support.[1]

Like most Indians, the Flatheads and Kutenais loved their children without restraint, and pampered them as much as was practical. To begin with, the youngsters were not often weaned until they were several years

[1] Compare Turney-High, *Flatheads,* 72, and Teit, *Salishan Tribes,* 381, on cradleboards.

old; and they went blissfully naked perhaps longer than
this – except when outside in extra severe weather. They
learned to avoid obvious dangers, to be patient and pro-
tective with younger brothers and sisters, to listen re-
spectfully when the elders of the family and the village
spoke. Children played like children everywhere, dancing in a circle hand in hand, dancing about squatting,
playing blind man's bluff, competing in hoop and ball
games, sliding down snow banks or on the ice in winter.
As a woodsy quirk to chasing games, the Kutenai children used to force the gift of a live snake upon the child
caught.

Little girls played with toy dishes and tiny lodges,
and with dolls, or often used puppies as their "babies,"
carrying them on their backs in little cradleboards. The
boys learned how to handle miniature tools and weapons and (with the Kutenai) canoes, and played war
with realistic savagry. At six the Kutenai boy was expected to kill birds regularly and to furnish part of his
own food, as training.

Kutenai children were spanked on occasion, but according to Turney-High the Kutenais had no official
camp child-scarer, such as the Flathead Spotted Face;
nor was there a child policeman to keep ambulatory
children out from under foot, as among the Flatheads.

GROWING UP

Of special interest to the girls was the unending
round, in prosperous times, of private and public gatherings, requiring much chatter and scurry of preparation. At any party, the food of course would be extra
good and as plentiful as the hosts could manage. With
her mother's help, a girl might hurry to finish a new

dress for herself – the simple Plains type "shift" of cured skins bleached white for "best" dresses; or she might be busy helping to finish new shirts or leggings – also Plains type garments – for her father or brother. In the days before trade beads, the Flatheads often used porcupine quill decorations for their garments, but the Kutenais used only fringe, which was cut very long on dress-up clothes for both men and women. The Kutenais at least did not adopt the trailing Plains headdress until modern times.

The speeches at community doings, though sometimes too long to suit the younger boys and girls, or the frivolous-minded of any age, were often high-class entertainment, memorable for their musical intonation, imaginative figures of speech, dramatic accounts of the speaker's experiences with animals and enemies, and rousing appeals to tribal pride.

Occasionally both men and women took part in the dancing, and at small informal gatherings the children performed, learning the steps and the stage presence they would need when they grew up. When a naked or gaudily-costumed tot showed talent and perseverance, Mom and Dad would glow with greater pride than if they themselves were holding the stage. At festivals, however, the dancers were most often men.

By the time a girl reached puberty she was well aware of what was expected of her as a woman: the tireless industry and devotion to her husband and children. The customs she must observe at the time of her first menstruation were apparently simpler among both the Flatheads and Kutenais than among peoples either to the east or west of them – at least in remembered times. She was required to purify her body with repeated baths, and to work hard performing chores for her family lodge and for relatives or neighbors. Sometimes she carried stones to build a votary heap or ring on a hilltop. She might pray to a tree: "Make me as strong as you are."

Boys on the verge of adulthood already knew pretty well what was expected of a man: that he should use his energy for hunting, counting coup upon the enemy, procreating a family, and performing ceremonials; that he should not dissipate it by swaggering around loudly declaring what a great fellow he was, nor by chasing promiscuously after girls, nor by quarreling and fighting with his own people. To be a success in his world, a Kutenai or a Flathead man must have personality power – an air of steadiness, fearlessness and confidence bred by health, hard work, self-discipline and faith in his guardian spirit. In very early times, the emphasis placed upon war by these tribes was lighter, and certainly did not approach the pitch characteristic among more southeastern natives.

GUARDIAN QUEST

It is true that when a mountain boy ventured upon his spirit quest at puberty, one of his strongest motives in known times was the need to store up supernatural help for the time when he might face a tribal enemy. Yet his sister also was expected to seek a guardian spirit. A Kutenai woman told Curtis that in her girlhood "I had done some mischief, and my mother told me to go out and camp alone, to see if I could not get some help." She spent the night in the woods, and a spirit gave her a song which she used for help and protection all her life. The practice of going out alone was begun gradually from the age of five years, when a child might be

LOWER KUTENAI TIPI
AND DRYING RACK
Courtesy of
British Columbia Archives.

KUTENAI SWEAT-BATH FRAME
Photo courtesy of Clara Graham.

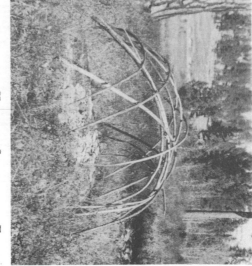

A KUTENAI CANOE
Frame of white cedar, cover of bark;
average length about twelve feet.
Photo courtesy of National Museum of Canada.

THE YOKE DESIGN OF A FLATHEAD DRESS
From Bureau of American Ethnology, Report, 1930.

sent to bring an article of his father's from the woods. At last came the time for the longer venture alone, the achievement of receptiveness, and the communion. "In general, the spirit appeared in the guise of a human being, but after singing, and imparting its wisdom, it melted into the form of an animal whose spirit it really was, and vanished." [2]

The guardian spirit did not, however, always take an animal form. Young Coyote in Boas' "Kutenai Tales" had for his Manitou power "Moonlight just Touching the Ground," who or which helped to hide his trail. A Flathead man still living in the 1960s remembered how his spirit came to him.

> When I was about nine years old I went huckleberrying in the Missions with my mother and my sister. They left me all alone one day; night came on; I cried and cried, I was so much afraid; afraid bear would bite me, afraid coyote would bite me. I cried until maybe four o'clock in the morning, when I heard the singing of this spirit. I cannot explain the name. You know in a burn how the dead trees rub together and talk? This is the spirit of the Wind-in-dead-timber speaking. He told me I was soon to be a man and would no longer be afraid; I would always be protected if I sang this song which he taught me. I used this song all my life. Sometimes I used it for curing other people who had been injured.[3]

Pictographs on rock surfaces of the Flathead Lake region are often said to be sites of spirit quests, the animal pictures representing the spirit acquired, the row of vertical lines representing the number of days spent at this spot in fasting and prayer. A unique haven for guardian-seeking youths on Tobacco Plains was one of the deep pot-holes north of Eureka, Montana, left there long ago by lingering small masses of glacial ice.

---

[2] Curtis, *op. cit.,* VII, p. 129.   [3] In-cas-ho-la, interview.

Tradition has it that two boys, one from Camas Hot Springs some hundred miles south and one from the Cranbrook area seventy miles north, arrived at the pothole on the same night, each hoping for his vision. The accepted procedure was to race around the rim of the pit several times before daring to go down. It seems that on this night the two boys were running in opposite directions, and met head-on in the darkness. Intent on acquiring prowess, they wrestled mightily, until one of them was thrown. They resumed their circling of the hole, again met, again wrestled, and the same youth was again thrown. This was no ordinary defeat; the loser immediately had a premonition that he would meet with ill fate. Though he joined the other boy in the bottom of the pit for fasting and prayer, he could not break the spell; he died not long afterwards, while the victorious wrestler lived to a very old age.[4]

Another rare site for communion in the Upper Kutenai range was at White Swan Lake, east of Canal Flat.

The shores are precipitous and the mountains are elevated to a great height on either side. A small stream breaks over a precipice and falls in a cloud of mist below. Just west of the mouth of this little creek is a remarkable submarine cave.

The Indians came to regard the cave as of supernatural origin and attached a religious significance to it. To enter the cave, one must dive from the overhanging cliff, descend below water and then enter an orifice below the cliff. A long, rising, sandy bottom leads upward to a large chamber, ventilated by fissures in the rock. Here when Indian youths reached a certain age they spent a number of days, sometimes as many as five, in fast and prayer. On the completion of the trial they were judged to have reached manhood and were accorded the duties and privileges of warriors.[5]

---

[4] Dennis, interview.   [5] Iverson, *op. cit.*, 7. See also herein pages 192-93.

The song, dance, body-painting pattern or other rite revealed to a youth as his or her personal medicine (Flathead, *sumesh,* Kutenai, *nupeeka*), and the corresponding objects for the medicine bag, were privately sacred and not to be revealed to anyone else in the world. Often, however, supplementary songs and dance routines were also given them, either on this first communion or later, and these might be demonstrated at tribal celebrations. Private song and medicine bundles were never sold as among the Blackfeet, though they might occasionally be passed on to a son or daughter or an intimate, usually when death seemed near.

Of course not every boy and girl became entranced at the time of the vision quest. "Luison, a Flathead, when less than fifteen years of age, remained in the mountains five days, during which he ate nothing, although he did not abstain from water. Nevertheless he experienced no vision." [6] Many youths were able to make do with "visions" copied from what they had heard others describe. But in this case their power in crisis seldom equaled that of the inspired. Medicine bags may seem to outsiders mere pink pills, but the assurance they gave the true believers could often be more effective than drugs in treating illness, more powerful than weapons in time of danger. The guardian spirit idea was older than American settlement, and came down from primitive hunting people who necessarily spent a great deal of time alone. The "battles" in which such people engaged, with man or animal, would be personal encounters with crude weapons, where harmony of body and spirit, and fearless confidence, could easily be the critical factor.

---

[6] Curtis, *op. cit.,* VII, p. 120.

TO GET A WIFE

Flathead youths in the nineteenth century sometimes lived apart in groups with their own lodges. This may have been a custom borrowed not so long before from the Plains tribes, where the young men belonged to clubs or societies for the various age groups. When a mountain boy killed his first big game animal, the meat, or part of it, often went for a feast in his honor given by the family.

Young men and women did not "date" for parties; but inevitably the various get-togethers were opportunities for acquaintance of a sort with other young people of the camp or band or tribe. Girls were chaperoned by their elders at festivities, and carefully watched over during the day-by-day round of work, for chastity was a cherished virtue. However, a girl often had to go out by herself digging roots or picking berries or carrying water or wood, or to answer the call of nature after nightfall; clandestine meetings could and of course often did result. Willing or unwilling, some girls were caught, and became pregnant before marriage. Nearly everyone deplored the circumstance, and if the man responsible did not offer to marry the girl, she was subject to ridicule; but neither she nor the child was disgraced for life. Though a virgin bride was desirable, the typical young husband was not too agitated if his woman had previously had experience with another man. There is no evidence, however, that any of the Flathead or Kutenai women in early times regularly sold their favors.

What the average young man wanted was a capable young woman to keep his lodge and mother his children; a woman who if possible would do him proud in the village by her looks and her ways – as well as make his nights pleasurable under the marital robe. He could scarcely expect to win such a prize until he had proved himself good at bringing in game; in known times he must also count coup against the enemy before his suit would be considered seriously by the girl's family.

Coup counting had originated at least as far away as the Midwest, where the tribes held the ancient regional idea that war was the greatest of sports. The term "coup" is the French word for "blow;" the Flathead term was *yes-koutiem* (verb). A warrior who touched an enemy with his coup stick, or struck him with his hand, achieved the ultimate triumph. Or the actual, symbolic blow for a brave deed might be struck on a ceremonial post during warrior boasting. It obviously took more guts to touch a live enemy than to kill one from a distance with an arrow; from this premise coup counting became so formalized over the generations that among many tribes, when a warrior killed an enemy with arrow or bullet, not he, but his companions who rushed up to touch the body – "presumably surrounded by his fellows defending his scalp," [7] – were allowed to count coup. Each coup entitled a brave to important new honors and privileges. Such individualistic motivation did not lend itself very well to organized military maneuvers. Most prehistoric Indian warfare in the region of the United States consisted of skirmishes; mass bloodshed was rare. This condition of martial affairs suggests that the continent was never crowded.

---

[7] Underhill, *Red Man's America,* 163. (Copyright, 1953, by University of Chicago Press; quoted by permission of Univ. of Chicago Press.)

A young warrior who went home with a notch on his coup stick, or at least with an accepted record of having touched an enemy – more than the equivalent of a letter on his sweater, a medal on his chest, or his name in the paper – could pursue his courting with considerable confidence. Ordinarily he asked the hand of his chosen girl through a mediator from among his own relatives, though with the Kutenais the process was less prescribed. Without doubt a girl was impressed by her wooer's battle record, but being human and feminine, she was also sensitive to his other qualifications. Kutenai and Flathead girls must have been very much like the Blackfeet girls whom McClintock heard singing, "My lover looked like an eagle from a distance, but alas when he came near I saw that he was nothing but a buzzard;" and, "Some young men appear well at a distance, but when you are close to them they smell like skunks." [8]

Flathead and Kutenai men and women were supposed to bathe every morning. It is doubtful whether any except perhaps the hardiest youths persevered in extreme winter weather. The men might then dress their hair in two braids doubled and tied, with bangs rolled under with a hot stick, or they might use four or more braids to hold the hair more securely. Women commonly wore two braids, though some early explorers spoke of the native women's hair falling loosely about their faces. The women did not use the headband so often seen in festive Indian costume today, but instead wore a sort of skull cap; such caps in older Basin-Plateau times were woven like baskets.

If all the persons concerned were agreed, the young

---

[8] McClintock, *The Old North Trail,* 411.

Kutenai or Flathead man brought presents to the parents of his intended, and came to sleep with her in a traditional location in her family lodge. This did not mean he had purchased her or that she became his property.[9] There were also marriages by simple rite in connection with certain traditional ceremonials. Flathead marriages were not always as simple. The bridegroom in a wedding described by Cox was only part Indian, but the girl was Flathead, and the ceremony took place in a Flathead camp near an early fur post. The bride "received a lecture from the old man [the chief], her mother, and a few other ancients, on her duty as a wife and mother. They strongly exhorted her to be chaste, obedient, industrious and silent; . . . She then retired with the old women to an adjoining hut, where she underwent an ablution," and was dressed in new garments. "A procession was then formed by the two chiefs, and several warriors carrying flaming flambeaux of cedar, to convey the bride and her husband to the fort." The men sang of the bridegroom's bravery; "some of the women were rejoicing, and others crying."[10]

FROM CYCLE TO CYCLE

Death before old age was as familiar to these people as to most aboriginal Americans. Their shamans and shamanesses knew a good deal about curing with herbs, but they were just as apt to treat illness with charms, or by prayer, or by dancing or smoking as directed by their guardian spirits. Such methods were effective in some types of illness, but often did not help. Sweating in the sweat-bath lodge, where steam was created by

---

[9] Turney-High, *Flatheads,* 89. [10] Cox, *op. cit.,* 128-29.

sprinkling water over heated stones, was common; usually the patient dashed out of the sweat bath to jump into the icy water of a stream or lake.

Storms, cold, starvation or malnutrition, disease, accidents, attacks by bears, buffaloes or enemy peoples, all took their sad toll. Mourning was loud and unrestrained, and therefore good therapy for the mourners.

The mountain folk were leery about the dead, or at least about the spirits of the dead. A lodge where a death had taken place must be destroyed or moved, and the spot purified and always thereafter avoided. These feelings and practices were a moderate version of the ghost terrors and death taboos among the primitive, wandering Pah-Utes of the Great Basin. The dead were buried, never cremated. In historic times at least they were not mounted on scaffolds as the Blackfeet dead usually were, the bones to be interred later in a secondary rite. There is the suggestion of Plains influence in a Lower Kutenai tradition relating that their earliest well-remembered chief, Three Moons, insisted that his body be buried, and that he was the first of their tribe (or band) whose body was not mounted on a scaffold.[11]

Some of the Kutenais told Turney-High that the bodies of their dead used long ago to be buried in flexed position. Ordinarily the Kutenai dead were disposed of with little fuss and bother. Among the Lower Kutenai, according to one report, everyone formed a

11 Causton, "The Kootenai Indians," Feb. 2. Reports of more recent burial scaffolds still standing in the Kutenai and Flathead country after White occupation evidently referred either to burial frames for slain Blackfeet invaders, or more often to scaffolds for food caches or blinds for deer hunting. See *Kalispell News* (Mont.), correspondence from seventeen readers, various issues Feb. 5 through May 13, 1948.

line and shook hands with the dead person, which sometimes frightened the small children. The bodies of both
men and women were dressed for burial in a kind of
robe, then wrapped and sewed in a blanket or hide or
tule mat, which covered the head. Kutenai mourners,
Boas said, cut off their hair and buried it with the body
of the deceased. When a warrior died, they painted his
face red, buried him between two trees, the trunks of
which were peeled and painted red. The hands of a
dead chief were placed in a certain position, the body
was covered for a few moments and then the cover was
removed; the position of the hands revealed on un-
covering was prophetic.

The Flatheads seem to have prepared each grave
with some care. They held a wake, and afterwards a
death feast or mourning feast, at which the property of
the deceased was ceremoniously given away. In later
times at least, the relatives provided as many additional
gifts as they could afford, and food for several days'
feasting. In a sense this was payment to the mourners,
and of course did honor to the deceased, and strengthened the prestige of his family. Elizabeth Heidelman
heard an old woman at a wake loudly complaining that
she was not being generously treated.

The "Happy Hunting Ground" for the souls of Indian departed is probably more the White Man's
Christian notion than the Red Man's tradition, although certainly the Red men believed that the spirits
of their ancestors persisted and hovered about. All Indians, according to Lowie, believed in the survival of
the soul after death. Interrogators of the Flatheads and
Kutenais did not always get this impression, though the
Kutenais told Turney-High that "The soul departed

for the West upon death. At the end of the world it would return from the East. When this happens, all souls will go to another and better world, but where this is no one knows." [12]

The Flatheads and their western relatives of the Plateau had a similar feeling that souls traveled in the same direction as the sun, the moon, and the Great River (the Columbia). The Plateau Good Spirit, Amotkin, was usually thought of as dwelling in the sky, while Amtep, the spirit of darkness, dwelt underground. Informants of the Flathead-Kutenai region who told Teit that the souls of good people joined Amotkin after death, while the souls of the wicked were assigned to Amtep, had probably been influenced by Christian teaching. Other Flathead informants said bad people went to a place of perpetual winter.

In the midst of the sound of mourning might be heard the cry of a tribes person "new-born. . ."

---

[12] Turney-High, *Kutenai,* 120.

Horseback

The Kutenais and Flatheads, hidden in the wild heart of the Northwest, were unconscious of the stray visits of old-world sailors to American lands or waters in the tenth to the fifteenth centuries. They could not hear during the first half of the sixteenth century the stricken voices of their far-southern fellow-Indians as the Spanish Conquistadores crushed them – the Conquistadors with their horses and their fire-arms. They could not glimpse the great white-winged canoes guided by other Spaniards and by the English adventurer Sir Francis Drake as they cruised along the north Pacific coast before the century closed. They could not dream of the landing of the strange English colonists on the Atlantic coast in the century that followed, nor of the arrival of French settlers to the north of the English, and soon to the south (New Orleans, 1718) ; nor could they imagine how the expansion of these adventures would turn the eastern Indians into cheated trappers and deceived allies of warring European rivals for the new world – and inexorably force their retreat toward the Great Plains.

With Spaniards to the south of him and Russian fur men to the north, the Britisher James Cook in 1778 cruised the coast opposite what is now the Pacific Northwest, and traded with the Indians at Nootka Sound (Vancouver Island) for furs which his men, after their leader had been killed in the Sandwich (Hawaiian) Islands, sold in China at immense profit. The expedition's search for the Northwest Passage was fruitless, but a new source of wealth had been touched; it was the British, not the Russians, who really made the Spaniards back down, leaving the north Pacific waters open to all comers, including the upstart Americans who had so lately been British colonists, and who were also trading at Nootka by 1788 – and looking for the mouth of the rumored Columbia River. And in Canada it was the British who defeated the French, and whose rival fur companies, Hudson's Bay and North West, were pushing westward to the very Rockies.

Prophets and story-tellers neither white-skinned nor red-skinned could foresee the drama that would begin to swing into movement as the more eastern Plains Indians demanded guns in exchange for their furs and buffalo products, and as the Indians in the Southwest wangled horses from their Spanish overlords.

THE SUPERNATURAL DOG

Presumably the natives in the Southwest managed to steal or bargain for a few Spanish horses here and there, now and then, during the century after Coronado reached them and began their enslavement. Then in 1680 a surprise rebellion by the Pueblos in the New Mexico area temporarily broke the Spanish rule, and loosed all the horses the Indians could desire. In the Pacific Coast region, wild horses straying from Spanish estates in California reached the Umatilla tribe in southern Oregon by 1730. These fleet new conveniences were doubtless designated "supernatural dogs" because both before and after their coming, the American natives used dogs as beasts of burden, by packing them and hitching them to loaded sleds and travois. Teit noted that the common Salish name for horse was related to their common name for dog. The Kutenais, to make their word "horse," combined their word for elk, *khil-kuhla,* with their word for dog, *kahalchan,* to make *kula-kahalchan,* or horse.[1]

As horses spread northward, the mounted hunters of tribe after tribe met on the buffalo plains to skirmish or trade. From packhorse to packhorse, from hand to hand, the White men's axes and knives and needles and kettles and fire flints were coming to them from the east and northeast. When "the arm that flashes fire" was added to the other miracles in iron, the warriors who got some first were the immediate victors in any clash with surprised bowmen. Even as late as 1813, a mountain trader who shot a wolf at a distance measured by the Indians as five arrow shots, observed that "nothing but their wonder could exceed their admiration of this effect of fire arms."[2]

Horses spread northward on both sides of the Rocky Mountains, but apparently earlier just west of them than just east of them. The Flatheads told how they were in southwestern Montana pursuing some Snakes who had killed two lodges of their people, when they observed from a distance some strange big animals mingling familiarly with the Snakes at their camp, and saw the men there climb upon them and ride! After hesitating for some time in their amazement, they managed to drive off the animals in retaliation for the killings. But the first young fellow bold enough to mount

[1] Smythe, *Tales of the Kootenays,* 46.
[2] Ross, *Fur Hunters of the Far West,* I, p. 168.

one got dizzy as soon as his steed began to trot. The Snakes were in touch with friendly language-relatives to the southeast and the southwest; from them horses passed to other upper Columbia tribes, including the Nez Perces.

The Flatheads thus had horses earlier than some of the Plains people, notably the Blackfeet, and perhaps even earlier than the Crows. Some of the Kutenais may have gotten horses east of the mountains from the Shoshones; Barbeau said they caught wild horses at the sources of the Missouri. Other Kutenais had them from the Pend d'Oreilles, who had got them from the Flatheads, Shoshones or Nez Perces. The Lower Kutenais didn't have many horses until sometime after the upper bands were well supplied. By the early years of the nineteenth century there were bands of wild horses on both sides of the mountains in the Upper Kutenai country.

AND GUNS AND TRADE GOODS

Horses had automatically begun to change the ways of these old buffalo hunters, the Flatheads and Kutenais, before they had much contact with other Plains people (if we except the Shoshones), and before they possessed any firearms. It was not long, however, until their hunting parties on the prairie began to meet the Blackfeet and Assiniboines and Crees from the north, and from the east and south the Siouian Dakotas, the Hidatsas and Crows, and even the Algonkian Arapahoes Chippewas and Cheyennes who only recently had been trapping and farming in Dakota, Minnesota and Wisconsin (later so named). Any of these people who were still on foot would kill for horses; the Blackfeet were soon giving "more honor to the successful horse thief than any other tribe."[3] All these people owned a certain number of guns. The mountain folk were forced to back up. The desperate longing for guns became a constant motivation in their lives.

Mounted on horses and carrying muskets, the Plainsmen knew a triumphant new mastery of the bison. Within a few decades after they first learned to ride, horses were not only providing them with high-speed passenger and freight service in peace and war; they had become each man's bank account and medium of exchange; his bride-"price" and gambling stake; his better half for races and parades; and a prime source of beauty and pride. Class distinctions became more sharply defined, for a man could be arbitrarily rated by the number and quality of the horses he owned. A man of many horses literally had everything. A man who owned only one horse or a very few, on the other hand, was forced to pack it or them, and go ignominiously on foot himself when camp was moved or when he brought in buffalo meat. "A man had to have a fast horse for buffalo," says Peter Andrew. "Some men who didn't have fast horses, would stay at home or help dress and carry the meat. Some men stayed home just because they were lazy."

The conical skin-covered tipis of the northern hunters, which evidently originated in Siberia, had spread across the Plains to the borders of the Southwest by the sixteenth century. With horses to carry or drag the lodge poles and the heavy cover, the tipi soon became taller and more imposing. This skin lodge "is without doubt one of the most picturesque of all shelters

---

[3] Wissler, "The Blackfoot Indians."

and one of the most practical movable dwellings ever invented." [4] Even the White frontiersmen of early settlement times testified that a good skin lodge was a very comfortable thing to live in. The Flathead and Kutenai skin lodges, adopted only after contact with Plainsmen, did not have the inner "wainscoating" of the typical Great Plains dwelling. Thousands of rings of stones once used for anchoring the tipis may still be seen on the western borders of the Plains. Larger rings were for ceremonial lodges; some were for defense or lookout.

Dog travois now became horse travois, upon which sizeable children, and the sick or aged, could ride atop the luggage. Neither the Kutenais, who used to pack their dogs, nor the Flatheads, who didn't pack dogs or use dog travois, adopted the horse travois as a regular means of transportation. They traveled too much in rough country. Some present-day Flatheads insist that their fathers or grandfathers did use the horse travois – a romantic object to the Whites – but probably they did so only once in a while. The Kutenais used it in emergencies, when conveying sick people or the bodies of the dead for short distances. [5]

When the mountain horsemen did not ride bareback, they used saddles of stuffed deerhide or of bone or wood covered by buckskin. Women's saddles might have a pommel of deer antlers. Sir George Simpson told of seeing a Pend d'Oreille youngster "about four years old, tied on his saddle on a steed of his own, managing his reins and whip in gallant style." [6] The

---

[4] Laubin, *The Indian Tipi,* 5. A true tipi, say the Laubins, is a *tilted* cone, steeper at back, with two flaps for the asymmetrical smoke hole (p. 3).

[5] Gravelle, interview. For an instance of transporting a wounded man by travois, see Hamilton, "A Trading Expedition."

[6] Simpson, *Journey around the World,* I, p. 140.

Upper Kutenai Camp with Horses, in Later Days
Courtesy of British Columbia Archives.

UPPER KUTENAI MOTHER WITH BABY IN CRADLEBOARD
In Later Days at Invermere, British Columbia.
Courtesy of British Columbia Archives.

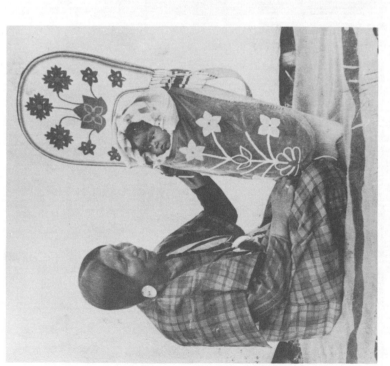

YOUNG FLATHEAD MOTHER WITH BABY, ABOUT 1900
Photo courtesy of Elizabeth Heidelman.

Flathead Insula, also called Little Chief or Red Feather, was observed on the Plains in the days of early White contact.

He threw himself upon the back of a wild horse recently taken, holding in one hand a small flag, and in the other a hoop covered with skin, after the fashion of a tambourine. On being turned loose, the animal dashed off, rearing and pitching, and using the most vicious exertions to disengage himself from his fearless rider, who, clinging with his heels, maintained his seat, in spite of the efforts of the horse to throw him. When he wished to check the speed of the animal, he blinded him by throwing the flag across his face; while he guided him by striking him with the tambourine, on the one side or the other of the head. This exercise he continued, scouring the plain at full speed, and directing the course of the furious steed at will, until the latter was wearied and subdued.[7]

The experience of Lieutenant Thomas Blakiston, a traveler among the Kutenais in 1858, countered the usual impression that all Indians treated horses with callous cruelty. He wrote that they treated their animals with kindness and intelligence, and remarked that they were experts at throwing the lasso.

A WORLD TRANSFORMED

Killing by bullet from a distance in battle posed a new difficulty: how could a man be sure which was his rightful corpse to be scalped, without his marked arrow to identify his victim? A similar difficulty developed in hunting game.

Midwestern warfare traditions reached a fresh stage of glorification as warriors were mounted and armed, and as they constantly met with strange tribesmen usually bent on horse stealing. Horse stealing under dangerous circumstances soon became an occasion for

---

[7] McKenny and Hall, *Indian Tribes of North America,* II, p. 278.

triumphantly counting coup. On the great grasslands, tribes of five language families were mingling, though their homes in the past had been thousands of miles apart. "We can hardly imagine a more dramatic melting pot than this," remarks Ruth Underhill. "Each [group] brought its own customs which were mixed and changed in the general brew." [8] With so much news to tell – the excitement mounting as the White men themselves began to appear in the wake of their traded horses and goods – the tribes rapidly perfected a sign language that spread across the continent. Along with the gossip, ideas both material and spiritual traveled north and south, east and west. Naturally such information as the pattern of a moccasin, or the way to cling to the side of a horse by means of a circingle and fire at the enemy beneath the animal's neck as from ambush, were more readily communicated than a religious ceremony and its significance.

The Crees, coming southwestward across the prairie from their earlier Canadian ranges, had to leave their canoes behind them, but they taught the more southern tribes how to make snowshoes. Evidently the Kutenais, and probably the Flatheads, had used snowshoes long before. The war bonnet originated by the Sioux, or perhaps used even earlier by the Crows, began to replace the simpler headgear of the other tribes. The dramatic splendor of this headdress exactly suited the newly rich show-offs of the Plains.

Horses not only allowed the Plainsmen great mobility; they enforced mobility, since they had to have grass. But during the intervals – frequent in the beginning of

8 Underhill, *Red Man's America,* 157. (Copyright, 1953, by University of Chicago Press; quoted by permission of Univ. of Chicago Press.)

the era – when both meat and grass were plentiful at a camp, there was leisure for such arts as painting motifs on tipi covers according to the directions revealed in visions, or relating upon them the picture history of the owner's exploits. What little tipi decorations the Kutenais and Flatheads used, however, was very simple. The mountain women did follow the Plains women in developing designs with the fascinating new trade beads; shirts, dresses, moccasins, parfleches and smaller personal bags of soft skin, and saddles, stirrup flaps and other horse gear, all were richly decorated. Early Flathead beadwork patterns were an outgrowth of the straightline patterns of the older porcupine-quill embroidery. The Kutenais sometimes used curved-line or floral designs of eastern influence.

The art basic to all this was dressing the skins to perfection. This arduous women's work was never done.

Womenfolk

WILLING WORKERS

Indian women have been thought of by the Whites as drudges and slaves. Ewers writes that the Blackfeet men "were the undisputed lords of their households. They expected their wives to wait upon them hand and foot. Some men beat their wives unmercifully."[1] Nevertheless the Plains women were more respected than generally supposed. "A good woman enjoyed the esteem of her husband and the community at large."[2] Her work was appreciated, even if it was secondary as a survival factor for the tribe. Kutenai and Flathead women also contributed directly to the larder by digging roots and picking berries. The fur trader Alexander Ross said that although the women of the mountain tribes possessed little or no influence, they seemed perfectly contented.

When a Flathead man came home from hunting or war, his wife "rushed to remove her husband's moccasins and the strips of fur he wore for socks. These she dried as well as his feet, out of pride if he had been successful, out of compassion if he had failed."[3] A Ku-

---

[1] Ewers, *Blackfeet,* 100. (Copyright, 1958, by University of Oklahoma Press; quoted by permission of Univ. of Okla. Press.)

[2] Lowie, *Indians of the Plains,* 80. (Copyright, 1954, by McGraw-Hill Book Company; quoted by permission of McGraw-Hill Book Co.)

[3] Turney-High, *Flatheads,* 91.

tenai man "provided his wife with the fruits of male work as a favor to her, as a means of acquiring and retaining her good graces. She too sought to grant him favors in the shape of good meals and clothes. Politeness in contrast with duty kept people in line and made mates happy with each other." [4]

As among White pioneers, a woman's work seemed endless; but the Indian man's work was much more strenuous while it lasted, and often terribly dangerous. It included not only hunting and warfare, but dancing at prolonged ceremonials, sometimes with self-torture.

In this society made highly competitive by the White man's horses and trade goods, the Plainsmen dressed up their women, as they did their horses, to flaunt their own positions – but also to please their beloveds.

> One of the first affectionate duties which a young [Flathead] husband was proud to do was to take care of his wife's cosmetic arrangements. On their first morning together he combed her hair carefully and plaited it into two braids for her and painted her face and hair part. If he had any affection for the lady at all, for the rest of her life he would be very careful of her toilet and be sure to set her on his best prancing horse and parade through the village on every ceremonial occasion. [5]

Women also had their own horses in which they took pride, and might use for commercial gain. Hudson's Bay's governor, Sir George Simpson, wrote that his party in 1841 met some Kutenais and bought a horse "from a female chief." There were supposedly no women chiefs among the Kutenais or Flatheads, but obviously this woman had at least an air of authority.

---

[4] Turney-High, *Kutenai*, 133-34.

[5] Turney-High, *Flatheads*, 91. See McClintock, *op. cit.*, 282, for a description of a thrilling holiday occasion involving a Blackfeet horseman and his wife.

The deal was for "a fine mare, with colt, two years of age," for which the White men gave in exchange "one of our own horses, a blanket, twenty rounds of ammunition and a fathom of tobacco. When we were all ready, however, for starting on our march, the lady, who had doubtless come to the conclusion that she had sold her favorite too cheap, tried to jockey us into paying for the foal which the mare was to produce next spring. This demand, though seriously meant, we treated as an excellent jest." [6]

Daily talk of sex, as of all other bodily equipment and functions, was usually so open with both men and women of these tribes that many White men coming among them were repulsed. But this does not mean that these people had no exalted feelings about mating. Most sins of the flesh were known among them, but they occurred as exceptions. It was said of the Flatheads in the early days of contact that "Chastity is particularly esteemed, and no woman will barter her favors with the Whites upon any mercenary consideration. Their morals have not yet been sufficiently debauched and corrupted by an intercourse with people who call themselves Christian." [7] Even long after the Whites had taken over the land, Turney-High said that "one gains the impression that the Kutenai were not only a straightlaced people in contrast with their neighbors of either the Plateau or the Plain, but that they were somewhat repressed." [8] A primitive preoccupation with the process of food intake, digestion and waste elimination frequently crops up in the Kutenai legends recorded by Boas and others, as in other regional legends. The sex-

[6] Simpson, *op. cit.*, I, p. 135.   [7] Coues, *op. cit.*, 710.
[8] Turney-High, *Kutenai*, 127.

ual urge, though mentioned either matter-of-factly or slyly, is nothing like as pervasive a subject in these folk tales as it is in popular White literature of today. None of these fleshly subjects occupies as much attention as more imaginative goings-on.

Love songs of the Flatheads have been recorded in recent times. "The wooing songs of many Indian tribes are plaintive, mournful, but among the Kutenais they become positively lugubrious," Curtis wrote.[9] This of course is stating the emotional reaction of a White listener whose musical experience had been very dissimilar. Turney-High notes that love charms and potions were eagerly sought by many Flatheads of both sexes.

Marriage was not a religious bond, and was quite easily dissolved; but faithfulness was so much preached and revered that most marriages were permanent. A later-day Kutenai chief remarked acidly that if a Kutenai man did his share of hunting and fighting, he did not need more than one woman. But there was no serious objection to a man's having several wives. In a modern Kutenai version of the Lame Knee legend, the chief has half a dozen wives. Lame Knee, the chief's assassin and successor, took the one he had killed for, and gave the other five wives to his friend and ally. Turney-High even states that among the early-day Flatheads, only the poor, lazy, unskillful or unfortunate men were monogamous. The early missionary accounts of the prevalence of polygamy among these people are contradictory. On the whole, it was a simple matter of mathematics and economics: because of the hazards of hunting and warfare, there were almost always a lot

---

[9] Curtis, *op. cit.*, VII, p. 121.

more women in the band than men. How could all the lone women be provided with game and protection unless some of the men took more than one into their lodges?

Among the Flatheads in particular, a man who could afford it often married his first wife's younger sister or sisters as they grew up, or her older sister or sisters if they were widowed. He might also keep war captives as slave girls or concubines; it is not clear how commonly this occurred.

ROLE OF ROMANCE

Most Plainsmen were virile, democratic and imaginative; their lovemaking would not be hesitant nor hum-drum; but neither was it unduly promiscuous. A Blackfoot man who cut off the nose of his unfaithful wife and thrashed the guilty man, or the Flathead husband who shot his wife's clandestine lover in the leg, did not always do so merely out of resentment or wounded pride; and presumably the two guilty parties had to be passionately attached before they took such risks. David Thompson probably was not being very realistic when he wrote that among the Flatheads adultery brought death to both parties, but the implication of marital rectitude is there. Although the Kutenais were "mild to their women, and particularly attached to their children," [10] a Kutenai man whose wife was unfaithful could take almost any revenge he wished. If the male offender was a formidable warrior, "A husband's only recourse would be to go to war and excel the wife-thief's coup. In such a case he would walk right into his rival's lodge and take his former wife

---

[10] Coues, *op. cit.*, 707.

back home. A man had to love a woman very much to get her back this way." [11] Chamberlain, however, noted that adultery was not severely punished among the Kutenai and that divorce was common.

The widespread legend of the Indian girl who fell in love with a star and lived in the sky as his wife was told by the mountain folk too; so was many a legend involving ardent wooings or extraordinary faithfulness in married mates. The War on the Sky, as recounted by Kutenais and neighboring Salish, was set off by Musk-rat when he shot his brother's widow because she repulsed his advances, using a strange arrow which her people believed to have come from the sky. During the war, the fish person Sucker fell from the sky to the earth and was so badly smashed up that not even the Manitous could revive him. "There was Sucker's brother's widow. He always wanted her to touch him. Then she also went to him and touched him. Then he was well again   .   .   ." though his bones always remained as though broken. [12]

McClintock knew of a Blackfeet maiden who jumped off a cliff singing a song to her dead lover, and of a brave who voluntarily died of starvation because his wife ran off with another man. Cox told of a Flathead man whose wife was captured by the Blackfeet: "He would not take a second wife;   .   .   .   he retired into the deepest solitude of the woods to indulge his sorrow, where some of the tribe informed us they often found him calling on her spirit to appear, and invoking vengeance on her conquerors." [13]

---

[11] Turney-High, *Kutenai,* 129.

[12] Boas and Chamberlain, *Kutenai Tales.* Later-day Flatheads also told this incident (in part) ; see Weisel, "Animal Myths of the Flatheads."

[13] Cox, *op. cit.,* 123.

Women were active in the Plains ceremonial life. The men's societies or lodges usually had their women's auxiliaries. Women took fiendish leading parts in scalp dances and the torturing of captives, and sometimes fought with the warriors in battle.[14] Kutenai women long ago had an organization of their own, the Crazy Owl Society, formed, it was said, to ward off epidemics. In this tribe, a woman as well as a man could sponsor a Sun Dance. Society among the folk of the mountains and plateau tended to be matrilinear, to the extent that a man marrying into another group very often went to live among his wife's people.

---

[14] See De Smet's account of a battle, *Oregon Missions,* 332.

Devotions

SPIRITS THEIR GUARDIANS

Natives of Siberia used to receive personal messages from the Unseen, promising the protection of particular guardian spirits in return for specified devotions. It can easily be imagined how these visions at first came unsought, when the recipients happened to be relaxed and receptive to nature, or when under fearsome or exciting circumstances they were keyed up to an acute pitch of awareness. It is easy to understand how the inspired one needed the definite associative focus of a particular person-spirit or object-spirit in order to recall the mood as needed.

Inevitably some individuals were more apt to get visions than others; or were more eloquent in expressing them; or more clairvoyant, sagacious or lucky in prophecy; these persons became the somewhat priest-like "shamans," a Mongolian term. Of the Indians of the United States, only the Pueblos did not seek personal guardian spirits. "Without guardian spirits an Indian is like a fish without fins," Barbeau was told by the mountain folk of the Flathead-Kutenai region. "He cannot live very long; he is nothing but a fool. For it is through them that we really know the sun, the moon, the mountains, the dawn and the night; it is from them that we get the strength of earth, of all nature." [1]

---

[1] Barbeau, *Indian Days in the Canadian Rockies,* 180.

Each member of a typical Plains tribe, if he was worth a whoop, belonged to at least one secret society, and conformed to its highly-organized traditions. Such social groups, so often military in purpose, had milder counterparts among the Kutenais, notably the Crazy Dog or Reckless Dog Society for young warriors who acted as shock troops, and also sometimes as entertainers. The medicine of the Crazy Dogs was not however secret. The Flatheads seem to have taken over almost none of the Plains secret society customs. Neither the Flatheads nor the Kutenais had tribal medicine bundles as the Plains folk did.

Sometimes a boy or girl received such strong power at the time of his or her spirit quest that on the spot he or she became a shaman or shamaness for life. Kutenai and Flathead shamans and shamanesses were combination doctors, feature singers, dance leaders, spiritual specialists, seers, magicians, mind-readers, hypnotists, prophets, moralists. However, the powers of these spiritual leaders differed from the powers of the layman more in degree than in kind, for anyone who had obtained the cooperation of a guardian spirit had some of these powers himself. Far from being hereditary, as was the priestly office under more formalized tribal religions, the position of shaman could be attained by anyone who demonstrated a strong influence with the spirits, through his accurate prophecies or effective cures, the superior quality of his revealed songs, paint patterns and dances, or his miraculous escapes and accomplishments on the hunt or in battle. The people gave a shaman both traditional and spontaneous reverence, which on the whole he felt was payment enough for his services. Of course if a shaman's claimed power were repeatedly ineffective, he might be discredited; in rare cases he might even be killed. A White settler observed that "most of the medicine men were sagacious old fellows and managed to keep their positions unless the tribe had a very hard run of luck." [2] We can grant that the shamans were shrewd, but this does not mean that they were commonly insincere, or that they were never in tune with the Infinite.

SUN DANCE

For some twenty tribes of the Plains the supreme ceremonial was the Sun Dance, in which everyone in the group had some part. Origin of the Sun Dance is ancient and obscure, and its details and interpretations are as varied as the number of tribes that practiced it. The time for the dance was not regular; among most tribes this depended upon the need of some individual sponsor who had vowed to stage a Sun Dance either in appeal to the spirits for a particular favor, or in thanksgiving for a favor granted.

The active communal rites began when chosen axemen felled the tree which, like a maypole, was to center the great Sun Dance lodge, becoming the focus of the speeches, prayers and dancing. Though the sponsor and the Sun Dance shaman were the leading celebrants, many of the warriors were drawn into the observances as they appealed to the spirits to grant them new dreams and powers. Part of this process was the self-torture of the sponsor and his fellow ritualists, inflicted by passing skewers through the flesh just beneath the skin and attaching these by thongs to buffalo skulls or to the tree

[2] Stuart, *Journals*, II, p. 40. See Ray, "The Plateau," 236 et al, for comparative Guardian Spirit beliefs of our tribes and others.

or pole. Applicants either dragged the skulls behind them as they danced, hung suspended from the pole, or pulled away from it in their frenzy. Only weaklings and those without favor among the spirits gave up before they were freed by the tearing of the skin and flesh, though some repeatedly lost consciousness from fasting, exhaustion, excitement and pain.

The Kutenais had their own simpler form of the Sun Dance, which they claimed they had always known, and which later-day tribesmen testify was without self-torture.[3] In some accounts the Kutenai Sun Dance chief seemed to hold office continuously; in others, he was a person especially honored by a particular Sun Dance, for outstanding services to his people. The time and place for the dance were revealed to the chief in a dream. He then directed helpers in detail how to make and dress the Sun Dance doll, to which he would pray in his own special lodge perhaps for many weeks before he was ready to lead the seven-day ceremony. The Sun Dance chief is said to have directed:

> You must fashion the doll in the form of a little boy about three feet tall. The head you must shape well for the spirit of the Sun will enter the head and there it will stay until the worship is finished. The body, arms and legs need only be made of sticks tied together. Build the image in secret and allow no one to see it until the dance begins.[4]

---

3 Sources consulted on the Sun Dance include Curtis and Causton, *op. cit.;* Graham, *Fur and Gold in the Kootenays;* Turney-High, *Kutenai;* Ewers, *Blackfeet;* Ray, *Cultural Relations in the Plateau;* informants Gravelle, Francis and Malouf; and Stuart, *op. cit.* Stuart's description of the Sun Dance, included in his undifferentiated discussion of the customs of the Shoshones, Bannacks, Flatheads, Kalispels, Spokans, Kutenais and Nez Perces, gives the Plains torture sequence. His "Sun Dance" (II, pp. 41 et al) seems to be a composite ceremonial; perhaps it is the account that is composite, and put together partly from report, rather than from observation.

4 Causton, *op. cit.,* Apr. 13.

Another source describes the doll as a six-inch male figure of buckskin stuffed with grass or deer hair, wearing two eagle feathers in its hair.

Chosen assistants then went into the woods to cut the particular tree indicated to them by the Sun Dance chief through clairvoyance from his lodge. Women hacked the trunk of the fifty-foot tree until it fell onto the shoulders of the men. At the exact spot indicated by the Sun Dance spirit, the dedicated workers, after a session in the sweat lodge, rested the tree on a frame, peeling and painting its lower trunk in alternating bands of prescribed colors. Now the call went out for people to bring gifts, which were tied to the branches before the tree was raised. By some accounts these were valuable gifts, to be later distributed to the needy; by other accounts they were only symbolic offerings of no value except as prayers, often consisting of strips torn from clothing.

For the ceremony of raising the frame of the Sun Dance lodge, a tripod of three poles was first raised, with the Sun Dance chief perched upon its apex. Stripped to a breech clout, he stood up there straight as a growing pole, arms widespread, facing the east solemnly, before he lashed the tripod poles to the Sun Dance tree as it too came into position; he then descended the sacred pole to be ready for further rites. When the framework had been completed, the members of the Crazy Dog Society, their faces painted in grotesque designs, went about camp begging to be fed; people who could or would contribute lodge covers or mats for the great lodge were excused from providing the Crazy Dogs with treats.

The lodge at last readied, the Sun Dance doll was

placed reverently upon an altar to one side, a fire was lighted between the image and the pole, another was lighted between the image and the lodge entrance, and the first day of dancing began. Leading the dancing under direction of the dance chief were the two whistlers, whose faces and bodies had been painted in traditional colors and patterns as part of the opening ceremonies. These celebrants, whose whistles were of bone, were expected to dance for afternoon-long and night-long sessions, clinging to a rope bar before the altar, without food or respite; other individuals joined in as they felt moved.

The days and nights of intensive dancing were interspersed with rest days of only desultory activity. No one taking part in the ceremonies could indulge in sexual activity nor in any frivolity until after the hushed moments when the Sun Dance doll was taken from the lodge by a guardian, to be hidden where it could never be found.

At this moment of leaving the lodge, the spirit of the sun departed the image, taking with it the prayers of the participants. After the very last Lower Kutenai Sun Dance held some fifty years ago, it was reported that when John David, the caretaker of the sun image, took it from the altar, he "walked from the Lodge in the air about three feet above the ground."[5] Now that tension of solemnity and reverence eased, the people built fires in the lodge for feasting, and laughed and shouted as the members of the Crazy Dog Society, acting just like crazy dogs, led the way in bringing gifts for distribution to the village poor.

There is a live question as to the antiquity of the

[5] *Ibid.,* May 4.

Kutenai Sun Dance. The Curtis field students, who talked to Kutenais many years before Turney-High did, described a spring festival held by them as directed in a personal vision, using an effigy, a tree-pole ceremonially cut and erected, two whistlers who clung to a rope while dancing, and other features almost identical with the leading features of the Kutenai Sun Dance as described by Turney-High. Curtis reported the occasion as the Health Festival. The effigy represented *Kuklukinam,* guardian of the tribal health.[6] The climactic prayer to the image by inspired dancers was interpreted: "Kuklukinam give me good luck! Let no sickness be in my family! Give me abundance of food! Give me horses and clothing! I wish that I may see you again in this lodge, Kuklukinam!" This concluding plea was the theme of the festival, since it was a supplication for health and survival. A similar farewell festival prayer is mentioned by the Flatheads. Following the final appeal, all the dancers wept as the effigy bearer, who had also been dancing, stopped, raised the image high, went outside through a line of celebrants, and hung the image on the east side of a tree. Then the feasting began, and after that the war dancing and coup recounting.

A contemporary informant among the Kutenais – laughing at the inquirer's attempts to pronounce the name of the Health Festival spirit – said, "Yes, the dance of Kuklukinam is the same thing as the Sun Dance, the Medicinelodge dance." Whether these rituals were derived from the Sun Dance of the Blackfeet or other Plains neighbors, or whether the Kutenais long ago had some such celebration which became altered

---

6 Cf. *Yayukuekan* of Boas and Chamberlain's *Kutenai Tales.*

by the knowledge of the Plains rites, cannot now be said. Even the Blackfeet may have learned the Sun Dance as recently as the early part of the nineteenth century, probably from the Arapahoes; at least three old Blackfeet legends were incorporated into its symbolisms. Turney-High commenting on the Kutenai "Song of the Erection of the Sun Dance Lodge," said, "This ritual song is in some ways remarkable, and to some extent is un-Kutenai."[7] Dr. Malouf says in comparing the Blackfeet and Kutenai sun dances that the song styles are identical. "The Blackfeet used a large doll stuffed with hair, while the Kutenai doll seems to have been carved out of wood. The dance circle was different, but the routine was similar."

Considering some of these differences and similarities, and considering how many tribes farther south knew the Sun Dance, it seems unlikely, though possible, that the festival might be descended from an ancient northern tradition, without any intervening Mexican influence.

There is also a debatable relationship of the Kutenai Sun Dance with the Flathead mid-winter festival, which was "concerned with the creation of a more intimate bond between a man and his tutelary, the impersonation of spirits, and a symbolic recall of mythological times."[8]

THE MID-WINTER FESTIVAL[9]

The Flatheads did not practice the Sun Dance, though they reverenced the sun. The seasonal ceremonials of the Flatheads were connected largely with

---

[7] Turney-High, *Kutenai*, 84.   [8] Ray, *Cultural Relations*, 123-24.
[9] This section abstracted largely from Turney-High, *Flatheads*, 38 *et al.*

food-getting and the renewal of guardian spirit powers. Their mid-winter festival included a typical Plateau theme feature – the Camas Dance, and the ecstatic Blue Jay Dance which Turney-High remarked "may be another link with the Northwest Coast" where celebrations sometimes became orgies.

Winter life for the mountain people was a continual struggle to keep warm and well-fed; it included the strenuous and dangerous winter hunt for bison cows. For long periods the women and children and the old and sick, and sometimes even the ablest hunters, were lodge-bound. So the first part of the Flathead Mid-winter Festival, an occasion of emotional thaw, a sort of week-end party where the guests got high on unleashed spirits, was good therapy. Though the opening rite of the Camas Dance was "primarily a prayer in the dead of winter for an adequate supply of vegetable food in the spring," soon after the attendants entered the long-house dance lodge, "all bars of dignity went down. Each person dropped his true name and was called by one not of his choosing. These names were ordinarily so completely and descriptively salacious that even the most case-hardened were embarrassed upon hearing them mentioned at any other time." Both men and women took part in the simple ring dance, and between songs the men might "grab the women and indulge in all manner of familiar horseplay." This was one of the festival occasions when young people liked to marry.

In spite of all the frivolity, and the marrying tradition, the body of the Camas Dance was the renewal of communion with the guardian spirits. Each dancer presented his sumesh song or songs (though not his most private one); some persons were inspired with new songs on the spot. After the Camas Dance had gone on for four days, the villagers were allowed a four-day period to rest and sober up. By the time they entered the Bluejay lodge they were thoroughly in earnest. The Bluejay shamans, who had been fasting and praying, and purifying themselves in the sweat lodge, now appeared in breechclouts, their faces charcoaled dead black, and began a fervid dance to the rhythm of deer-hoof rattles and chanting. All night in the firelight the people did their best to increase the hysteria of the shamans, who danced up and down in rows, awaiting the entry of the Bluejay spirit into their own.

On the second night, sick persons were brought to the lodge, where the shamans danced about them, each treating the ailment in which he specialized. Disorders involving fears and tensions, if no others, might be relieved. The hysteria in the Bluejay lodge mounted with the passing hours, until the dramatic denouement when the fires were suddenly beaten out, and in the pitch darkness the shamans became Bluejays, talking jay-jibberish and climbing the lodge poles. Any intelligible words they now uttered were carefully noted by the audience, as material for prophecies. After a while the Bluejays tried desperately to escape from the lodge, and when finally allowed to do so, they ran off into the woods and climbed trees, from which they had to be rescued, and restored to their human senses by the application of sweet-grass smoke. Now, in the fullness of their powers, they again treated the sick.

The Kutenais so admired the Bluejay dance that they learned it too, but in comparatively recent times. A contemporary woman of mixed Flathead, Kutenai and White blood, says that a shaman who had been possessed by the Bluejay could do wonderful things. "One of them when bitterroot was boiling over his fire, used to wash his hands and plunge them right into the boiling water to stir the stew. His brothers who were also Bluejay medicine men could put a hex on people they didn't like." [10]

Ray, after first remarking that there are few similarities between the Flathead Mid-winter Festival and the Kutenai Sun Dance, then points out a number of parallels: in both instances the leader receives his commission in a vision; the preparations in both cases include sweating; on both occasions the fourth day is devoted to erection of a central pole for the dance lodge; the dancers for both festivals use whistles; the sick are treated as part of the ceremony in both the Sun Dance and the Guardian Spirit Dance. He concludes that these resemblances may be coincidental, or that there may be an ancestral relationship; or that a haphazard exchange of elements may have occurred.

Ray considers the Sun Dance less unified and meaningful than the Mid-winter Festival; Lowie remarks that the mis-named Sun Dance, in which sun worship had little part, seemed to lack any central spiritual significance. Perhaps the significance had faded or had become confused since the creation of the source festival long ago. Or perhaps this apparent lack is only the reaction of intellectualized, traditionalized and dogmatic White men, who seem not to be satisfied that a

[10] Marengo, interview. The mid-winter festival dance was known in later times as the Jumping Dance. One informant remembers that the ceremony lasted ten to twelve days and was held at the Post Creek ranch of Tinum Finley (or Tanum-Anthony, apparently a son of Jocko Finley's son Nequam). In-cas-ho-la says that whiskey put an end to the Jump Dance; the dancers would just get drunk and drop out.

religious event should lift souls out of their distracting everyday cares, relax and harmonize their bodily equipment, and inspire them with a sense of beauty, timelessness and communion with the Unknown. Both charity and hilarity could be natural conclusions for such an occasion.

PERSONAL POWER

Parts of the traditional Kutenai and Flathead festivals were rather formal, ordained and undeviating; but on almost all such occasions there would come the relieving variations introduced by personal spirit songs and the personal pantomimes of boasting warriors. "Even if you were outside the lodge or building in the dark, you could tell who was singing inside, by his own song he always sang."[11]

The personal songs or prayers of shamans might be used in prophecy or curing, or in magical feats achieved by trickery, illusion, mind-reading, entrancement or hypnotism. Convincing examples of clairvoyance in Flathead shamans have been recorded.[12] An enthralling specialty of Kutenai shamanism was "going behind the blanket" (or robe, hung up like a curtain) where the practitioner was possessed by his guardian spirit and thus endowed with supernatural power. Going behind the blanket could be an entertaining combination magic show and seance, but it could also be in deadly earnest. A mixed-blood reservation grandmother of today tells of calling in Kutenai medicine men when she was younger:

[11] In-cas-ho-la, interview.

[12] See especially Turney-High, *Flatheads*, 31; Malouf and White, "Recollections of Lasso-Stasso."

I had the flu and lost a baby, and had been very sick for a long time; my flow [urine] stopped. I sent for Kutenai medicine men, not telling my mother [who was Christian-trained] because she wouldn't have approved. My mother had left a White woman to take care of me and she was there when the medicine men came but they asked her to leave as she was not sympathetic with their powers. So she went outside. The medicine men could always tell when anyone present was not a believer, and would make them leave.

Now the leader came to my bedside and said to tell him what was the matter and he would tell me whether it could be cured. When I told him my water had stopped he said he thought he could help that. He and the others went behind the blanket and sang and danced and got more and more excited. I was so sick I hardly knew what was going on. At last the leader came out from behind the blanket with eyes very bright, and came and put his hands on my head, feeling for the right place. Then his hands came away from my head clasped together, stuck tight — the evil was inside. He cried, his hands were stuck so tight; he cried for help; it took several of the strong men from behind the blanket to pull his hands apart and let the Thing loose. At that minute in my bed I was swimming wet, then after just a little time I was perfectly dry again, and I soon got well.

Other contemporary women informants insist that some medicine men could correctly foretell the sex of an expected child by studying the mother's body profile.

Ka-tse-kate, in the modern version of the Lame Knee legend as told to Bert Davis,

. . . sang a very powerful song. Then followed many strenuous signs and exhortations which so exhausted him physically and mentally that he fell to the ground unconscious. At last he partially revived and fell into a troubled sleep or trance, and a vision of everything that had ever happened passed before him in proper sequence. It was as though he had two minds: his own mind which he used every day was trying to understand all these things; he was trying to comprehend why he had this other wonderful mind that had never been active before. Then slowly the understanding came. This great mind was not part of *Ka-tse-kate* at all; he was part of this mind – or was it mind? Now he knew that it was really the Great Spirit itself, and he should be able to learn all the things he wanted to know.

MUSIC

Personal demonstrations in song and dance, and audience-participation in many rites, are typical of the democratic and individualistic religion of these people. "One who has seen [such] dances about a blazing fire can testify that one frantic, half-naked dancer, ornaments streaming in the firelight, can be quite as imposing as a file of perfectly costumed masks [masked dancers] in the Pueblos." [13]

At dances, the music – drum, voices, flute, rattles – seemed the very sound of the body movement's sure, quick rhythm, of the body paint's gleam and the glitter of ornaments. All these enchantments varied according to the personal taste of the individual celebrants, ostensibly according to the dictates of their guardian spirits. The gestures of the dances, though diverse, were seldom loose-limbed or abandoned. They often imitated symbolically the movements of birds or animals, or of men hunting and fighting. Their power was in repetition, in concentration and restraint that could build up to an ecstatic or explosive climax. The mimicry of such performances as the Prairie Chicken or Crazy Dog dances was as much for entertainment as for prayer; other dance routines were solemnly purposeful, especially if the camp or tribe were hardpressed for food, afflicted

[13] Underhill, *Red Man's America*, 256. (Copyright, 1953, by University of Chicago Press; quoted by permission of Univ. of Chicago Press.)

by disease, or in danger from an enemy. War dances grew in importance with the Great Plains influence.

Practically all Flathead and Kutenai rites were conducted to music. Of Flathead music the Merriams wrote: "There are distinct kinds for sweating, love, scouts, victory, various types of dancing, etc. These musical categories were never confused." In general, this music is "bold, open . . . down-sweeping." [14]

The "songs" as heard by White men are mostly chants, sung without words, or with wording the informants themselves cannot interpret; how many of them once had definite verbal meanings is not known. Turney-High asserted that "the Kutenai have no poetry." As most songs have been sung in late times, the note pattern itself is the message. The voice may be the solo instrument, or there may be accompaniment from drums, flagelots or flutes, deer-hoof rattles or, in later times, bells worn by the dancer.

Few intimate personal medicine songs have been recorded. Turney-High printed the note patterns for two of these. One was obtained from an informant who explained: "I have kept this secret all my life. I have not sung it for three years. I will die not long from this time, so I will put this on record for my descendants." [15]

Music with these native Americans was not a detached incident of entertainment, or a limited interval in Sabbath services; it was the harmonic sound of living, intensely enjoyed for its own sake yet functional in the strongest sense, for it could bring persons and tribes their luck, including their economic luck.

---

[14] Merriam, "Ethnology of Flathead Indian Music," 6, 10.
[15] Turney-High, *Kutenai,* 108.

From Where?

THE SALISH GET ABOUT

This is the stage of the story when it is most enlightening to compare the Plains and Plateau traits of the Flatheads and Kutenais, in order to conjecture as reasonably as possible their pre-history. In Flathead legends, according to Turney-High, Coyote and other heroes are often described as fishing for salmon, and rarely as hunting for bison. Teit decided that the Flatheads had possessed all the material culture traits of the Great Plains for two hundred years or more. But he also observed that "The social organization of the Flathead tribes appears to have been in general of the same kind as that common to other interior Salishan tribes, [and] the Kutenai, Nez Perce and Shoshoni." [1]

Further countering any claims of an eastern origin for the Flathead is the legend telling how they migrated long ago from somewhere in the vicinity of the present California-Oregon boundary, on the fringe of the Great Basin. The particulars of this tale are not considered likely history, but La Farge does say that Salishan and Shahaptin culture "looks like Great Basin culture as it would develop in better surroundings." [2] Individual vision seeking by both men and women was very strong in the Basin; and the women, who were co-partners in

---

[1] Teit, *Salishan Tribes,* 373. [2] La Farge, *op. cit.,* 182.

the food-getting, took part in Basin dances similar to some the Flatheads used. The mid-winter festival was also of great importance in the Basin.

The Great Basin Pah-Utes lived in dwellings of grass, brush and earth. The Flatheads and Kutenais, like many of their Plateau neighbors, once used to build pole-framed longhouses, excavated a foot or two below the surface of the ground, and covered with bark, or mats of tule or Indian hemp *(Apocynum)*. A prehistoric village might be made up of half a dozen such longhouses, one for celebrations, one for the young men to live in or dance in, the others for family groups – several to eight or more – with a lodge fire to each couple of families. Just when conical lodges were adopted, and whether they were always covered with skins like the Plains tipis, or at first covered with mats, remain questions. The Lower Kutenais never used skin lodge covers; [3] their lodge-cover bands or mats resembled those of their Salish neighbors, the Coeur d'Alenes and Okanogans. The Spokans and Kalispels continued to use vegetable covers for their lodges to a certain extent, even during horse times.

Horse mobility out-moded the longhouses as regular residences, but such structures were put up for festivals until fairly recent times. Lewis and Clark saw them among the Flatheads. Tobacco Plains Kutenai elders remember a great longhouse constructed with skin covers borrowed from the tipis, used to house a memorable celebration on the site of the "69" Ranch near Eureka, Montana.

Many of these similarities between Plateau and Basin culture could be coincidental, but it seems clear

---

[3] Or almost never. See Causton, *op. cit.,* March 23.

that aside from the horse-buffalo complex, the Flatheads were more like other far-western interior people than they were like the Plains people, who had a more highly organized social and ceremonial life and tighter tribal discipline, and who were more devoted to warfare.

Both the Flathead and the Kutenai informants consulted by Turney-High were dumbfounded or greatly amused at the idea sometimes put forward that the Flatheads came from the east. Probably the Flatheads who talked to Teit some thirty years earlier were still so much in the grip of their resentment against the Blackfeet who had driven them from their prairie hunting grounds, that they stressed their claim to being Plainsmen. Actually, it is quite possible that the Flatheads never hunted on the Plains until the buffalo disappeared from the western valleys, which may have been not so long ago.

Supposing that the Flatheads were far-westerners, then why the apparent Algonkian elements in the Salish language, and how did these people get to the mountains?

If the ancestors of the present Salish tribes came south together, and if the final lap of their route was down the Fraser River as indicated for the Coast Salish, it is of course possible that they all crossed the Rockies at the head of the Columbia or the Fraser; or more likely that their supposed association with Algonkians took place further north. It is also possible that they never knew the Plains at all; the claimed Algonkian cast to the Salishan language may be only apparent, or the connection so remote that it originated in Asia or Alaska.

Dr. Malouf's feeling that the ancestral Salish group probably lived at one time in the central position of the mid-Columbia seems the most reasonable assumption. In this case some Salish people may early have gone into the borders at least of the Great Basin, only to turn north as the post-ice age drought seared this region. When the drought also reached into what is now central Oregon and Washington, some of the people would naturally seek the Coast for relief, and others the mountains. Boas speculates that the Interior British Columbia Salish had separated from the Coast Salish at a time when the culture of both was much simpler.[4]

All the Salish had in common a free, informally organized society with no rigid laws nor disciplinary controls. But the richer environment found on the Coast by the once-Plateau Salish brought about a settled village life with more involved social traditions, and finer arts and crafts; at the same time many ceremonials and legends were borrowed from neighboring non-Salish peoples. One whale brought in by an organized party was a village bonanza for weeks, and the abundance of salmon and other sea foods, together with vegetable foods, plus the mild climate, made living comparatively easy. The Flatheads, who had to hike and scramble over so much rough territory in such extremes of weather to make a living, were a different breed of men. Even compared to the Plains Indians, David Thompson found the mountain folk more energetic and willing to work.

Just as Plateau culture seems like a later development of Basin culture, changed by more favorable living conditions, so the Coast Salish acted a lot like

4 Boas, "Salish Tribes of the Interior of British Columbia."

BASSOO GOOSE HUNTER
A later-day Kutenai, in regalia.
Photo courtesy of Fred E. Peeso.

THE KUTENAI SUN DANCE
A cardboard diorama distributed by the British Columbia
Department of Education, Vancouver.
From *British Columbia Heritage Series, I*, vol. 8, 1952.

ROCK WITH WHAT MAY BE A CARVED SUN SYMBOL
Found by George Young near the junction of
the Yaak and Kootenai rivers. See text page 147, fn. 18.
Photo courtesy of Glenn Frisbie and George Young.

Plateau Salish who had for some time been living better still – even too well. Curtis rated the North Pacific Salish as "inferior to the average interior type." Long hours of squatting in canoes had affected their form and gait; their faces were "expressionless and apathetic;" bathing was not regularly practiced; sex relations were lax and prostitution carried on under management of fathers and husbands; slavery was firmly established; there was constant internal strife, thieving and assassination.[5]

In contrast, the Salishan Flatheads were "a brave friendly, generous and hospitable tribe strictly honest, with a mixture of pride which exalts them far above the rude appellation of Savages when contrasted with the tribes around them."[6] Father De Smet wrote that even among their enemies, the Flatheads (including the Pend d'Oreilles) were known as "a nation of Chiefs." Such eulogies are conspicuously frequent among the writings of the early explorers.

It is believed that the Flathead peoples are fairly recent residents in western Montana. They themselves testified that the Kutenais were there before them. To more than one observer, Indian and White, the Southern Flatheads, who first received this name from the Whites, have seemed the leading or mother group of the Plateau Salish, if not of all the Salish. They may have remained a long, long time somewhere on the mid-Columbia, while groups split away in various direc-

---

[5] Curtis, *op. cit.*, IX, pp. 41, 80-85. See also Drucker, *op. cit.* It must be noted that these reports do not correspond very closely with the testimony of Charles Hill-Toute, in the *1905 Archaeological Report*, Minister of Education, Ontario.

[6] Osborne Russell, *Journal of a Trapper*, Portland: OHS. 1955, p. 33. Note also Thompson, *op. cit.*, 422.

tions, some of these coming early to the present Flathead Valley where they left ancient artifacts, and then died out or moved away. The easiest route east would have been up the Spokane River and then south up the Clark Fork. If this was the way taken in the later migrations, and the Southern Flatheads were in the advance, they would have been longest in the range where the White men found them. Although Turney-High rated the midwinter festival as a leading Flathead ceremonial, Curtis wrote some forty years earlier that "Among all the interior tribes of the Salishan stock, *excepting among the Flatheads* [the Southern Flatheads], there was observed a winter ceremonial for all persons under the protection of guardian spirits,"[7] which was similar to Shahaptian and Chinookan practices. This suggests that the Upper Flatheads, whether or not they had once known this festival, learned or relearned it from the Pend d'Oreilles in recent times.

KUTENAIAN CROSSINGS WEST

When the Blackfeet began to push southwestward around 1700, the Tunaha and the northern Shoshones were the first buffalo hunters in their way. Although the Plains Kutenais when met by Alexander Henry at the opening of the nineteenth century, had "the reputation of a brave and warlike nation,"[8] so many of them were killed or enslaved by the Blackfeet, and so many more were destroyed by a cruel epidemic, sometimes but not always referred to as smallpox, that the survivors scattered and took refuge with other tribes, mostly west of the mountains. According to information given to Curtis, one of these refugees went with his mother

---

[7] Curtis, *op. cit.*, VII, p. 86. (Italics the author's.)   [8] Coues, *op. cit.*, 707.

among the Flatheads, and became their chief, named
Big Hawk. Big Hawk's successor, Three Eagles, was
said to have been the chief in Lewis and Clark's time.

The epidemic that scattered the Tunaha may well be
the same one that nearly wiped out the Lower Kutenais, according to a narrative they believe to be history.
Informants told Rose Causton that long ago their people moved from the Bonners Ferry site, down river to
Innias Creek near what is now Copeland, Idaho (midway between Bonners Ferry and Creston, B.C.), in an
effort to escape the ravages of a "measle epidemic."
Several generations later, disease again struck these
people, this time following an all-tribe Sun Dance held
at the Innias Creek village. This second epidemic,
described as "a big belly ache," was so swift and drastic
in effect that some of the visiting celebrants from the
Upper Columbia never reached home. The stricken
band at Innias Creek moved up-river to the mouth of
"Belly Ache Creek" near what is now Leonia, Idaho,
in hopes of leaving the disease behind. But the deaths
continued until none was left except one woman and
her grown daughter. Canoeing their lonely way down
the river, the two found only corpses at the camps
where they stopped. Sometime later the two women,
known to descendants as "Singing Through" and
"Traveling On," were joined at Kootenay Lake by a
man from Windermere, said to be the only Upper Kutenai survivor of the same sickness, who by marrying
these women fathered all future Lower Kutenai people.[9]

Both the chief of the Bitterroot Flatheads and the

---

[9] Causton, *op. cit.*, Feb. 2, May 11, 18. A similar legend is recorded briefly
by Boas and Chamberlain, with no tribal band specification. (*Kutenai Tales,*
325.)

chief of the Pend d'Oreilles at the Treaty Council in 1855 had Tunaha blood in their makeup. Teit was told that the last Tunaha-speaking person had recently died (around the turn of the century). Turney-High several decades later was told that there was still "much tunaha blood around."

The trail of Plains artifacts leading westward from Sun River suggests that this migration went on for generations, and began even before the Blackfeet came south. More northern Tunaha crossed westward by more northern passes, into Upper Kutenai country.

In many ways the Kutenai folk seemed to belong more to the Plains than the Flatheads did. Part of them at least resided early on the prairies and were friends of the Blackfeet and the mountain Crees in pre-horse times. Boas decided that "The Kootenay are in type similar to the Indians of the Plains; they are much taller than the Indians of British Columbia." [10] "The realistic figures which they painted on their garments, their tents and even their persons followed the style of painting among the Plains Indians [particularly the Crees], not the styles of the Pacific Coast." [11] The Kutenais also were "Prairies" in that they made pottery, danced the Sun Dance and grew tobacco. Kutenais told Turney-High that they had borrowed the Plateau Midwinter Festival from the Flathead, and did not think much of it; on the other hand they said they got the Sun Dance, which they celebrated with much serious-

---

[10] Boas, "Physical Types of the Indians of Canada."

[11] Jenness, *op. cit.,* 358. Dr. Malouf, however, believes that naturalistic designs in western Montana were derived from the Southwest through the Shoshone. Not long after the advent of trade beads, designs were exchanged among the tribes until original characteristic distinctions were lost. Note the Flathead cradleboard pictured herein on page 104.

ness, "from across the eastern ocean where the Sun Dance Spirit lives." [12]

SACRED TOBACCO

Native Americans over most of the East and Midwest grew tobacco for ceremonial smoking. Various species of *Nicotiana* are native to the continent; tobacco was a gift of the new world to the old. Before pipes were known, prehistoric people around their campfires – literally the light of their lives, next to the sun itself – used to place themselves or parts of their bodies, or certain meaningful objects, in the midst of the smoke that arose from different aromatic fuels, for cure, purification or sanctification; they used sweet grass smoke as incense on primitive altars. [13]

The Kutenais were no farmers. Neither they nor their neighbors raised anything except tobacco. Tobacco planting probably came to them from the Blackfeet, Gros Ventres or Sarsi to the north (or even from the Snare Indians, who were rumored to have raised crops), or from tribes to the east who farmed for food, and many of whom revered the calumet as a religious object. In Kutenai legend, Coyote institutes the peace pipe after a quarrel with Buffalo. The stories of Lame Knee, who because of his disability became the guardian of the tobacco garden, are told both among the Blackfeet and the Kutenais. With the Siouian Crows one of the most honored clubs was the Tobacco Society, in which a novice could buy a place only at a very high

[12] Turney-High, *Kutenai*, 187, 184.

[13] "An unusual characteristic of the Kutenais is their keen appreciation of agreeable smells. They customarily fill their pillows with aromatic plants, and throw large quantities on their lodge fires solely for the pleasure of the aroma." Baker, *op. cit.*, 12.

price; the elders of the society supervised solemn and intricate sowing ceremonies that lasted for many days.

The traditional tobacco garden on Tobacco Plains was near the east bank of the Kootenai River about three miles below where it flows into Montana from Canada, along the north shore of the pond formerly known as Lake Livermore. In remembered times the little individual plots marked off for the different teams of men or man-and-wife (as with the Crows) could still be traced. Other tobacco plantations in the Kutenai range were near present-day Fortine, on a branch of the Tobacco River; in the range of the Middle Kutenais at McGinnis meadows or at the junction of the West Fisher with the main Fisher River; and at Spotted Bear far up on the South Fork of the Flathead River. The Lower Kutenais had no tobacco garden, but sent delegations to Tobacco Plains at planting time.

Before the sowing, the people gathered to enjoy a feast that included meat of a certain cut from a certain species of game animal, after which the leaders smoked and offered the pipe in prayer to the four directions, asking for a favorable crop and for good luck in general for the tribe. In the version of the Lame Knee legend told to Davis, the head grower or tobacco shaman used his medicine to "make the seeds fertile and make the soil give up its food to the plants." Sticks and elkhorn hoes were used to work the soil. Certain taboos were in force until the seed was known to have germinated. When the Tobacco Plains people went to hunt buffalo during the growing season, a few persons were left to watch the garden.

Exactly what plant the Kutenais raised, the natives in settlement days could not indicate. Some think it came from across the mountains; most, however, claim that the plant grew wild near a hillside spring at Canal Flat, and that here the seed was collected for the tobacco garden. Once or twice a year, wrote Smythe, the Kutenais and their guests met in the Elk River Valley for games – horse-racing, wrestling, running, jumping, bow and arrow shooting. The prize commonly awarded was a packet of the coveted tobacco raised by the Upper Kutenais.[14]

Neither Kutenais nor Flatheads went to the trouble of making elaborate pipes. According to what the Flathead Lake Kutenais told Thain White, their pipe designs were admittedly borrowed from the east or south,[15] perhaps before the horse era but probably not too long before. Another present-day informant says that tobacco growing by his Kutenai wife's people goes back eight generations. Yet Turney-High was told that smoking was so ancient with them that it is mentioned in legends of the pre-human era. It is possible that they first smoked tobacco obtained by trading.

The Flatheads probably had their pipes from the Snakes, who apparently did not grow their tobacco, yet among whom Ross reported "a fabulous story that they were the first smokers of tobacco on earth!" It is worth remarking that language-relatives of Shoshonean-speaking Snakes lived far to the south, where some of the tribes were farmers.

WERE THE KUTENAIS MOUNTAINAIRES?

It used to be taken for granted that the Kutenais borrowed their Sun Dance in horse times from the

---

[14] The plant used was most likely *Nicotiana attenuata*.
[15] T. White, "Kutenai Pipes."

Blackfeet or the Crees, but their own claim to have had it long ago may be more than tribal ego. Significantly, the Lower Kutenais, who did not often go east to the Plains even in horse days, seem to have been just as devoted to the Sun Dance as their upriver relatives; the whole tribe often came together for the performance. Simon Francis today even indicates that the dance was customarily held in Lower Kutenai territory, although Joe Dennis of the Upper Kutenai doesn't think it was ever held at Bonners Ferry until recent times.

Rose Causton was told by Lower Kutenais that according to tradition their people originally came to Idaho from the shores of Lake Michigan six hundred years ago, having been crowded westward by more powerful and warlike tribes. But it is hard to picture the northern Great Plains, with their semi-nomadic populations following the caribou or reindeer or bison, as the locale where a people could live isolated for enough generations to develop so unmatched a vocal expressiveness as the Kutenais did.

Even Upper Kutenais have sometimes said that the tribe once lived on the north shores of Pend d'Oreille Lake, near what is now Hope or Sandpoint, Idaho, or at the locality of Cusik, Washington. In fact, Curtis gives the range of the Lower Kutenais, referred to by the place name *Akuklahlhu,* meaning "swamp" or "The Place of the Red Willows" *(Cornus stolonifera),* as "Bonners Ferry and the north end of Pend d'Oreille Lake." And Chamberlain listed a group of "Lake Pend d'Oreille Kutenais" as *Aqkiyenik* or the People of the Leggings, which suggests that the Middle Kutenais, known by a similar native name, and sometimes called the Thigh people, came to the Kootenai River from Pend d'Oreille Lake.[16]

Informants Gravelle and Baptiste Mathias, however, agreed with Curtis that the Middle Kutenai were of Tunaha stock. It can of course be imagined that Tunaha crossing the mountains westward by the Sun River route,[17] were on their way to an ancient homeland at Pend d'Oreille Lake, when some or all of them digressed up the Thompson and down the Fisher, finding this a country rich in fish and game. Kutenai from all the bands used to go, in remembered times, on periodic pilgrimages to the vicinity of Hope as sacred ground. At stopovers along the way the celebrants offered prayers to the sun, made up their quarrels with relatives and fellow tribesmen, and subjected themselves to placating self-torture, for they believed that eventually the spirits of their ancestors, who went to the sun upon death, would return to the earth at Pend d'Oreille Lake. Clara Graham suggests that the Kutenai Sun Dance was held here.[18]

---

[16] The Kutenai words for leg, leggings and thigh begin with the same *ak* sound as the word for arrow; see here p. 52. Bert Davis was told that the oldest station in the Middle Kutenai country was on the Fisher River near the mouth of Buck Creek – along the Thompson-Fisher route to the Kootenai from the Clark Fork. It must be noted that Chief Paul at Tobacco Plains told Turney-High that the Tunaha were Plainsmen whose original village known as The-Place-of-Red-Willow-Branches *(a'kik nuskánwuq)* was located east of the Divide (*Kutenai*, 18).

[17] See herein p. 142.

[18] See Chamberlain, "Kootenay Indians," 178; Jenness, *op. cit.*, 360. Max Campbell of Tobacco Plains and Libby writes: "There was a place below Bull Lake and not far from Hope, on the east slope, with stones placed in circles and about two feet high, and undoubtedly tipis placed within these circles. It is evident that many people have been to that place in worship of some kind, I would guess, worship of the sun."

A resident of the Bull Lake area, George Young, recently unearthed a mysterious carved rock which could be of Kutenai origin. A double circle about eight inches in diameter has been deeply incised upon a ninety-pound

So strong a place-veneration as this must have sprung from a long home-association, or from the emotional impact of some memorable event. Although many of the legends of the Kutenais resemble tales of the Blackfeet, Crees and other Plains peoples, just as many of them repeat in some form the olden stories of the Plateau Salish, particularly the Okanogan, whose range touched the known range of the Kutenais on the northwest.

Even if the Kutenais on their way south once ranged in eastern or northern Canada, they could have then migrated westward to be isolated perhaps for uncounted generations in the country centered by Pend d'Oreille Lake, with its ample supply of fish, game, camas and huckleberries, only going forth again to the prairies in fairly recent times, as the Salish crowded them from the west. Such a theory could only be authenticated by archeological evidence. Chief Paul's heretical insistence that the Kutenais "woke up at Tobacco Plains" [19] may have been partly band pride; what

---

rock. (See illustration, page 138.) As pointed out by another interested resident of the area, Glenn Frisbie of Troy, "It seems logical to assume such a heavy object was cached at some central meeting point." Frisbie also remarks that "Symbolic objects or emblems were used in the Sun Dance and other ceremonies." (*Western News,* Libby, Montana, Aug. 7, 1969). At the locality of this find, near the junction of the Yaak and Kootenai rivers, according to Young, he also found about thirty grooved hammers, along with a scraper and what appears to be a crude stone head. This suggests a village site, and may or may not have any connection with any ancient treks to Pend d'Oreille Lake. It also suggests that the Indian village or camp supposedly buried by a rock slide at nearby Bull Lake, may have been of this band or group. L. Caspar Berray, homesteader below Bull Lake in the 1880s, remembered meeting an Indian running along the trail away from the lake, who told him that there were evil spirits in the mountain across the lake (to the west), who had caused the death of his tribesmen. Berray related that somewhat later, during an apparent slight earthquake, a further section of the cliffs west of the lake disappeared with a roar.

[19] Turney-High, *Kutenai,* 18.

he was also supporting, however, was the *western* origin of the tribe. He said that Tunaha used to come *back* into the Trench (to Michel's Prairie) for the traditional tobacco sowing ceremonies. In this case it might be that the Sun River Tunaha once used the Spotted Bear tobacco garden, which would be directly over the Divide for them.

If as Chief Eneas Abraham says, "Tunaha blood is in all Kutenais," the Tunahas may be the truly ancestral people; and they can be imagined as having resided long ago in northern Idaho. It is interesting to remember that Boas thought the word Tunaha, or Ktunaha, referring to the Plains Kutenais of late prehistoric times, and admittedly the name applied to them by Athabascan or Algonkian neighbors, might mean "The People who Walked down a Valley," or "The People who Came out of the Woods," or "Those Going out of the Mountains."[20] The idea that the term Kutenai, shortened from Ktunaha, meant in Athabascan "Water People" is not out of tune with the idea that the Tunaha came to the Plains out of the valley, woods or mountains. Chamberlain as well as Barbeau said that the mountain spirit was especially featured in Kutenai myths and legends.

[20] Teit, *Salishan Tribes,* 297 fn. 4; 302 fn. 22; 306 fn. 30. The writer must confess that Dr. Malouf does not consider these speculations significant. It is hoped that new evidence will be unearthed to determine whether or not they represent more than a romantic notion.

Freemen

INDEPENDENCE

A Flathead or Kutenai man could do pretty much as he pleased as long as his activities didn't interfere with tribal strength and safety. In most matters he found that his personal well-being required the same behavior as the well-being of the group, though in the tense times before a buffalo surround or a clash with the enemy, the hot-headed young men – especially after they were mounted on equally excitable horses – could not always be kept in hand.

Superstitions and traditions were hard to oppose individually, as they are anywhere and at any time. Yet even a man who balked at becoming a hunter-warrior and chose a womanish role in tribal life, was evidently tolerated with as much understanding as we give to sissies or squares in our modern American society. Non-conformists usually acted, or said they acted, upon the advice of their guardian spirits; the public attitude toward them was compounded of respect for individualities and respect for the spirits. All this would not mean that variant personalities were never criticized nor ridiculed.

The Kutenais might in known times be more Prairies than they were Mountainaires, yet on the whole they lived even more informally than the Flatheads did, probably because the bands were small, and because food getting in the mountainous part of their range was so much a matter of each man for himself. "Democracy" and "individualism" probably had no precisely equivalent indicators in the Flathead and Kutenai vocabularies, but they were down-to-earth realities for the tribespeople.

CHIEFTAINSHIP

The head chief among the Flatheads had unquestioned power, but he traditionally knew enough not to test it by behaving ignobly as an individual. The son or grandson of a chief usually succeeded him if worthy. Turney-High says the Flathead chieftainship, typically Plateau, was "stable and rather dynastic," and that there was no way to depose an unpopular leader. But according to Teit, "seldom did a member of the same [Flathead] family hold a chieftainship for over three generations." Ray corroborates the informality of chiefly succession among both the Flatheads and the Kutenais. On the whole, neither heredity nor wealth prevailed against a candidate with a spectacular record of public service.

Of six Upper Flathead chiefs listed by Teit, two were unrelated to their predecessors; one of these, Standing Grizzly Bear (Paul or Big Face), was "more than half Pend d'Oreille and Kalispel in blood," while his successor Victor was said to have been partly of Tunaha descent. The Pend d'Oreille chief Alexander of the time of the Stevens Treaty had both Tunaha and Snake blood. De Smet mentioned a Kalispel chief of Nez Perce blood. Descent of the Tobacco Plains or head Kutenai chieftainship, according to Gravelle, "was from father to son or through daughter to her son;

two women were involved in the last eight generations."
Of Columbia Lake chiefs named by informants, most
but not all were in direct blood line; the same was true
of Lower Kutenai chiefs. Reservation chiefs in the
Flathead Valley included the Flathead chief Arlee
who was part Nez Perce, and the Kutenai chief Eneas
who was part Iroquois.

No single chief of these peoples wielded autocratic
power. The head chief of the Flatheads had immense
prestige and his decisions were seldom questioned, but
he invariably consulted his sub-chiefs and leading warriors on matters of import; among the sub-chiefs were
the band chief, the hunting and berrying chief, the
scouting chief and the battle chief.

Each Kutenai band had its own head chief who
acknowledged little or no allegiance in historic times
to the head chief of the Big Village on Tobacco Plains.[1]
The Upper Kutenais, who were nearer the Great Plains
than the Lower Kutenais and in horse-and-gun years
often had to fight the Piegans, found themselves considering their war chief as their head chief; in more
peaceful intervals, however, the camp or guide chief
exerted the most authority.

The people listened to their chief not alone from fear
of discipline (by the chief in person, by his delegate or
by the public); they were inclined to heed his wishes
because they admired his personal qualities and achievements, and felt that he was a real father to them; and
because like the modern monarchs of Britain, he sym-
bolized the group as a whole. His proud "I" used in

---

[1] Present-day Lower Kutenais have told Paul Flinn that there never was an
all-tribe chief. "They say that when a chief visited the grounds of another
chief the visiting chief was just another Indian with no special privileges"
(Flinn, correspondence).

speaking of his tribe to outsiders was the voice of all his people. "The great chief Michelle of the Kootenais," wrote Father De Smet in the mid-nineteenth century, "recalls in the midst of his tribe the life and virtues of ancient patriarchs. His life is that of a good and tender father, surrounded by a numerous family of docile and affectionate children."[2] (The Kutenais were here of course on their best behavior!)

All these forces for loyalty were in most cases fused and exalted by the chief's spiritual power. Besides being an active leader chosen or approved by the people, he was a shaman, or at least a man of strong medicine, chosen by the spirits through their revelations to him.

"The Flathead village arrived here today," wrote one frontiersman, "The chief rode out into a spot that suited him and dismounting stuck his spear into the ground and sat down beside it. The squaws came up, unsaddled his horse and led it away, while others undid their packs and set up the lodge over his head. Some style about that fellow!"[3]

DEMOCRACY

Weighty or critical affairs were considered by the tribal council, where sat the chiefs and the important warriors. "Elections" and "council decisions" were not formal processes of law; the members conferred until they had come to a concensus *feeling* – actually the firmest basis for enforcement. Everyone usually knew without official debate which young men were deserving of a voice in tribal business, and which had earned advancement. Coup-counting records were the critical consideration, but qualities of day-by-day dependability

---

[2] De Smet, *Letters and Sketches,* 172.   [3] Stuart, *op. cit.,* I, p. 246.

and charm had their influence. "After all the speeches were made, everybody all at once came to the same opinion," a Spokan informant told Curtis. De Smet said of the Flatheads, "I know not of any government where so much personal Liberty is united with greater subordination and devotedness."[4] The chief was as much a persuader as an administrator. All this did not mean that there were never any disagreements, minority opinions nor political conniving.

The Flathead chief had a whip (a switch before the whip was adapted from the Whites) which he wielded, sometimes after consultation with the council, when such a means was thought necessary.[5] In most cases the chastising chief actually felt that "this hurts me more than it hurts you," for his people were both his children and the members of his tribe, which existed perilously and could afford neither disrupting influences nor very much deadwood. Except for occasional incorrigibles, the punished persons dreaded the public shame and the chief's tongue-lashing as much as the unsparing lash of the whip.

From the time they could understand anything at all, Kutenai children were instructed and lectured day and night by their parents, elder relatives and the village leaders, very often through story and legend, on how to act for their own good and the good of the group. This instruction, and the very real force of public opinion, particularly the merciless ridicule of offenders which

---

[4] De Smet, *Letters and Sketches,* 172.

[5] Curtis heard that whipping and tying in a "jail house" were introduced among the Flatheads by Spokane Garry, after his training in Canada, and that the Kutenais learned whipping from the Catholic missionaries. Palladino, however, asserts that whipping was not introduced by the missionaries (*Indian and White in the Northwest,* 79).

recalls the Blackfeet, commonly kept citizens in line. The Kutenais interviewed by Turney-High claimed that their chiefs never needed to resort to whipping like the Flatheads; they said that his lectures, sarcasm and appeal to group opinion were control enough. Nevertheless, Father De Smet reported the practice of flogging seducers among the Kutenais. Early settlers at Bonners Ferry observed the Kutenais at that time using the whip for tribal discipline. "One young mother when huckleberrying stood her baby in its cradleboard against a tree, and a bear killed it; the Tribe sentenced her to lashing; it was a pitiful sight. When Isadore was chief, he got drunk on one occasion and sentenced himself to five lashes from each woman in the family." Rose Causton also relates the latter incident, adding that "this cured the chief of drinking." [6]

In both these tribes, family trouble was left largely to the family to manage, and this was even more true of violence and murder than of lesser offenses. A murderer usually had to make his get-away as best he could if he expected to escape full vengeance by relatives of his victim. On occasion, the relatives could be satisfied by heavy fines of property arranged by the chief. This attitude toward murder and intra-tribal violence was rather typical also of the Plains. Flathead chiefs insisted that if a life had to be taken for a life, the retaliation must be immediate.[7] This prevented feuds and false justifications for violent acts in the future. Since the guilty person could go into hiding for a time, even initial revenge was often forestalled.

[6] Leslie, interview; Causton, *op. cit.,* Feb. 16.

[7] Turney-High, *Flatheads,* 46.

Contact

THE PUSH FROM THE EAST

Native resentments, frustrations and fears bred of White occupation in the eastern part of the continent were being progressively communicated westward during the eighteenth century. The once rather mild Sioux became the traditionally terrible enemies of the Assiniboines and Chippewas whom they forced deeper into the Plains. Farther north, Cree and Blackfeet groups were ranging nearer and nearer to the Rockies.

Certainly what bison the Flatheads and Kutenais could take in the north would not have left any other peoples hungry in that early era. But when these small and unaggressive but dauntless tribes dashed to the hunt on horses, before some other northern tribes were mounted, the Plains people who were still on foot, or partially on foot, naturally raised their voices in battle song and set forth on their raids. Among the raiders were the Blackfeet – who "developed hatreds for which there is no accounting – "[1] including the Piegans, Bloods and Blackfeet proper; it was the Piegans who most often clashed with the mountain people.

In the early years of the nineteenth century, the Kutenais were "generally in amity with the Piegans, who are their nearest neighbors on the east. They have

[1] Greenbie, Sidney, *Furs to Furrows,* 286.

fought many desperate battles, but the Piegans now consider it their own interest to be at peace with them, to be better enabled to encounter the Flatheads, from whom they plunder the vast number of horses they possess. Wild horses are also common, and frequently seen in large gangs."[2] A peace with the Piegans, however, was always a dubious state, and this one would not last.

If the Plains people fought in spite of the abundance of bison, so the Kutenais and Flatheads continued to cross the mountains seasonally to hunt and fight, even though they could probably have subsisted on food obtained west of the divide. Fish and vegetable food could have been used in greater quantities; but of course a man cannot fish from the back of a horse; nor was it so easy to hunt deer, elk, moose and caribou on horseback, for they often ranged in rough or heavily-timbered country. The mountain men became like the typical Shoshone man, who, Lewis and Clark reported, considered himself degraded if he was compelled to walk a little distance.

The core of tribal vitality and discipline among the Flatheads and Kutenais was the brave young man, sustained by faith in his guardian spirit. Contact with the other Plains hunters magnified the importance of fighting in comparison with mere game-getting, though the source of the complex was already there. Upper Kutenai informants said there were usually lots of caribou around, but they were too easy to kill; the young men needed the constant threat of the Piegans and the seasonal defiance of the buffalo hunts to keep them strong, alert, unselfish and patriotic.

---

2 Coues, *op. cit.*, 707.

APPROACH OF WHITE-SKINNED STRANGERS

In 1793 the North West Company's Alexander Mackenzie crossed the continent via Peace River and the uppermost reaches of the Rocky Mountain Trench, and reached the Pacific some distance above the mouth of the Fraser River (later so-named), which he considered to be the Columbia, and thus marked it upon his map of the new Northwest. Also marked upon Mackenzie's map was a rumored tribe of Indians called the Cattanahawes. Three years later – 1796 – Duncan McGillivray of the same company noted in his journal at Fort George on the North Saskatchewan River that a tribe from the southwest (the Kutenais), "had determined to force their way to his trading post or die in the attempt. These Indians had already made several efforts to visit this fort in order to trade but each time had been prevented from doing so, with loss, by their enemies the Plains tribes. This time, it was reported, they hoped to obtain immunity from attack by trading horses in return for a guarantee of safe passage." There is no evidence that the Kutenais were ever able to reach the fort.[3]

Four years later a third North West trader, David Thompson the great map-maker, met a party of Kutenais at Red Bear River near the Divide. He persuaded them to go with the traders to Rocky Mountain House where he obtained from them in trade the skins of 110 beaver, ten bear, two wolverine and five fisher. This western outpost of the company was located on the Saskatchewan River between today's Alberta cities of Edmonton and Calgary. Since the Kutenais already had

---

[3] Graham, *op. cit.*, 3.

traps when Thompson met them, they must have had earlier contact with White traders at Rocky Mountain House (as T. C. Elliott believed), or with mixed-blood free trappers who had already crossed the Rockies; or they had been trading traps and skins with the Black-feet. At any rate, the Kutenais were the first tribe of the mountains and Plateau to deal directly with a White trader.

"When [the Kutenais] first saw the White men they thought they were the inhabitants of the sun or from the spiritual world. This idea was soon confirmed as one of the White men took up a gun, a stick as they thought, and pointing towards a flock of geese flying overhead, the stick spoke and two geese fell to the ground to the great amazement of the natives, at the power of the White man, thinking the power came from his body and going through the stick killed the two geese." [4]

FLATHEAD CONTACTS

It was in the upper Bitterroot Valley, probably just below Lost Trail Pass, that the Flatheads in 1805 met Captains Meriwether Lewis and William Clark and party, likely the first White men they had ever seen.

The Shoshones, among whom Lewis and Clark had been camping just before they met the Flatheads, had Spanish trade goods, and scolded because the Spaniards would not let them have guns. A very early North West Company trader named M'Tavish is said to have met a Spokan woman "who told him that she had seen men ploughing the earth, and that she had also seen churches, which she made him understand by imitating the sound of a bell and the action of pulling a bell-rope, and [she]

---

[4] McLaughlin, "The Upper and Lower Kootenai."

made the sign of the cross." She may have been a Snake
prisoner traded to Spaniards of the Southwest or more
likely of the San Francisco Bay area.[5] Such an experience would have been rare among the Flathead peoples.
Palladino and other early historians believed that Flatheads had been contacted by the Verendryes who penetrated the Missouri country from French Canada in
the eighteenth century. Present-day students do not feel
that the Verendryes ever saw the Rocky Mountains.
There was an old legend among the Flatheads that their
hunters after a long absence east of the mountains
brought back tales of white-skinned, blue-eyed men;
possibly these were the Verendryes.

Captains Lewis and Clark had just crossed the east-
west extent of Louisiana, the land recently purchased
from France by the United States through the visionary
strategy of her second president, Thomas Jefferson.
Now, on Jefferson's orders, they were pressing on
toward the elusive Columbia – that river which had
nonchalantly continued to mind her own considerable
business during the century and more when White men
of varied nationalities were jockying up toward her
from all directions. None was successful until the
American Captain Robert Gray – and the Englishman
George Vancouver right after him – sailed into the
river's mouth from the sea in 1788. Even after that, the
world's great geographers were hopefully speculating
that the Columbia originated in some lake of the Great
Plains; those Rocky Mountains where the Kutenais
and Flatheads had their homes might be prairie or
swamp for all the White world knew until close to 1800.

---

[5] Franchere, *Voyage to the Northwest Coast,* 271. More surprising, if true,
is the account of a parchment roll written by Spanish explorers or traders, for
delivery at Fort George by the Kutenais who turned up there in 1796.

Gun Men

EXPEDITION FROM THE UNITED STATES

As Lewis and Clark with their party of some thirty men approached the Rockies in the summer of 1805, they were told that once over the Divide they would find themselves among the Flatheaded people. They were well into the mountains, and anxious to find horses to replace their canoes, before they met near the Three Forks of the Missouri a small party of the northern Shoshones, who in early September led them toward the Bitterroot Valley. In the mountains, probably at Lost Trail Pass, they encountered their first Flatheads, who, Clark wrote, "threw white robes over our shoulders and smoked in the pipes of peace. We encamped with them and found them friendly. The chief harangued until late at night, smoked in our pipe and appeared satisfied. I was the first white man who ever were on the waters of this river." [1]

Clark's journal of the next day, September 5, noted that "we assembled the chiefs and warriors and spoke to them with much difficulty as what we said had to pass through several languages before it got into theirs, which is a gurgling kind of language spoken much through the throat. These people possess elegant horses," numbering five hundred head. [2] Lewis was given some

---

[1] Thwaites, *Journals of Lewis and Clark,* III, pp. 52, 53.   [2] *Ibid.,* 53.

boiled roots to eat, which he found unpleasantly bitter, though the Indians seemed to relish them. Coues believed that from this incident the Bitterroot Mountains received their name.

Flathead guides assisted the expedition down the Lolo Fork or Travelers Rest, for the crossing westward at Lolo Pass. Lewis and Clark did not know at this point whether the Continental Divide was east or west of the Bitterroot Valley, but at any rate they had found that its inhabitants were not flat-headed, and that they called themselves the Salish. Lewis and Clark first wrote of the tribe as the *Oat-lash-shoots,* a band of the *Tush-she-pah* nation – Shoshone terms, the latter evidently including the Pend d'Oreilles and Kalispels, and the Spokans and Colvilles.

After the expedition had wintered at the mouth of the Columbia, among the non-Salish Chinooks and other native peoples, Lewis could describe in his journals how these Coast Indians flattened the foreheads of their babies by strapping their heads tightly to the cradleboards, using stiff pads in front, or a special compressor lowered from above, to give the skull a peaked effect.

Some of the interior Salishan people, as the Coeur d'Alenes, told Teit that they used to strap the heads of infants to the cradleboards, and that some mothers may have tightened the straps enough to cause a slight flattening of the forehead. But the so-called Flatheads of the mountains, though even the French voyageurs called them the *Têtes plattes,* vehemently denied that they ever practiced head-flattening. How could we have done this, they asked, when our cradleboards before the mothers had horses to ride were too short for

binding babies' heads to? Dr. Malouf says this Flathead claim is borne out by the normal frontal bones of
all the skulls excavated in the old Flathead range. The
term "flat-headed" may have referred to the gesture
used to indicate this tribe in the sign-language – the
placing of both palms to the sides of the temples; or it
was most likely a generic name used by the Plains Indians when speaking of any people west of the Rockies.[3]

After a dark, cold, wet, wind-whipped winter at the
mouth of the Columbia, lightened only by the satisfaction of actually setting foot on Cape Disappointment,
and by the glimmering realization of what this journey
and claim might mean to their young nation, Lewis and
Clark in the spring returned up the Columbia to the
Rockies. Not content with their already epic achievements, in the Bitterroot Valley they divided their
forces in order to look over even more of the country.
Clark and his crew started off south toward the Yellowstone. Lewis, after his Nez Perce guide had turned
back with dire warnings to look out for Blackfeet,
traversed the mountains further north to the headwaters
of the Dearborn River by the defile since known as
Lewis and Clark Pass, and crossed to Sun River which
he followed to the Missouri. Later while exploring the
Marias River, the party met the region's inevitable
hazard, eight belligerent Blackfeet, who camped over-

[3] The English artist Paul Kane in 1847 painted a portrait of a peaked-
headed Indian woman holding a baby who lies in a carrier with attached
apparatus for artificially flattening its skull. Copies have frequently been published as the portrait of a "Flathead Woman," often misunderstood to refer
to the Montana Flatheads. Original portrait is at Royal Museum, Ontario. For
a print, see La Farge, *op. cit.,* 184. Actually, the artist's model was a woman
of the Cowlitz tribe, Salishan neighbors of the Chinooks on the Coast. According to the La Farge caption, this custom of head flattening existed among
the Mayas of Mexico and Central America!

night with them. The White men set up a night watch;
but with what some historians regard as surprising
neglect, only one man at a time kept his eyes open, and
the dawn guard for a moment laid down his gun. Like
panthers, the Blackfeet in a breath had all four guns
and were off. In the pursuit and struggle that followed,
and the fight to save their horses, one Blackfeet was
knifed to death, one fatally shot by Lewis; the others
fled, and the White men raced to the Missouri in fear
of reprisal by a larger party of the natives. Here the
expedition members were reunited for the safe return
trip eastward with their boatloads of maps, geographical records and scientific information.

It took more than ten months for the news of the
unfortunate killing of the two Blackfeet – or at least
for the news of schemed revenge – to travel the several
hundred miles north to the Piegans around Rocky
Mountain House on the Saskatchewan, where David
Thompson was trying to get off for his second attempt
to cross the mountains into Kutenai country.

THOMPSON TACKLES THE DIVIDE

The initial attempt had been made in 1801, the year
after Thompson met his first Kutenais on the east slope
of the mountains. The Northwester was acting on
orders from his superiors in the company, who directed
him to go over the Rockies and locate the headwaters
of the Columbia. But this 1801 endeavor to get over
the Divide was dogged by disaster. The leader first
chosen became ill; the Kutenai guide engaged was
murdered within a mile of Rocky Mountain House,
presumably by the Blackfeet Piegans, who were grimly
determined that no arms should leak through to their

good trade customers and usual enemies, the Kutenais and Flatheads; the substitute guide was a craven Cree. Thompson himself at last took charge of the party. Bogs, fallen timber, high water and rough rock blocked their way; the Cree and his wife got drunk on a small amount of weak rum administered in hopes of putting a little heart into him; sobered, he still could not find a way across the Divide. Turning back to the fort, Thompson concluded that at least he had learned a thing or two: not to employ an eastern guide, not to use horses to the passes unless a trail were first cleared, not to delay in the spring until the melting snows had become flood waters.[4] But he was unable to try again until 1807. Meanwhile Lewis and Clark had left their terse record at the mouth of the Columbia, declaring, in effect: we got here first by land, as our Captain Gray got here first by sea. But Great Britain did not thereupon politely quit.

David Thompson, of Welch parentage, had come to America as a Hudson's Bay Company apprentice in 1784, when he was fourteen years of age. During the next twelve years of assignments about Canada, he learned a great deal of astronomy and surveying, and absorbed all the practical know-how of trapping trail, trading post and Indian camp. Young, practical-minded, hardened and adventurous, he left Hudson's Bay in 1797 for that brash new competitor of the august concern – North West Company. Thompson's compact but broad-shouldered figure, his shock of straight black hair and his large features centered by an oddly short nose, added up to no air of elegance; but his keen gaze and direct manner, and his remarkable fund of

4 Howay, "David Thompson's First Attempt to Cross the Rockies."

hard-earned knowledge, proffered with no show of egotism, inspired respect among the lowly and the mighty. In 1799, at Isle de la Crosse Lake, he married Charlotte Small, the fourteen-year-old daughter of the Scots trader Peter Small and his second wife, a Cree or Chippewa woman. It was at Rocky Mountain House in 1801 that their first child was born – a son, on June 10, four days after Thompson had set out with his small party to try to storm the ramparts of the Rockies.[5]

Before Thompson faced up once more to the fearsome challenge and allure of the Divide, in 1807, he had become a partner in the company. He was determined to take Charlotte and their three children with him this trip. The trouble was, the Piegans were keeping them all practically prisoners at Rocky Mountain House. The Piegan war chief, Kootanae Appee, an old friend of Thompson's, was peaceably inclined, but most of his men were bold and suspicious.

Now it was that "the murder of two Peagan Indians by Captain Lewis of the United States drew the Peagans to the Missouri to revenge their deaths." Apparently a tribal call to arms had been issued. Perhaps because of promises and predictions voiced by members of the expedition or because of premonitions in their bones, they realized that more White men would follow the Lewis and Clark trail. Already that fabulous business man John Jacob Astor and his ruthless rival Manuel Lisa, were mustering their forces, intent on western beaver hides.

Thompson, thanking God for this favor, acted fast.

---

[5] Only a woman story-teller would wonder at this point whether Thompson's failure to complete this hazardous mission, a failure which critically affected Great Britain's claim to Oregon, may have been subtlely conditioned by his desire to return to his wife!

He sent Finan McDonald, a frightening red-haired, red-bearded giant of a Scotsman, his second in command for the current expedition, off upriver May 10 with five men and a boat, to Kootenay Plain. Big Finan, who was probably related to other McDonalds of the fur trade, had been a Northwester since 1804. Thompson with two men, ten horses and supplies, went overland to join them. He seldom mentioned his wife and children in his business-like journals nor in his *Narrative,* written late in life; but as the journey began they were doubtless with him rather than with McDonald.

By relaying, back-tracking and juggling his men, horses, canoes and inadequate supplies, through snow and icy flood waters, Thompson in late June collected his party on the divide at what was later to be known as Howse Pass. Before setting off down Blaeberry Creek (since so named), he knelt to pray: "May God in his mercy give me to see where these waters flow into the ocean, and return in safety." [6]

"Rarely could even the trace of a Road [trail] be discerned," Thompson wrote. "It is clearly seen that Jaco Finlay with the men engaged last summer to clear the Portage Road had done a mere nothing. The Road was nowhere cleared any more than just to permit Jaco and his family to squeeze through it with their light baggage." [7]

June was on its last day when the group reached the mouth of the creek on the Columbia, near present-day Golden, B.C. Thompson noted that this river flowed north. Knowing that the mouth of the Columbia was

---

[6] Coues, *op. cit.,* 692 fn. 9.
[7] Elliott, "Discovery of the Source of the Columbia," 34.

much to the south, and believing that Alexander Mackenzie had discovered the Columbia further north and flowing south, he called this river the "Kootanae" for the Indians whose land it traversed. He was impressed by the "romantic bold scenery" of the Trench here; but everyone was hungry, there was no game in sight, the trout refused to bite, and when he located the canoes Jaco Finlay had made for them according to plan, they were in such poor shape that new ones had to be built.

J. FINLAY

Chronicled also as Jacco, Jaccot, Jocko or Jacquot, Jacques Raphael Finlay was the son of James Finlay, an early Scotch emigrant in the fur trade, and an Indian woman, probably a Chippewa with some French blood. James Finlay was the first independent English trader to reach the Saskatchewan; he wintered in 1768-69 far up this western river at "Finlay's House." The Montreal fur trading firm which he helped organize was at one time a business threat to the North West Company, but both his part-Indian son Jacques and the two sons of his Montreal wife, supposedly a White woman, became Northwesters. The James Finlay for whom the Finlay River was named, after he reached it via Peace River in 1797, was probably Jocko's half-brother, his father's namesake.

Born adventurous by the blood of both his father and his mother, Jocko had only a little schooling before he joined North West Company. In spite of Thompson's opinion of him at this point, Finlay had been a valued employee for many years before 1807. In 1794, when in charge of the company's post on Bow River, he and a lone companion fought off a party of "Missouri

Indians," probably Blackfeet, and rescued the single
man not dead of arrows and bullets in the nearby Hudson's Bay fort. For this service he was rated in company
reports as "a man of courage." Restless of restraint, and
ineligible for top career status in Montreal, Finlay was
inclined to branch off on his own when trading with the
Indians, so as to make a middleman's extra profit.
Nevertheless the company was paying him well for his
services in 1800. He is thought to have had three wives,
the first a Cree, the third a Spokan; many of his large
family of sons and daughters were blue-eyed.[8]

KOOTENAY HOUSE

Foraging south up the Columbia River that first June
west of the Divide, Thompson killed nine swans for his
hungry and discouraged crew. They met a few Kutenais, but the natives either had no food or would not
trade. Most of the Kutenais here had probably already
met men who were at least part White. Among the
mountain men mentioned by Thompson was Jacques
Hoole (Houle), said to have been in the West since
1743 as a free trader dealing with Hudson's Bay; he
was nearly ninety years old in 1807, a tough old white-
haired adventurer respected by French and Indian
alike. Kutenais in the Libby, Montana, area told old-
timers that the first White man in their country – at an
approximate date which figures before Thompson's
time – was known as Whitehead from his white hair;
he may well have been Père Hoole. This first-known
White resident of the Flathead-Kutenai country was

---

8 See Meyers, "Jacques Raphael Finlay," 163; C. White, *David Thompson's
Journals Relating to Montana,* 227; Oakshott, "Koo-Koo Sint, Red Hair and
Jocko."

killed by Blackfeet about 1814 – a tragically appro-
priate ending to his long career of war and hardship
and trouble.[9]

Thompson, who enjoyed spending a whole day on
some mountain eminence mapping and sketching the
view, was keen to explore this great virgin valley. But
hunger threatened to sour the adventure. Only a few
Kutenais were about; they said they expected their Old
Chief with all the rest of their countrymen, in company
with a large band of Flatheads, in about ten days.
(These were likely Pend d'Oreille Flatheads.) Meanwhile the Northwester came upon the river now named
Kootenay, and called it the McGillivray for William
McGillivray, a founder of the North West Company,
who had a number of relatives also in the company. He
sometimes referred to this stream as the Flat-bow, after
the Lower Kutenais.

Two more Kutenai men came up the river; one of
them was a brother to the Old Chief. They allowed
Thompson and his party a little food, discovering probably with some surprise that these supposedly superior
beings were no great shakes as rustlers. They advised
the White men that their fish weirs would not hold in
the strong current, which proved true. In awe over the
axes that made this wooden shelter possible, the natives
nevertheless shook their heads gravely over the choice
of a building site,

> . . . as it was so far from water, and open to the insults of
> the Peagans, who seldom fail every year to make a visit and steal
> horses. I had long thought this myself but was at a loss where to
> find a better place. After much looking about, at last found an
> elegant spot on the Kootanae River, in a commanding site, the

9 See Cox, *op. cit.*, 171-72.

water quite near, a rapid river in front, with a small, nearly surrounding lake, that precluded all approach but on one side, and
pines enough at hand; these advantages decided me to change the
place of my building.[10]

Here near the mouth of today's Toby Creek, on the
west side of Lower Columbia Lake, Thompson in the
latter part of July commenced building a sixteen-by-
sixteen foot building for Kootenay House. To add to
the general satisfaction with the new location, one of
the hunters killed a bear. "This gave us life again,"
Thompson wrote. A Kutenai messenger arrived with
news of the death of the Old Chief's son, and Thompson
was impressed by the people's grief. The young Kutenai had been killed by the Piegans, often called by
Thompson the Meadow (Prairie) Indians. The Flatheads, Thompson was told, had "all pitched away to a
military post of the Americans, except ten who were
still with the Old Chief." These Americans, the Kutenais said, had arrived to set up a post at the confluence
of the two southernmost branches of the Columbia, and
several of Lewis and Clark's men were with them. This
was evidently Jeremy Pinch's outfit, possibly sent out by
Manuel Lisa of the Missouri Fur Company, who had
engaged several of Lewis and Clark's men, including
John Coulter. "The establishment of the Americans
will give a new turn to our so-long delayed settling of
the country," Thompson noted.[11] But the suppositional
Pinch post, whether it was at the mouth of the Clearwater or the Snake, or somewhere on the Clark Fork or

---

[10] Elliott, "Discovery of Source of the Columbia," 41.

[11] Thompson received from the Indians that season two letters purportedly
from American traders, telling him how he ought to behave in country
claimed by the United States. None of the several names signed to these letters
appears on the records of American fur companies.

Spokane, was not continued. Fort Manuel, Lisa's own location in the fall of this year, was not on the Columbia side of the Divide, but at the Three Forks of the Missouri; it too was only temporary. If we discount the possible temporary quarters of Pinch, Kootenay House was the first fur post in the Columbia basin.

During August Thompson's small crew worked on the house and a hall for the men. The main building was strongly stockaded on three sides, the fourth resting on the steep bank of the river. On the 29th, the men speared five salmon, the largest weighing twenty-six pounds. Into this peaceful and picturesque wilderness valley now intruded the plague of its people in the persons of forty Piegan warriors who seemed determined to lay seige to the fort. They sent word that they would have the rare red scalp of Finan McDonald. Thompson's position was well fortified and the party had ten guns, but they had very little food. At night two brass kettles were let down the steep bank for water. This grim situation was suddenly resolved when a large party of Kutenai hunters appeared; the brave Piegans forgot Thompson and hurried home. When they got there, however, they faced tribal censure for their retreat. The civil chief ordered Kootanae Appee to lead a party of three hundred men across the mountains to crush the Whites and Kutenais before they became too strongly established.

Appee accepted the charge reluctantly. "I shall lead the battle according to the will of the tribe," he said, or so reads Thompson's account; "but we cannot smoke to the Great Spirit with success, as we usually do, for it is now about ten winters since we made peace with them [the Kutenais]." Kootanae Appee, as Thompson described him, was six feet and six inches tall – a little taller even than Big Finan – "appearing to be of bone and sinew with no more flesh than absolutely necessary," a skilled diplomatist, but of mild and kindly manner, father of twenty-two sons and four daughters by his five Piegan wives.[12] Thompson does not say whether his name meant that he had Kutenai blood. Appee is believed to mean "leading man."

When Kootanae Appee approached the little outpost with his force, he sent two emissaries to ask Thompson to withdraw from the territory of the Kutenais and Flatheads. Thompson carefully allowed the couple to observe the strength of the fortifications, and pointed out what they could themselves lose by antagonizing the Northwesters, upon whom they depended for guns, tobacco and goods for their own trading activities. He then played his ace: he proffered a bribe of trade tobacco, which the natives could seldom resist. The messengers returned to Appee with the offer, and he and his leading warriors in council decided to accept. The whole expedition, they reminded each other, was the idea of the foolish civil chief, Sakatow, "who himself never goes to war," and had stayed safely across the mountains in the home camp.

After the appeased Piegans had departed, Finan McDonald could make the trip to Rocky Mountain House for supplies. When he returned, the folks at Kootenay House had settled in for the winter. More of the Kutenais were learning the use of traps. In March of 1808 James McMillan took a load of furs over the mountains by dog sled, and returned. He was to be much among the Kutenais during the next few years.

---

12 Thompson, *Narrative,* 346, 381.

TOBACCO PLAINS – AND BEYOND [13]

On April 20, 1808, a stormy morning, Thompson said good-bye to his family, left Finan McDonald in charge, and headed south from Kootenay House by canoe with four men. They traveled up-lake to Flat Bow River Portage (Canal Flat) and crossed to the Kootenay (present name). Making good time in the rapids, they passed before evening the point where half a century later the United States-Canadian boundary line would be designated across the river, and came into lower Tobacco Plains.

The wide gravel flats and the sandy hills and terraces left here by glaciers and glacial lakes were softened everywhere by bunchgrass and spring flowers, prompting Thompson to call them "beautiful meadows." Because the Indians spoke so much of growing tobacco here, he and his men called the spot Tobacco Meadows. Two days later, entering the most hazardous water yet encountered, they "shot it on the left; it may be run close on the right with less danger." [14] Just below the canyon, at the mouth of Fisher River, which Thompson called Rock River, a branch trail led south to the head of the Fisher and down Thompson River to the Clark Fork. Thompson was to explore this route later; for now he continued down the Kootenai.

He must have been told of the famous *Gran Portage,* which he approached two days later; but he was unpre-

---

[13] This section abstracted largely from C. White, *op. cit.,* beginning with the journal entry for April 20, 1808.

[14] This by the description was the canyon above Jennings where ninety years later steamboats would be facing the same problems, sometimes with disastrous results, until the largest of the rocks in mid-channel were removed by blasting (See Olga Johnson, *Story of the Tobacco Plains Country,* chapter on "Steamboating").

pared for its magnitude. Landing on the south bank above the terraces and thundering of Kootenai Falls, he sent men ahead to reconnoiter. The returned scouts vehemently declared the way

> impracticable on this side from the mountain coming down perpendicular to the river.[15] I immediately with three men crossed the river and we spent three hours in examining the north side. We found it very bad indeed, but practicable with much care and precaution. I sent the men to bring all over to this side. We began carrying at quarter after three with light loads and went about a mile over terrible road along side of a mountain nearly perpendicular, walking wholly among the fragment of broken rocks that had rolled from the summit, to a brook [Falls Creek, known also as Koot Creek]. Each trip took one and a half hours.

On the morning of May 8, as the Kootenai widened and calmed, they approached the river's northward turn, the site of today's Bonners Ferry, Idaho, and found ten lodges of Upper and Lower Kutenais. As soon as they landed, Thompson smoked with the leaders. The chief of the Flat Bows, Ugly Head, "so named from his hair curling," made the big speech, explaining that they were without furs or food, because they had been engaged in a war with the Piegans. Thompson managed to keep the ceremonies as brief as possible, and got one of the Indians to set off directly to the Old Chief who was camped with some of the Flatheads.[16]

---

[15] The Great Northern Railroad now passes here.

[16] This is a rare mention of Lower Kutenais being involved in conflict with the Plains people.

There was a Flathead "Old Chief" in those times, but this was the Kutenai Old Chief, probably Chief Whitehead; one of Chief Whitehead's sons, Chief Moiese, is said to have "helped David Thompson;" he may have worked with his father before he himself became chief. Andrew Mishel of St. Mary's Reserve, and Jim Eneas of Windermere, list apparently in common the four earliest remembered chiefs of their people: Standing Elk, Blanket Yoke Neck (Stand Mettler?), Sitting Near Rock (Go Sit Down Bank – who thus escaped

From this natural stopping place, one way led north down the river to Kootenay Lake, and from there west, north or east by trails not so much used. Another continued west along Deep Creek and over the low pass to Pend d'Oreille Lake; this was Thompson's "Great Road to the Flatheads," or "Lake Indian Portage." At Pend d'Oreille Lake, the Great Road joined the north-south travel route along the Clark Fork.

Thompson in 1808 went only as far as Kootenay Lake, where he arrived May 14, after spending about a week at Bonners Ferry. As related in his *Narrative,* he was surveying the valley, trading and talking with the Indians, laying plans for the future. It seems as though he must have here been told that the outlet of Kootenay Lake reached the Big River by a comparatively short, but rough and unnavigable, course, and that he must have sensed that the Big River was the Columbia. He probably felt that the company would not want him to neglect his trading for a doubtful exploration of the Columbia at this time. His crew was small; extremely high water delayed his business with the Indians. On May 19, having retraced his route to Bonners Ferry and

Blackfeet arrows in an engagement), and Leo Whitehead, son of the last named. Mishel's wife traces her genealogy all the way back to Standing Elk, well before the opening of the 19th century. These informants and others claim that these chiefs were of Middle Kutenai stock (see herein page 297). Gravelle says the "super-man Chief Whitehead" was a Tunaha; this agrees with Curtis' claim that the Middle or Jennings Kutenais were Tunaha.

The earliest Kutenai chief known about by the late Kutenai leader, Mathias, at Flathead Lake, leader of Middle Kutenai stock, was Feather, who was said to have left the Upper Kutenai country to reside on a Kootenai River island near Bonners Ferry. (He could have been formerly a Tunaha.) His successor was Going Grizzly Bear, who also was searching for a new home site (Malouf and White, "Early Kutenai History"). Earliest Lower Kutenai chiefs, according to other informants, were Big Chief, succeeded by New Big Blanket, predecessor of Three Moons, the chief of 1828-1840 (Causton, *op. cit.*).

On the Flathead chiefs, see herein, page 292, fn. 7.

MICHELLE TEE-MO, NATIVE BONNERS FERRY KUTENAI
Still proud of his firearms, nearly a century after Thompson.
Photo courtesy of Edgar B. Stephenson.

MONUMENT AT THE SITE OF KOOTENAY HOUSE. ON THE BANK OF TOBY CREEK.
Photo courtesy of British Columbia Archives.

KOOTENAI FALLS DURING HIGH WATER
Discernable is the north bank trail – the route used by Thompson.
This trail has been maintained in later times by the Forest Service.
Photo by Winton Weydemeyer.

CABINET GORGE ON THE CLARK FORK OF THE COLUMBIA
Along the canoe route from Kullyspell House to Salish House.
Photo by Ross Hall.

A Downstream View of the Kootenai River Valley

On the flat in the left foreground, opposite the mouth of the Fisher River, and on various benches not far downstream, the *Akayenik* camped; and here winter fur posts were maintained by Hudson's Bay Company, and in 1810–12 also by the Northwest and Pacific Fur companies. Photo by Winton Weydemever.

beyond, he and his men switched from canoes to horses and took off northeast across country for Kootenay House.

The natives often traveled up the river by water, as well as down; whole flotillas of canoes used to carry visiting Upper Kutenais to Bonners Ferry and return, or visiting Lower Kutenais to Tobacco Plains or Columbia Lake and home again. But Thompson had found the down trip difficult enough; he chose to return by the overland route which led up the Moyie River, and past the site of today's Cranbrook, B.C. Ugly Head was their "manly, humane guide." None of his fellow tribesmen would take the job for they were afraid to go within reach of the Piegans. Streams were high, timber dense, rocks rough. Of the three hundred pounds of prime furs acquired from the Indians, sixty were lost at a river crossing. "On June 5th at 5:00 p.m.," Thompson wrote, "we had all crossed to McGillivray's Carrying Place to the source of the Columbia River." [17]

It was still June when Thompson and his family, with Finan McDonald and several of their men, left Kootenay House on the way eastward with the furs. Climbing up the rocky, wooded course of Blaeberry Creek, Thompson reported: "One of my horses nearly crushing my children to death from his load being badly put on, which I mistook for being vicious, I shot him on the spot and rescued my little ones." [18]

BRIEF MONTANA POST

From Kootenay House that fall (1808), Finan McDonald and two or three assistants were sent down the Kootenay to set up winter quarters for trading in the vicinity of Kootenai Falls. Unseasonal cold set in; even

---

[17] Thompson, *Narrative,* 390-94.   [18] Coues, *op. cit.,* 693 fn. 9.

Big Finan, whose feats of strength were traditional among the Flatheads for generations, was temporarily stymied when his canoe froze in the ice of the river. But he stubbornly returned to the upriver fort for horses, transferred his load, and continued his assignment. Further down, after crossing at the mouth of the Fisher (unless he traveled the north bank all the way – there were trails on both banks), he and his helpers built a crude log warehouse near the river, and passed the winter there in two "leather tents."

It is impossible to discover from Thompson's journals and *Narrative* exactly where Finan built this temporary fur collection post – the second or third in the area that later became Montana. Both Lisa's quarters and the possible Jeremy Pinch quarters of the previous year were equally makeshift, but they did antedate this one of Thompson's. McDonald's location has been indicated at various spots along the Kootenai from the mouth of the Fisher River to Bonners Ferry. The most probable site is somewhere near Libby, Montana. Going down this way the next summer, on the day after passing the mouth of the Fisher and the day before reaching Kootenai Falls, Thompson chronicles: "went down to the hangard of last winter." "Hangard" was a term often used by the Northwesters to indicate a shed or shelter.[19] The Bonners Ferry station marked on one of Thompson's maps (undated) may refer to the trail camp made there in 1808, or to a later camp set up for trading. On August 29 the party arrived at the Great Road of the Flatheads, where, Thompson said, "we

---

[19] C. White, *op. cit.*, journal entry for Aug. 26, 1809. Old-timers of the Libby area claim that the discovery of old guns, axes and hearth remnants at a site between the mouths of Bobtail Creek and Quartz Creek south of Libby, indicate that a very early trading post was located here.

must procure horses to take up to the Flat Head River [Clark Fork, also called by Thompson the Saleesh] where we hope, please Heaven to pass a good quiet winter." [20]

KULLYSPELL HOUSE AND SALEESH HOUSE

On the Clark Fork Thompson selected a site near present East Hope, Idaho, on a peninsula near the mouth of the Clark Fork River, and ordered the building of Kullyspell House. Here at Indian Meadows tribesmen collected each fall to fish, hunt and gather berries.[21] It required four or five men to lift the heavy logs for the seven-foot walls. The roof was of cedar poles chinked with clay and long grass. For living and trading quarters, uprights were set into the rocky ground, and horizontal logs dovetailed into place in grooved slots, making a tight, weatherproof dwelling.[22]

This was Kullyspell House, the first permanent structure with roof and fireplace in the present Pacific Northwest of the United States. Lisa's man Andrew Henry did not set up his temporary post on Henry's Fork of the Snake River until 1810; John Jacob Astor's Pacific Fur Company post at the mouth of the Columbia was not founded until 1811. Most of the trading at Kullyspell House that fall was with the Pointed Heart or Coeur d'Alene Indians.

That man Thompson! Already this year he had twice crossed the Continental Divide; he had canoed up the upper Columbia and some hundred and fifty miles

[20] *Ibid.,* Aug. 28, 1809.

[21] See Jim Parsons, "David Thompson," in *Spokesman-Review* (Spokane, Wash.), Oct. 12, 1958. Parsons gives the location as east of Sheepherder's Point, just opposite Memaloose Island. (Cf. Coues, *op. cit.,* 673.)

[22] Peltier, "Thompson Built Trading Post."

down the Kootenay; had crossed to Pend d'Oreille Lake through unknown country, and built a substantial trading post; in late October he had explored the lower Pend d'Oreille River as a possible way to the Columbia, but had been turned back by the falls. Now, although it was getting late in the season, and he had promised himself an easy winter, he set off up the Clark Fork, crossed overland to the mouth of the Fisher River on the Kootenai, circled back down his previous course to the new Kullyspell House – and re-ascended the Clark Fork to build a second post before the year was out!

The new post, Thompson wrote, "is in a small bay of the river, close to us is a spur of hills which come on to the river in a cliff sixty feet high. The Saleesh when hard-pressed always made for the rock, as a natural defense."[23] Eventually this post was to have seven buildings of hewed logs. In early November, according to Thompson's account: "We fasted, except for a chance goose or duck among us, until the 14th, when Jaco, a fine half-breed, arrived and relieved us. From him we traded 28 beaver tails, 40 pounds bear meat and 30 pounds of dried meat, and now, thank God, enjoyed a good meal."[24] This was Flathead House or "Saleesh House."

The new location was especially convenient to the Middle Kutenais. Ugly Head of the Flat Bows also came up the river to hunt for the White men; with him were two companions, Deceitful Dog and Large Kidney. Other Kutenais came and went during December,

---

[23] Thompson, *Narrative*, 542. This location according to Coues was "between Eddy and Belknap stations, close to the mouth of Ashley Creek" (*op. cit.*, 674 fn. 17).   [24] Thompson, *Narrative*, 417.

bringing a few beaver plews, and assuring Thompson that many of their tribesmen were "working beaver." But on the fourth of January, 1810, Thompson's man Beauleau came into the post and reported that the Indians had no beaver and that they were all gone to buffalo.

The Kutenais and Flatheads were learning readily enough the tricks of trapping. The beaver, weasel, muskrat, all these small residents of their land, they had been accustomed to watch for fun as often as they killed them for meat and fur; and their legendary personifications were as familiar as their present selves. Now, when a small animal was sighted, it was apt to look to the native woodsman less like a fellow creature, and more like a price; in the gleam of eye and fur could be seen the gleam of a musket barrel or a brass kettle or a hank of beads; on the forest air the trapper could almost sniff the potent fragrance of the White man's tobacco, waiting in ropes to be clipped off for his pipe. Even bears, who already seemed a little less awesome, because of their vulnerability to bullets, the Indians began to regard not so much as reverenced fellow beings, but more as wearers of hides for which the traders might give good exchange.

Bucking the elements was nothing new to the native mountaineers. But the traders seemed to expect that a man should set his traps and walk his line on schedule, even when he was over-hungry, or over-fed. Suppose he and his companions were not in the mood for hiking that day; suppose they were in the mood for horse-racing or gambling. Suppose there was company in camp, a new wife in the lodge, or a little son ill unto death. How could they bring the furs to the post at a specific time if these intruders set dates that coincided with a traditional tribal festival, or a regular seasonal buffalo hunt? To rush and worry, always to be frustrating the natural flow of a man's impulses, to break the nerve of tradition leading back down the years through all the ancestors, wounded the spirit or soul — "that substance with which a man is lined." [25] What ailed the spirits of these White fur men that they insisted on overworking, quarreling, cheating, suffering such hardships and losing their lives in the mountains, to possess animal skins which, apparently, neither they nor their people needed to keep them warm? Yet what was the chance of staying alive at all in this terrible, fascinating modern time, without firearms? And the women. Once they had set eyes on those trade goods, they seemed to lose their usual good sense. Often they seemed to lose their hearts as well, if White men so much as beckoned.

GUNS TELL

In February the Kutenais were around again for trading. One day Thompson obtained a hundred beaver skins from five men, a lad and two women. Going up-river during March, he traded further with Kutenais, Kalispels, and Flatheads (Pend d'Oreilles were not commonly distinguished by Thompson) in their camps, taking in buffalo tongues, dried meat, a horse, deer hides, as well as skins; passing out tobacco, powder and balls, a limited number of muskets, shirts, blankets and trinkets. On "the Onion plains" (Camas Prairie) he found Jacko Finlay camped. He was back at the "Saleesh camp" near present-day Dixon, when word

---

[25] Turney-High, *Flatheads,* 27.

arrived that a party of Meadow Indians had been seen
to the north of the Saleesh (Flathead) Lake.

Rumors multiplied, and tension spread in the village
like a contagion: "everything was now suspended."
Tracks of mounted warriors had also been seen near by,
but the informants

could say nothing of the number as they did not dare to examine
too much the tracks of the enemies, [who had] entered the
woods. A young man went off to alarm the Kutenais to the eastward and my men. About noon Jaco Finlay arrived; having seen
a band of people of suspicious appearance, he gave information. . .

About one hundred men now mounted their horses, proud of
their guns and iron-headed arrows to battle with the enemy; they
soon returned, having found these cavalry to be the Kutenais
under their Old Chief, who had quitted hunting the Bison, and
were returning to their own country. But [it] gave me, as well
as the old men, great pleasure in seeing the alacrity with which
they went to meet the enemy, when before [before they were
armed with guns] their whole thoughts and exertions were to get
away from, and not to meet, their enemies.[26]

[26] Thompson, *op. cit.,* 420.

Scalps

THE FRIENDLY TIMES

Before horses and guns, peace was pretty much the order of the seasons in the country of the Kutenais and the Flatheads – if the testimony given Teit by these and the surrounding tribes is accurate. The Flatheads mentioned only occasional quarrels with the Snakes, when some blood was shed. The Kutenais according to later testimony, oftener knew the peace broken. Chief Paul of Tobacco Plains told Turney-High: "My enemies all surround me. When one throws food to a dog all the other dogs will fight him. I have always had fine food in a fine country and all the dogs wanted it." It is natural that as their people appeared less important in the sweep of White settlement, the elders were inclined to magnify the ancient combats as a signal of tribal importance and strength. Jim Eneas of Windermere, reminiscing in 1960, said, "It was fight, fight, fight. Fight with Shuswap and Okanogan too, not just with Piegan."

Teit was told that the Crees had once been the enemies of the Kutenais, but that the two tribes made peace at least three hundred years ago. Gravelle says the Coeur d'Alenes used to harass the Lower Kutenais in particular, but that the two groups became friends before horse days. The Upper Pend d'Oreilles always seem to have been amicable neighbors with both the

Kutenais and the Southern Flatheads. Members of the Kalispel branch are said to have been more pugnacious, some quarrels resulting.

Several involved stories are told of warfare on a small scale between Flatheads and Lower Kutenais, terminating finally in a peace through intermarriage.[1] Gravelle, who speaks for the Upper Kutenais, says these people and the Flatheads "were enemies for a while, but that didn't last. The Flatheads won the engagement once, the Kutenais twice – after the Kutenais got their power back."[2] Curtis was told that Bad Road, one of eight young Tunaha who had fled across the mountains on account of the epidemic, married a Kutenai woman, and the others married Flatheads. While staying with his brothers and the Flatheads, Bad Road went with them on a war party to steal horses from the Kutenais (as apparently was their habit), and was the sole survivor among the raiders, because he called out to the Kutenais in their own language, asking mercy. After this he lived with his wife's people for a year, "then returned to the Flatheads to prepare them for a messenger of peace. He was soon followed by a Kutenai bringing tobacco from his chief, and its acceptance instituted a peace that was never interrupted."[3]

A STORY OF CIVIL WAR

There is a legendary account of intra-tribal warfare among the Kutenais, after a warrior of the Lower Kutenais ventured to violate the subterranean cave at White Swan Lake, which was sacred to the Upper

[1] Causton, *op. cit.*, May 25 to June 22, inclusive. The final peace-making was an elaborate process.　　　　　　　[2] See herein p. 208.

[3] Curtis, *op. cit.*, VII, p. 119.

Kutenais. The people camping at the lake, at first unaware of the presence of the intruder, were mystified by the disappearance of food and other property from the camp, and by the regular midnight call of a loon sounding across the water. A son of their chief, suspecting that the loon call was faked, watched at night and followed the nervy young Canoe Indian back into the cave after he had raided the camp on shore. When the outraged local youth saw the thief at ease on a ledge with his loot, he struck him, cut off his head, and took the trophy back to the display in the village.

When the Lower Kutenai boy failed to return to Kootenay Lake, his father (or according to one version, a young warrior son of Chief Suckermouth) came east for a visit, and quietly listened until he heard someone talking of what had happened. He then took leave of his hosts and started for home, but circled stealthily back, and watched until he saw the chief's son start up the mountain toward the little source lake where he was in the habit of meditating upon the island.

At dark on one of the peaks of the west arose a signal fire and immediately there came a premonition of disaster. For this among the Kootenays was a signal that an enemy had been killed. The Upper Kootenays ascended the mountain to the isle in the mountain-top lake and were horrified to find the headless body of their chief's son. They flew to arms, descended in fury upon the Lower Kootenays and waged a bitter battle. Though the struggle continued for three days, neither side could claim the victory, and the remnants of the invaders returned to their home little appeased in vengeance.

Time healed the scars of enmity and after several generations the two branches of the tribe were reconciled.[4]

---

[4] Iverson, *op. cit.,* 8; also told by Dennis and Gravelle, interview.

THE ARM THAT FLASHES FIRE

These occasional clashes among the region's residents left most of the days of the year free for making a living, and for living. By the time the White men knew the Kutenais and Flatheads, their relentless wars with the Blackfeet had made the older conflicts seem unimportant.

Guardian spirits were needed for peace time living as well as for warfare, but it is not clear whether the Kutenais or the Flatheads practiced coup counting before the wars with Plains tribes began — as they habitually did afterwards. There was no conscription of soldiery; public opinion and the honors accorded a coup counter roused sufficient volunteers for most military expeditions. For immediate need, the leaders of a proposed war party went about camp stopping before each lodge to beat upon a piece of stretched hide (later, canvas) until one or more of the able men within emerged to join up. Then the prospective combatants stripped, painted, and danced themselves into the necessary fierce enthusiasm, to the sound of drumming and high-pitched cries of approval from the women watchers. On the actual eve of battle, the music was more mournful.

Honors accorded Kutenai men, say Lower Kutenai informants, were celebrated at "drummings," of which there were four kinds: the hide drumming to recruit a war party, known among the Flatheads later as the Canvas Dance; the war drumming before a battle; the scalp drumming or victory drumming; and the Sun Dance drumming. It was said that only one of the Lower Kutenai men, Chief Three Moons, was ever accorded all four drummings, as a leader on four such occasions. Taken captive as a boy by a tribe to the southwest, Three Moons according to legend made his way home when a young man, led Kutenai warriors on a successful expedition of revenge, and followed this by many other victories in battle.[5]

To these natives, the introduction of shooting arms was a revolution as sharply defined as that of the first atom bomb explosions in our own day. David Thompson was told by a very old Flathead man how when he was a youth he "made a heavy war club, with which he felt himself confident of victory." The Flathead warriors then "formed a very large party against the Peegans, and hoped for success, when for the first time their enemies had two guns, and every shot killed a man. 'We could not stand this, and thought they all had bad spirits with [them], we all fled and hid ourselves in the mountains. Constant war parties now harassed us, destroyed the Men, Women and Children of our camps and took away our horses and mules, for we had no defense.' "[6]

When the Pend d'Oreilles first got some guns, they attacked the still gunless Coeur d'Alenes and started a little war in which the Southern Flatheads had a small part. It was these Southern Flatheads who led in the peacemaking, at a large council attended also by Spokans, Kalispels, Colvilles and Kutenais.[7] The Flatheads were located closer to the Blackfeet than most of the others, and probably already realized that the Plateau folk had better stick together.

The Blackfeet, having guns and needing horses, at first fought the mounted Mountainaires on foot. Even after the Prairies had good war horses, they usually

---

[5] Causton, *op. cit.*, Feb. 2. [6] Thompson, *Narrative*, 436.
[7] Teit, *Salishan Tribes*, 123.

fought on foot if they were in mountain territory; they
weren't used to fast riding in rough and timbered country. Thompson said that the mountain Indians, accustomed to firing at deer at a distance, were much better
shots than the Plainsmen, who were used to shooting
buffalo at close range.

It was the distance a bullet could travel, and its
penetration power, that counted. As for firing speed,
bows and arrows were still superior to the early muskets,
and were much used in warfare until the middle of the
nineteenth century.

CAMPAIGN ON THE FISHER

According to Kutenai tradition, the first "war" between the Blackfeet and the Middle Kutenais or
"Neek," sometime in the eighteenth century, was a
running campaign of successive skirmishes. The tale as
here told is pieced together from the Bert Davis story
of "The Campaign on the Fisher," and supplementary
information collected by Harold Odle who lived as
neighbor to contemporary Flathead Lake Kutenais. It
seems that the Neek were camped at the mouth of Bad
Rock Canyon when they were attacked by a large party
of Blackfeet, part of whom, at least, were mounted
(perhaps on horses stolen earlier from Upper Kutenais
or Flatheads on the Plains). It is not clear whether the
Middle Kutenais had horses of their own at this time.

Instead of going into hiding, the Kutenais circled
behind the Blackfeet and cut off their retreat. By
further maneuvering, they fought the raiders down
through Flathead Valley, edging toward the familiar
cover of their own Pleasant Valley country. But the
Blackfeet broke away southward and camped east of

Flathead Lake – a fatal blunder, for here some Flatheads (these would most likely be Pend d'Oreilles)
came to the aid of the Kutenais. Together, with grim
glee, the allies drove the Blackfeet horses into Flathead
Lake where they were forced to take refuge on Wild
Horse Island. (Father De Smet in 1841 noted that there
were many wild horses on the island.)

The Blackfeet, retreating northward on foot, were
nudged over Haskell Pass into Pleasant Valley (modern place names), and so onto a battle ground of the
Neeks' own choosing, where the Plainsmen must have
felt uneasy if not bewildered among the swampy
meadows, heavy timber, steep mountains and frequent
streams and lakes of the Thompson-Fisher country.

At the first battle station definitely indicated by
Davis' Kutenai informants, one of the heaviest engagements of the war took place near Dahl Lake when the
Blackfeet took a stand on a small butte. This station
was known to all future Kutenais as *Kalasmee,* the
name of the Neek chief who lost his life here.[8] "This

---

[8] Cf. "Kalasmi, named after a Kutenai man," in T. White, "Kutenai Place
Names." Stations listed by Davis (see map, page 14) are as follows: 1. *Kalasmee.* 2. *Neltope* – Antelope. 3. *Ya Kok mo In Ke* – Where they trapped the
fish that lived in the lake. 4. *Ak Ka No Mook,* Little clay banks. 5. *Kill Ko
Ka Ki* – Footbridge. 6. *Qu No Go* (or *Gho*) *Nook* – Top Creek (creek orig-
inating on a summit). 7. *Mook Wook* – Red willow. 8. *Ya Ka Kank Su Ka
Ki* – Flute rest (where they found the flute discarded by fleeing enemies).
9. *Ya Ka Kan Llam Ki* – Where the enemy's skull was dug up (by later Kutenai historians). 10. *Koom Ne Nee* – Sleeping place (enemy scouts caught
sleeping here were killed). 11. *Ya Ka Wis Ki Lok Po Com Ki* – Where the
root was floating on the water (root still attached to a tree). 12. *Yo Ka Kok
Me Nooki* (see text). 13. *Ah Kin Kom Lasin Nitok* – Big Circle (probably
refers to course of the rivers). 14. *Ya Ka Wis Ko Ka Lak Kanee Yom Ki* –
Where they used to soak up the rawhide buckets. 15. *Thk x(Gho) en nee tse
la lut* – Where the three flat places come together (joining creek valleys).
16. *Kik Qsuk Noo Ko* – Where the creek hits the lake (Loon Lake a number
of centuries ago evidently reached up to this point). 17. *Ky Ya Ka Nan Lin*

chief must have been much loved and respected by his people," Davis writes, "This death seems to have sealed the doom not only of this particular enemy party, but of any Blackfeet whom the Neek could get their hands on from this time forth." Davis continued:

Before the Blackfeet quite reached the Kootenai River, toward which they were literally herded by the Neek, they may have realized that they were getting into a trap. The head village of the Neek – *Ay Kaye Neek* – was on a bench across the Kootenai not far down river from the mouth of the Fisher. At any rate, the desperate invaders managed to elude the Neek warriors and to turn back by the way they had come. Near the mouth of Schrieber Creek is the station *Ya Ka Kok Me Nooki,* "Where the Rocks were Found Standing up in a Circle." [9] Mr. Zangros explained that the rocks had been stood up as breastworks. Evidently the Blackfeet were surrounded here. The survivors finally arrived by a bewildered route at Crystal Lake, and here at *Ya Kak No Kim Lam Me Lak Nam Ki,* "Where Many Skulls Were Found," the last big battle of the campaign was fought. Of the Blackfeet survivors, one was killed at *Ya Kil Nam Naan xe Nee Yom Ki,* "Where the Fish Were too Small." It seems that a certain very big enemy still wasn't filled up when

Klo Kts – Where they used double lodge poles (probably because pole trees here were small, or because of the weight of deep snow in this area.)   18. *Ya Ka Kis Sin Ka Woki* – Where they found two stakes standing up (no explanation.)   19. *Ya Kil al Ka Nu Kan Ki Nee Yom Ki* – Foot crossing.   20. See text.   21. See text.   22. *Ki Yuk x a Kim Lut* – Where the two mountains link together.   23. *Kuk Tsuk Nook Na Na* – The narrow lake. (?), not precisely located but said to be a point at the head of Boiling Springs Creek where two of the enemy were killed.   24. *Ya Kil Kal Ka Ki* – Human carcasses were found here.   25. *Ya Ka Kis Ka Ki,* Where two human carcasses were found (antedating the campaign under description. This was positively said to be the oldest station in the range, suggesting to Davis that the Middle Kutenais passed here en route to their home village on the Kootenai – number 27. See herein p. 146).   26. *Ki Mon Nok No Meen Na* – End of a small ridge.   27. *"Ah Kiye Neek* – translation refers to the human thigh. A high bench north of Kootenai River opposite Jennings. My informants stated that the Neek tribe lived at this place."

[9] Cf. *Yakakmoinki,* supposedly at Island Lake: T. White, "Kutenai Place Names."

his fellow-warriors finished their breakfast here on Elliot Creek;
he stayed to catch more fish – and was overtaken by the Neek,
who were crowding on the trail of their victims. At an unnamed
station near the head of Boiling Spring Creek, this war of ex-
termination ended when the last two Blackfeet were killed.

Odle's story, however, has a different conclusion
(which perhaps belongs to a different campaign). He
was told that the final engagement of the war took place
on Tobacco Plains, as the Blackfeet survivors who had
fled up the Kootenai were about to escape along the
Grave Creek Trail to South Kootenay Pass; and that
a stone monument once marked the spot, eight miles
from Eureka near the mouth of Grave Creek Canyon,
where the last of the raiders were slain. The battle
monument at this site is spoken of by early settlers.

The Kutenais and Flatheads may have felt that this
catastrophe for the invaders would discourage any further depredations. But there were plenty more Blackfeet men where those first ones came from, and most of
them were eager warriors. From now on, they would
have to be reckoned with not only on the Plains when
the Mountainaires hunted there several times a year,
but also almost anywhere in the Trench. Plains raiders
even on occasion attacked some of the Kalispels as far
west as Pend d'Oreille Lake.

The favorite passes used by the Mountain and
Plateau folk when they went east after buffalo became
favorite passes for the Piegans or other Blackfeet when
they came west after horses, scalps and captives. To
avoid bloody meetings, more difficult passes came into
use, until the Divide ranges were netted with trails.
Because the Indians in prehistoric times had no good
axes, their early trails often ran through high and rocky
country that was free of heavy timber. In the woods,

when blazed trails became blocked by blow-down or the wreckage left by snowslides, the natives simply cleared the way with fire. If the fire went wild and destroyed a few million trees, the Indians knew that the burn would soon grow up to grass and small brush, which made good grazing and browsing for deer and elk, and in later times for horses.[10]

WAR IN EARNEST

In the summer of 1810, a few months after the false alarm near Camas Prairie, the Flatheads "formed a camp of about 150 men," Thompson reported, to hunt on the Plains, for the bison bulls were getting fat, and the Flatheads now had about twenty guns, "with which they thought themselves a fair match for the Peegan." Thompson approved the expedition, partly because he wanted to obtain a supply of dried meat for Kullyspell House and Saleesh House. He sent with the natives Mr. Finan McDonald, Michel Bordeaux and Baptiste Bouche with ammunition and tobacco to encourage them.

They crossed the mountains by a wide defile of easy passage, eastward of Saleesh Lake. The Peegan were accustomed to watch this pass and it had been unused for many years. [It is difficult to infer which pass is here referred to.] [But] the case is now different, and they are determined to hunt boldly and try a battle with them. [Thompson's account continues from the report he had later of the events.] They were entering on the grounds, when the scouts came riding at full speed, calling out, "The Enemy is on us!" Instantly down went the tents and tent poles, which, with the baggage, formed a rude rampart; this was barely done, when a steady charge of cavalry came on them, but the horses did not break through the rampart, part of pointed poles.

10 B. Davis, "Notes on Indian Trails."

Each party discharged their arrows, which only wounded a few; none fell. A second and third charge was made; but in a weak manner; the battle was now to be to the infantry.

The Saleesh took possession of slightly rising ground about half a mile in front of their tents and lay quiet on the defensive. The Peegans, about 170 men, formed a rude line about 400 yards from them and from time to time through the day sent parties forward to dare them to battle; these would often approach to within sixty to eighty yards, insulting them as old women, and dancing in a frantic manner, now springing from the ground as high as they could, then close to the ground, now to the right, and to the left, in all postures, their war coats of leather hanging loose before them, their guns, or bows and arrows, or a lance, in their hands. Such was their wild activity, they were an uncertain mark to fire at.

The three [white] men had several shots discharged at them, but the violent gestures [of the Piegans] prevented a steady aim in return. The three men were all good shots, and as I have noticed the Indians allow no neutrals, they had to fight in their own defense. Mr. McDonald fired five shots, killed two men and wounded one.[11]

RED HAIR THE WARRIOR

"M'Donald was to be seen in every direction," Ross Cox wrote of what was apparently this battle, "in the hottest of the fire, cheering and animating his friends; and they at length succeeded in driving the Black-feet to take shelter in a thick cluster of trees, from whence they kept up a constant and galling fire on the Flat-heads, by which a few were killed and several wounded."[12] In this mood, six feet four inches tall and broad-shouldered, his eyes blazing from amidst a wild

[11] Thompson, *Narrative*, 425.

[12] Cox, *op. cit.*, 167. Cox places this engagement in 1812, but Cox was not always accurate. Note Alexander Henry's description of what seems to have been the same battle (Coues, *op. cit.*, 713).

bush of red hair and beard, Big Finan must have been a fearful figure, yet he could not inspire the Salish to a bold attack upon the woods. Too long had they feared the Piegans and their guns; longer still had they regarded warfare as a means of counting coup as best a man could without taking needless risks; once a warrior had shed blood, his vows for the current expedition were released. Thompson related:

> The evening ended the battle. On the part of the Peegan, seven killed and 13 wounded, on the part of the Saleesh, five killed and nine wounded. Each party took care of their dead and wounded; no scalps were taken, which the Peegan accounted a disgrace to them; the Saleesh set no pride on taking scalps. This was the first time the Peegan were in a manner defeated, and they determined to wreak their vengeance on the white men who crossed the mountains and furnished arms and ammunition to their enemies.[13]

Finan McDonald, born in Aberdeenshire, Scotland, in 1782, migrated to the New World with his father Angus Ban McDonald, and family, about 1786. He evidently had little if any schooling. "To the gentleness of a lamb he united the courage of a lion," Cox said of him. Finan's wife was Margaret, the daughter of a Pend d'Oreille or Spokan chief, *Chin-chay-naywhey*. The date of the marriage is not recorded, but their first child, Eleanor, was born at the site of Bonners Ferry in June 1811. In the best warrior tradition of his wife's people, Red Hair, as the natives called him, may have won his woman by his remarkable conduct in that hunting and military expedition of 1810 – even though he carried no coup-stick.

---

[13] Thompson, *Narrative*, 425. Perhaps the Salish at this stage took no pride in bringing home scalps, but they soon acquired the practice.

CONFEDERATION

As they got more guns, the mountain tribes grew bolder. In a series of engagements on the Musselshell River, the Flatheads told Teit, about 170 Blackfeet were exterminated by Salish forces. The mountain warriors also successfully fought parties of Crows, Sioux, Cheyennes, and Assiniboines. When it was the Flatheads and Kutenais who told the war stories, they naturally emphasized (and doubtless exaggerated) enemy losses. Thompson in 1812 noted that the Flatheads themselves had forty tents of widows and old women to maintain. There is proof, however, that the Piegans were becoming disturbed by the success of the Salish. As early as 1812 they sent a delegation to suggest a friendly peace with the Flatheads.[14]

A month's time was set for counciling before a firm reply was to be given to the Prairies. Word of the council was sent to all the surrounding Plateau tribes, for since they had obtained horses, even the Nez Perces went across the mountains to hunt. "From every tribe several of the most respected men came, and were now assembled" near Salish House, Thompson wrote. "Of the Shawpatins only two came but they were remarkably fine looking fellows, they said their tribe was hunting near the enemy and could spare no more. We were invited to attend. With Michel the interpreter and two men we took our place."

After some smoking and an introductory speech by the Flathead chief, a Spokan rose, showed his scars, and spoke bitterly, saying that the proffered Peace was but a pretense to put them off their guard, so that they

---

[14] The account following is from the *Narrative*, 546 et al.

would go in small parties and be destroyed, even women and children, as in the past. "Who is there among us that believes them?" he asked. "Do as you please; I now sleep all night, but if you make peace I shall sleep in the day, and watch all night." Others spoke more calmly but in like distrust, seeming not to heed the Flathead leadership. The Flathead chief said in conclusion, "You all know we are the frontier tribe; the enemies must break through or elude us, before they attack you; it is our horses they steal and our men who are slain in battle more than any other people's." [15] He said the Flatheads were anxious to make peace, even though they did not fear the Plains warriors as they used to; but they wanted to know the attitude of the Piegan allies. They asked the White men's opinion.

Thompson replied, "You are all of the belief that the Great Spirit has made the ground to look green, and hates to see it red with the blood of men," but he did not advise making peace with the Piegans only; the mountain men lost their lives also to Bloods, Gros Ventres and Sarsis. He suggested that they reply by asserting their ancient rights to hunt the bison, which they would gladly do in peace if allowed.

The young men protested so docile a reply. It was

---

[15] "War seems to be the Piegan's sole delight. . . They are fickle and changeable; no confidence can be placed in them" (Coues, *op. cit.,* 726-7). In fairness to the Blackfeet, it should be remarked that the early descriptions of their character were written mostly by White men who had suffered at their hands. More disinterested observers, instead of calling these people treacherous, might have called them passionate, impulsive and astute; instead of calling them cruel and warlike, might have called them brave, spirited and proud; might even have added that they were handsome, virile and imaginative. The occasions on which the Blackfeet were the recipients, instead of the perpetrators, of cruel treatment, did not get much historical attention. Nor are the Blackfeet the only color of men who have taken advantage of minority groups within their own race.

decided to make a show of their new strength as allies. In midsummer the mounted warriors gathered from all over the mountains and adjacent plateau, three hundred fifty strong, and crossed the Plains resolved to go in defiance even beyond the borders of the old Flathead and Kutenai buffalo grounds. With the allies were several of the White men.

Upon what Thompson described, from the accounts he heard, as a grassy ridge in the open, the westerners met a like number of Piegans. Horses were used

> only for the purpose of keeping watch of the enemy. After a series of slight attacks, the Peegans formed a single line with the men about three feet apart, and advanced singing and dancing. When within about one hundred fifty yards of the enemy, the Peegan rushed forward. The Saleesh, having meanwhile brought their entire force into line on the low ridge, met the attack gallantly. Several on both sides were slain and many wounded. With difficulty the Peegans carried off their dead and wounded, and quitted the battlefield, accounting themselves defeated.

BLOODSHED FOR PAINT

Once the Blackfeet got into the mountains, they discovered valuable sources of paint to which the Flathead groups laid claim. The Blackfeet used more paint than the mountain people for decorating their bodies, tipis and trappings. Duncan McDonald said that constant combat was waged over the right to use the iron clay on a ridge back of East Helena, which yielded a vermillion paint. This, McDonald said, was too far west for the fiercest fighting, which was inspired by a chrome-yellow clay found at Wolf Creek, called by the Indians Yellowstone. The clay occurred in deep caves in country contested by the buffalo hunters; the battles for the paint were as furious as the battles for the buffalo. A mineral deposit yielding green coloring was found by the Flatheads on the south fork of the Blackfoot River near Lincoln Gulch. This was not much disputed, for the location was kept quiet. "I suppose it was some copper stain. They used a great deal of green in their painting." Black paint was obtained in Canada and may have had a petroleum content.[16] Favorite Kutenai paint sources were at Sinclair Canyon on the Upper Columbia, or the Paint Pots on the Vermilion River near Marble Canyon.

EXCESSES OF ENMITY

From the Plains warriors the Flatheads and Kutenais took over the bloodcurdling scalp dances, and the Flatheads at least learned to light fires under their staked prisoners. Cox wrote of a Christmas day on the Clark Fork in 1813:

There was, however, in the midst of our festivities, a great drawback from the pleasure we should have otherwise enjoyed. I allude to the unfortunate Black-feet who had been captured by the Flat-heads. Having been informed that they were about putting one of their prisoners to death, I went to their camp to witness the spectacle. The man was tied to a tree, after which they heated an old barrel of a gun until it became red hot, with which they burned him on the legs, thighs, neck, cheeks and belly. They then commenced cutting the flesh from about the nails, which they pulled out, and next separated the fingers from the hand joint by joint. During the performance of these cruelties the wretched captive never winced, and instead of suing for mercy, he added fresh stimulants to their barbarous ingenuity by the most irritating reproaches, part of which our interpreter translated as follows: "My heart is strong. – You do not hurt me. – You can't hurt me. – You are fools. – You do not know how to torture. – Try it again. – I don't feel any pain yet. – We

---

16 Stone, *Following Old Trails*, 156. See also Teit, *Salishan Tribes*, 340.

torture your relations a great deal better, because we make them cry out loud, like little children. – You are not brave: you have small hearts, and you are always afraid to fight." Then addressing one in particular, he . . . said, "I killed *your* brother, and I scalped your old fool of a father." The warrior to whom this was addressed instantly sprung at him, and separated the scalp from his head. He was then about plunging a knife in his heart, until he was told by the chief to desist. The raw skull, bloody socket [from which they had scooped out an eye], and mutilated nose, now presented an horrific appearance, but by no means changed his tone of defiance. "It was I," said he to the chief, "that made your wife a prisoner last fall; – we put out her eyes; – we tore out her tongue; – we treated her like a dog. Forty of our young warriors –."

The chieftain became incensed the moment his wife's name was mentioned: he seized his gun, and, before the last sentence was ended, a ball from it passed through the brave fellow's heart, and terminated his frightful sufferings. Shocking, however, as this dreadful exhibition was, it was far exceeded by the atrocious cruelties practised on the female prisoners; in which I am sorry to say, the Flat-head women assisted with more savage fury than the men. . . We remonstrated against the exercise of such horrible cruelties. They replied by saying the Black-feet treated their relations in the same manner; that it was the course adopted by all red warriors; and that they could not think of giving up the gratification of their revenge to the foolish and womanish feelings of white men. Shortly after this we observed a young female led forth, apparently not more than fourteen or fifteen years of age, . . . we renewed our remonstrances, but received nearly the same answer as before . . . we ordered our interpreter to acquaint them, that, highly as we valued their friendship, and much as we esteemed their furs, we would quit their country for ever unless they discontinued their unmanly and disgraceful cruelties to their prisoners. This had the desired effect, and the miserable captive was led back to her sorrowing group of friends. Our interference was nearly rendered ineffectual by the furious reproaches of the infernal old priestess who had been conducting her to the sacrifice.[17]

---

[17] Cox, *op. cit.*, 118-20.

POWDER AND SPIRIT

In spite of bullets and gunpowder, personal power was still of critical value in a fight – as Finan McDonold had demonstrated, although his power did not come of any native guardian spirit, and was not articulate in any private medicine song.

> Once a Piegan boy named Kishanehn was adopted by the Kutenais and raised to manhood in the Upper Kutenai country. During a period after the smoking of the peace pipe between the Kutenais and Piegans, the Piegan boy, now a man, rejoined his people and began turning against his benefactors. When groups of the two peoples met, he was tough and took everything away from them that he could. He had them buffaloed.
>
> Two Kutenai youths, aged fifteen or sixteen, one of them called Unknown Bear, got mad and said, "Next time we see this Kishanehn we are going to kill him!" When going to buffalo, they met him at this creek now called Kishanehn, which runs into the North Fork of the Flathead. As usual he was going to take everything away from the Kutenais. The two teenagers told him to lay off, and threatened him. Kishanehn laughed; he thought he was a superman, and the arrows would bounce off of him. But Unknown Bear shot him and killed him, and this was the start of Kutenai Power again. After that, Unknown Bear did so many brave things they couldn't help appointing him chief. He took very good care of his people. The Prairies were so scared of him they wouldn't bother the Kutenais any more.[18]

Even in the 1850s and later, however, the Kutenais were still to be fighting the Blackfeet, who all this time were the implacable enemies not only of the mountain tribes but of the White men, especially the "Bostons."

These tales of intertribal warfare overshadow equally

---

[18] Informants Dennis and Gravelle.

important goings-on of horse days – intertribal visiting
and trade and exchange of ideas. John Jacob Astor's
overland party bound for the Pacific in 1810-11, for
example, met in the heart of the Big Horn Mountains
"a small band of savages, who reconnoitered warily
from the rocks before they ventured to advance. They
proved to be a mixed party of Flatheads and Snakes.
The Flatheads are described as simple, honest and hospitable. The band of Shoshones and Flatheads was
bound on a visit to the Arapahoes, a tribe inhabiting
the banks of the Nebraska [Platte]." [19]

[19] Irving, *Astoria*, 373, 377.

Oregon

DISPUTED LAND

The Kutenais and the Flatheads, now living west of the Continental Divide except for forays or camping trips on the Plains, were residents of that vast and vaguely defined northern area between the Rockies and the Pacific, coming to be known by the early nineteenth century as Oregon. European and American powers were still maneuvering for rights on the Pacific Coast; the United States and her former mother country had agreed upon no American dividing line west of Lake of the Woods; Oregon was still a free-for-all between them. This foggy cold war implicated the natives from St. Louis to the Pacific.

In late spring of 1810, when David Thompson journeyed for the first time up the Kootenai River past the Gran Portage, with the winter's furs from Saleesh House, Kulyspell House and Bonners Ferry, he still held the Kutenai-Flathead country for North West Company, undisputed either by American traders or by his British rival, Hudson's Bay. In late summer, after delivering his furs to Canada, he turned again westward, leaving his family at Winnipeg House. English interests were concerned with Astor's advance toward the strategic mouth of the Columbia; pressure was apparently put upon Thompson to try to get there first.

After long delay due to the besieging of Rocky Mountain House by allied Blackfeet,[1] Thompson managed with an Iroquois guide to cross through Athabasca Pass by dogsled in mid-winter, the first known crossing here by a White man. This route was to become a main trail of the traders through the northern Rockies, because it was out of the way of the Blackfeet. As Thompson proceded, he found the snow a depth of from seven feet to unfathomable and the temperature sometimes far below zero; during warmer intervals, avalanches threatened; the wolverines destroyed precious supplies. When the little party at last reached the Columbia at its far northern bow, the exhausted and hungry men refused to go any further. Thompson was forced to spend the remainder of the winter in near starvation at the mouth of Canoe River, at what was thereafter known as Boat Encampment, where he wrote, "We are pygmies in such forests; what could we do with 2-pound axes?"[2] In the spring, he helped build a canoe of thin-split cedar boards; but what few men he had left (many had earlier deserted) could not be persuaded to set off with him down this unknown section of the Columbia into a possible further hell of rough flood waters, gameless lands and hostile natives. He was obliged to turn upriver to Kootenay House, from where with a small crew he crossed to the Kootenay River by Canal Flat and embarked once more upon this now familiar waterway, hoping to meet some of the men from the western posts, or a free trapper or two. Instead

---

[1] The Blackfeet were bellicose from successes against the Bostons, and resentful of Finan McDonald's fiery participation in the campaigns against them by the Flatheads and Kutenais. This was two years before they became desperate enough to ask for a peace parley with the mountain tribes, as recounted in the preceding chapter.   [2] Thompson, *Narrative*, 452.

they met two Kutenais who said they had left most of their people and all the freemen at Tobacco Plains, bound for the Saleesh country. "They tell me the Hudson's Bay are in [at] the Lake," Thompson noted.

Hudson's Bay had the previous year (1810) sent a man into the Trench to see how Thompson of North West was doing, and what the prospects were of setting up a profitable competing post in the area. Joseph Howse (or Jasper Hawes), "with nine servants," in the fall crossed by the pass that bears his name – and North West promptly sent McMillan in turn to shadow the Hudson's Bay men. Howse, according to his correspondence, called at Kootenay House, "carried into the Flat Bow (by Canal Flat to the Kootenay) – descended to the most Southly Bight [evidently the Fisher River], crossed [portage poil de Caster] to Flathead River (above ye Lake) where we built." [3]

Howse on this trip is thought to have built a temporary fur collection post on the north bank of the Kootenai about a mile below the later town of Jennings, which would be at or near the main village of the *Ay Kaye Neek,* or Middle Kutenais. The station could not have been continued, for after completing his house on the "Flathead," Howse accompanied an Indian hunting party to the eastern Plains, and left for the Saskatchewan in the spring convinced that the route he had followed was not practicable for trading. The site of the Howse House on the "Flathead" is placed by many historians near Kalispell on today's Flathead Lake, but it seems pretty certain that Howse's "Flathead River" was the Clark Fork, and and his "Flathead Lake" the

[3] Robertson, *Correspondence Book,* 222, letter of Howse to Simpson, Feb. 9, 1843.

Pend d'Oreille. Henry's journal records that McMillan of North West and his companion Nicholas Montour left Kullyspell House on "Flat Head Lake" December 12, 1810, "where Hudson's Bay Company are also settled."[4] Howse House was the first Hudson's Bay post west of the Rockies, but was not continued.

RACE TO THE PACIFIC

After leaving the river at the Kootenai end of the Saleesh Crossing Place, Thompson this time passed to the Clark Fork by way of the beautiful chain of waters that includes Loon, Crystal, Thompson and McGregor lakes. He found both Saleesh House and Kullyspell House deserted for the time, but arrived June first at a new post built the previous winter by Finan McDonald or Jocko Finlay or both – Spokane House, at the junction of the Little Spokane and Spokane rivers. From here, along a well-worn Indian trail, the explorer continued to Kettle Falls on the Columbia. "After praying the Almighty to protect and prosper us on our voyage to the Ocean, early on the third of July we embarked," he wrote. With him were five French Canadians, two Iroquois and two Columbia River Indians; a British flag waved hopefully above them, and they were prepared to post exploration notices at strategic stops.

The various Indians on the upper river were friendly

---

4 Coues, *op. cit.,* 671-72. Coues notes that Thompson at different times called today's Pend d'Oreille Lake: Flat Head Lake, Saleesh Lake and Kullyspell Lake. An 1867 map in a manuscript by A. C. Anderson (B.C. Archives) shows a trail branching west from the main Kootenai River trail, the branch marked "to Howse River to Howse House." The chief evidence for the location on today's Flathead Lake is the Arrowsmith map referred to in the parenthetical insertion of the Howse letter (by Howse's own hand?). This could easily have been an error, though it is possible that Howse on his way out in the spring stopped for a time also at Flathead Lake.

and anxious to trade. Thompson observed with interest their dancing and singing, their longhouses of rush mats, the dimunition of bison hide products and the increase of shell ornaments as they proceeded. Most of the Mid-Columbia Indians had never before seen White men, though Chief Yellepit of the Shahaptins had a Lewis and Clark medal to show. At the salmon fisheries near John Day River they heard the first news of White men below. The Lower Columbia Indians Thompson found beggarly, hostile, "very sensual," and without the dignity of the Plateau and Mountain tribesmen.[5]

The British party reached the mouth of the Columbia July 15 – four months too late. There on the south shore stood the buildings of Pacific Fur Company's Fort Astoria, begun after the arrival of the ship, the "Tonquin," in March. The Astor crew included quite a number of former employees of North West who had been enticed out of Canada. When Thompson went back up the river, traveling with him part way were Alexander Ross, David Stuart and others of these "Americans," bent on establishing trade.

After Stuart and Thompson and their parties left, the Astorians heard the news of the destruction of the "Tonquin," which had apparently been blown up by a wounded member of the crew after Vancouver Island Indians had massacred most of his shipmates. Morale at the isolated fort of Astoria, surrounded by the unpredictable Clatsop and Chinook Indians, was as low as the bottom of the well when surviving stragglers of Wilson P. Hunt's overland party, including former Northwester Donald McKenzie, arrived at the post.

[5] Thompson, *Narrative,* 472 et al.

At heart a geographer, Thompson at least was taking his pleasure in mapping the Columbia Valley.[6] Accompanied by Finan McDonald, he did not leave the river until he had explored it all the way up past the mouths of the Pend d'Oreille and the Kootenay rivers, through Arrow Lakes, and back to the scene of his last winter's travail at Boat Encampment. He had been from there to the source in the spring. So he was the first White man – if not the first man of any race – to canoe the Columbia's whole magnificent distance of mountain cascades and icy lakes, the sweeping giant-land of open hills and buttes and prairie benches far below, and then the tall green timber and ferny canyons that opened out onto the coastal flats. Along the whole course of the river, none of the native tribes except perhaps the Nez Perce were as friendly and dependable as the Kutenais and Flatheads of the source country.

TO FLATHEAD LAKE

That fall, after crossing the mountains and plains to bring back trade goods, Thompson returned to the Clark Fork and worked at repairing Salish House, often referred to as Flathead House or Fort Flathead. Kullyspell House, however, was soon abandoned in favor of the new location at Spokane House.

In the spring of 1812 Thompson made his controversial trip to "Saleesh Lake" in today's Flathead Valley. Coues stated that Thompson never saw today's Flathead Lake, but Thompson's own journals seem quite definitely to prove that he did. On February 29 he

---

6 Franchere of the Astorians noted (*op. cit.,* 122) that Thompson "traveled, I thought, more like a geographer than a fur-trader." Coues in his introduction (xxix) to the *Journals* of Alexander Henry said that "Business was Henry's religion, and science was Thompson's."

"Engaged a guide and two horses for a Journey. The men are, please Heaven, to see the Saleesh Lake and country around it." On the afternoon of the thirtieth, he and his men "alighted on top of a knoll commanding a very extensive view of the lake and the country far around. Sketched off the lake, etc. The Saleesh River bears from me eighty degrees south of West for six miles, then makes a curve to the westward and bends around to the Bitterroot Rivulet" (Little Bitterroot River).[7] Thompson's sketch and description fit the view from a knoll not far southeast of present-day Polson. It is unlikely that he was the first all-White man to see the lake, for McDonald and McMillan, at least, had traveled over much of the country here; Jacques Hoole had been in the country even earlier; perhaps Jeremy Pinch or other early American adventurers had been here too.

Later in the spring Thompson took the furs out through Athabasca Pass. At Winnipeg he rejoined his family, including five children as of March 11, and took them with him to Quebec, for he had orders from North West Company to begin work on a great map of western Canada (later so-called) and Oregon. He was never again to cross the Rockies.

BRITISH-AMERICAN FEUDING

To the concern of the Kutenais, Rocky Mountain House was soon abandoned because of the pestiferous Piegans, and Kootenay House was afterwards little used. Nicholas Montour, son of a White trader and his Indian wife, dealt with the Kutenais after Thompson

---

[7] C. White, *op. cit.,* March 1, 1812. The sketch mentioned is included in the published *Narrative.*

left, but he worked further down the river. He was evidently the first trader at the modest post of "Fort Kootenay," located at this time on the north river bank, probably opposite the mouth of the Fisher River. (Angus McDonald believed that an earlier location at Bonners Ferry was the first "Fort Kootenay.") The pushing Americans of Pacific Fur Company, who had sent Ross Cox and his companion Russell Farnham to compete with Finan McDonald in the vicinity of Salish House, in the winter of 1812-1813 sent Francis Pillet and six men to deal with the Kutenais. The newcomers pitched their tent near Montour's cabin, and here the British-American war for Oregon was fought in farcical miniature during the winter, climaxing in a pistol duel between the two leaders; one was hit in the coat collar, the other in a trousers leg; "the tailor speedily healed their wounds;" in the spring they parted as friends.[8] Both these parties brought in rich returns in plews.

That summer Alexander Ross and John Clarke had the gall to set up Fort Spokane right next door to Spokane House. The British and the Americans here preserved a jaunty social relationship, but each in the

---

8 Cox, *op. cit.,* 106. See also Ross, *Adventures of the First Settlers on the Columbia,* 213. Jacob Meyers located what he believed to be the site of these "forts," probably around 1920. (He was writing letters of inquiry about the posts to John Campbell in the mid-teens.) Highway construction workers about 1950 discovered at the site a rock inscribed: "Forts, 1810-1812. HBC 1810 – NWC PFC 1812. J. Meyers, locator." The "HBC" doubtless referred to Howse's supposed set-up here for Hudson's Bay Company. The spot where the marker was found is some little distance down-river from a spot where a rancher earlier plowed up a large hearth stone with chimney rubble, an ancient bootjack in the form of a nude woman, and several jugs of alcoholic beverage reported to have been still palatable and potent. The fields of this ranch can be seen in the Kootenai River view on p. 182. Fort Kootenay was to be variously located along this stretch of the river.

field used any and every means to get the furs first. Cox
was still with Clarke at Spokane House in the spring
of 1813, when word was received from the trader
among the Flatheads that he was out of goods, including that supreme necessity, tobacco, and in danger of
losing the Flatheads' furs to Finan McDonald of North
West. Mounting a locally famous racer named Le Bleu,
Cox made a seventy-two mile trip to the Clark Fork
with tobacco in record time, and secured the Flathead
trade.[9]

The Americans were doing all right for themselves.
Then to Spokane House and Fort Spokane – months
late – came word of the new war between Britain and
the United States. Going anxiously down to Astoria
with furs, the Pacific Fur field men found Duncan
McDougall about to sell out to North West, in fear of
British warships then on the way – or so he and his half-
starved but hard-drinking men explained. Seventy-five
Northwesters, Finan McDonald evidently among them,
came down the Columbia for the transfer. Many of the
former Northwesters who had turned Astor men now
lightly shifted their services and loyalty back to the
British. Among these were McDougall, Ross and Cox.
Donald McKenzie was hired on contract to establish a
post among the Nez Perces.

For the British, possession of the Pacific post meant
the virtual abandonment of the overland route east
through Kutenai country and across the prairies, for
bringing in supplies and sending out furs.

Astoria gave way to near-by Fort George. Astor
was through on the Pacific Coast. But his career had
just begun. He next organized the American Fur Com-

[9] Cox, *op. cit.,* 216-17.

pany to compete with Lisa and his successors out of St. Louis. Meriwether Lewis, governor of Louisiana Territory, with acute vision advised Washington superiors to "govern the Indians by governing the whites," through a selective system of licensing traders. If this policy could have been consistently followed, the subsequent history of Indian-White relations in the Northwest might have been quite different, although even the most law-abiding and conscientious traders would have gone up the Missouri or the Platte with little understanding of the problems they faced.

NORTH WEST COMPANY ABSORBED

By the Treaty of Ghent, 1815, all territory taken either by the United States or by Great Britain in the recent conflict was restored. The North West men continued to occupy Fort George although they no longer owned it. On the Spokane River the company took over Astor's old Fort Spokane. Joint occupancy of Oregon by the two nations for a period of ten years was agreed upon, and later the arrangement was renewed. North West Company continued its interior posts, advancing into the Snake country to head off the Americans, who persisted with their rendezvous in spite of frequent loss of life to the Blackfeet.

Competition between the Hudson's Bay and North West companies had become murderous in the literal sense of the term. The consequent loss of face among the natives, and the need to unite forces against American competition, hastened the forced fusion of the rival corporations in 1821. Hudson's Bay's field governor, George Simpson, toured the Columbia district to acquaint himself with the difficulties that had been hold-

ing down profits here for North West, as compared to
its profits east of the Rockies. Among these disad-
vantages were the lack of a network of easy waterways;
reluctance of the comparatively prosperous tribes –
many of them salmon fed – to engage in trapping; the
necessity of crossing the Divide to procure buffalo meat,
and the excessive expense of supporting the posts with
long-haul supplies. These supplies included items
which Simpson denounced as unnecessary luxuries, and
food-stuffs which he declared the traders ought to be
raising on the spot. New posts were located with agriculture in mind – a move that would have its important
– if delayed – effects upon the Flatheads and Kutenais.

In many ways, the new unified regime closely resembled the old in operation. Most employees in
the British fur trade were wretchedly under-paid and
forever in debt to the company for their future wages,
so that they could scarcely quit if they wanted to. As
they paddled and portaged, the voyageurs sang as much
to forget their troubles as to express delight in their
work. When David Thompson protested because his
French Canadians consumed eight pounds of meat per
man per day, they protested in their turn, "What
pleasure have we in Life but eating?" [10] Many of the
engagés were accompanied by their wives and children,
which created problems for the traders; however, the
women were useful in camp, and their presence was one
way to keep the men better satisfied – and more firmly
tied to their jobs.

It has been estimated that at least half the trappers
and voyageurs who went into the West disappeared.

[10] Thompson, *op. cit.*, 443.

An early Episcopalian missionary to the Northwest from Canada thus assessed the role of the natives in the fur game: "God knows that I speak the conviction of my mind, and may he forgive me if I speak unadvisedly, when I state my belief, that the life of an Indian was never yet by a trapper put in competition with a beaver skin." [11]

Few company men had Thompson's attitude of implacable opposition to dispensing liquor among the Indians. Although the firewater issued to the natives was excessively diluted, commonly with water and red pepper, the yearly average amount of liquor dispensed during 1806-1810 was 9,700 gallons (apparently for North West Company alone). Sometimes opium or laudanum was given to dangerous Indians, drunk or sober. After the amalgamation of the two British companies, however, Hudson's Bay issued much stricter regulations (not always followed) about allowing the natives to have strong drink; no such restrictions prevailed among the American (United States) traders.

TRIALS OF THE TRADERS

The amalgamation of the two fur companies brought across the Rockies for the first time Dr. John McLoughlin, to act as head factor for the Columbia District. McLoughlin soon built new district headquarters farther up the Columbia, to be known as Fort Vancouver. Among the lesser employees there was little change of personnel. Finan McDonald was still keeping the post journal at Spokane House in July, 1822. That winter he was sent into the Snake River country,

---

11 McLeod, *Journal and Correspondence,* 136 fn.; quoted by Lewis and Phillips, *Journal of John Work,* 53 fn.

where the company was operating its own modified form of the rendezvous, a moving camp of hired hands paid according to their catches. Alexander Ross, who had the Snake expedition the following winter, noted that McDonald's trip "was as successful as could have been expected, for Mr. McDonald was a zealous and faithful servant [he never rose beyond clerk]; but in other respects it was rather an unfortunate trip. In a conference with a war-party of Piegan, one of his men got treacherously shot." [12]

This incident was only a sample of McDonald's misadventures that year. Forcing a fight with a party of Piegans, he lost eight men, and later was accidentally wounded by his own gun during a squabble with one of his Iroquois trappers. Heading north at last with his furs, he annoyed Ross by going to Spokane House, which Ross considered to be poorly located, instead of going to Fort Nez Perce, recently established by Donald McKenzie and later to be known as Fort Walla Walla. For big Finan McDonald, Spokane House and Salish House had become as much home to him as any place could be. Frontier amenities were observed there, including a festive ball each autumn when the men left for the winter ground.[13] "No females in the land [were] so fair to look upon as the nymphs of Spokane; no ladies could dance so gracefully as they; none was so attractive. [There were] fine horses also. The race grounds were admired, and the pleasures of the race." [14]

---

[12] Ross, *Fur Hunters*, II, p. 5.

[13] "Last night Mr. Kennedy give a ball being the custom of the place when the men leave for their winter grounds some of the men got a little intoxicated and wished to purches rum but we never sell them that article here." (McDonald et al., *Original Journal at Fort Spokane,* entry for Nov. 5, 1822, by James Birnie who kept the record after July 23.)

[14] Ross, *Fur Hunters*, I, p. 138.

George Simpson, that dynamo of a young opportunist who was the new field governor for Hudson's Bay, eventually inspected the post, stormed against its luxuries and agreed that it was located too far off the route of the Columbia brigades. He ordered a move to Kettle Falls; this was accomplished in 1825.

Nobody wanted the Snake district, but Ross was assigned to it the next season (1823-24), although he had sent in his resignation from the company and was anxious to be relieved. The critical Simpson characterized Scotsman Ross as a "self-sufficient, empty-headed man;" nevertheless he had risen rapidly in the fur business. Perhaps he was not too able an administrator; perhaps also he was too independent for Simpson's taste. His revealing journals, later published in Canada, Simpson said were "full of bombast and marvelous nonsense." [15]

Ross's party included "two Americans, seventeen Canadians, five halfbreeds from the east side of the mountains, twelve Iroquois, two Abanakee Indians from Lower Canada, two natives from Lake Nepessing, one Saultman from Lake Huron, two Crees from Athabasca, one Chinook, two Spokanes, two Couttanois, three Flatheads, two Collespellums, one Palooche, and one Snake slave." Accompanying this motley crew of adult males were twenty-five women and sixty-four children. En route south from *Prairie de Cheveaux* (Horse Plains near the Flathead post), the party camped successively at Camas Prairie and at two other locations in the lower Flathead valley. Near present-day Ravalli they killed a couple of wild horses for meat and were obliged as usual to pay the Flatheads

---

[15] Merk, *Fur Trade and Empire,* 45-46.

"four skins Indian currency" per horse.[16] They then proceeded to Hell Gate and the Bitterroot Valley. The Iroquois were always conspiring to go off hunting and trapping and trading on their own. Many of them had been Christianized in Canada; Ross said when he heard them singing hymns together of an evening, he knew well that trouble was brewing.[17] One day on a later expedition, Peter Skene Ogden's Iroquois sighted a small party of Piegans with some cheap trade goods; whooping, they stripped the Plainsmen of all they had, leaving Ogden to make settlement and keep the peace.[18]

In the mountains to the east the party ran into such deep snow that for days on end they worked their way yard by yard by driving each horse a few jumps ahead of the last one, to break a trail. A crude snow plow contrived by Ross proved almost as slow. The delay went on for agonizing weeks, with Ross at one time forestalling the desertion of a key man by threatening him at pistol point. Troublesome Iroquois were sent on a buffalo hunt; the fresh meat, and the festive fiddling of a Canadian, put some heart into the company. It was April 15 when they finally made their way through Gibbons Pass to more open country.[19] In the spring the expedition weathered repeated clashes with the Blackfeet, crossed into Idaho for the summer, and met up with a hazard less bloodthirsty but equally loot-hungry – an American trader. Jedediah Smith, coming upon some of Ross's Iroquois, who later claimed that they

---

[16] Ross, *Fur Hunters*, II, p. 6.

[17] Elliott, "Snake Country Journals of Alexander Ross," 372.

[18] Donald McKenzie's Iroquois on one expedition exchanged their horses, guns and traps to some Snakes "for their women."

[19] Ross, *Fur Hunters*, II, pp. 20-48; and Laut, *Conquest of the Great Northwest*, 249-255. Agnes Laut copied from the H.B. records in London: Ross' "Snake Country Journals," for 1824.

had been robbed by Snakes and were destitute, bought all their furs. Unashamed, Smith joined Ross and returned to Flathead House with him in November, looking over the country as far north as what was to be the Canadian boundary line and studying the position of his rivals.

In December he saw gathered at the post forty-two lodges of Flatheads, thirty-four of Pend d'Oreilles, thirty-six of Kutenais, twelve of Nez Perces and four of Spokans. Each tribe had its turn at trading; the men approached the post on their proudest horses, headed by their chiefs; their salute of gunfire was returned by the wonderful boom of the fort's little cannon – which the company was never obliged to turn against them. Ross complained in his journal that the total trade with the assembled natives amounted to less than three skins per Indian. (The natives had also brought in over 11,000 pounds of dried buffalo meat.) But four thousand pelts were turned in by the Snake expedition's free trappers in two days, and a thousand more had been taken by the engagés. On Christmas day the "2 gentlemen, 14 laborers, 4 women, 7 children" at Flathead House were joined by "considerable Indians; the peace pipe kept in motion. All the people a dram." The following day, Sunday: "No work today. Ordered the men to dress and keep the Sabbath." [20]

Peter Skene Ogden, who was to head the Snake expedition for the next five years, came in to direct the work of putting up the supplies for the pack horses. The 1824-25 party was to be larger than Ross's. Jedediah Smith learned that Hudson's Bay had taken no fewer than 80,000 beaver out of the Columbia district

[20] Elliott, "Snake Country Journals of John Ross," 388.

during the past few years. He left in the spring with
Ogden, to pass on his impressive observations to William
Ashley's men of the Rocky Mountain Fur Company.

During Ogden's first season on the Snake, Finan
McDonald traded among the Flatheads on the Clark
Fork with Scotch-Irish John Work, who had come west
the previous year. Work reported that they found the
Indians friendly and carried on a profitable trade.
Finan had requested a transfer to Canada, but he was
due for a final Oregon adventure. Previously he had
put in his turn north at Kamloops; now he was sent
with Dr. McLoughlin's step-son, Tom McKay, and a
small party to scout the headwaters of the Des Chutes
River to the south. Through this trip he became the first
known White man to contact the Klamath (or Clam-
ittee) Indians, and probably gave them their name.[21]

By September 1826, Finan was back at Kettle Falls.
Here, if not earlier, he must have met the scholarly
Archibald McDonald, to whom he was distantly related. Archibald had promoted the idea of the Kettle
Falls post, known as Fort Colville. Colville and Walla
Walla were taking over most of the business formerly
transacted at Spokane House. Archibald was in the
Kettle Falls area that summer with a party that included David Douglas, the Northwest's most famed
early botanist from Scotland, and Francis Ermatinger
of Hudson's Bay, both of whom went east that fall
when Finan and his family left for the Prairies at last,
via Athabasca Pass. En route to Canada, Red Hair was
horribly injured by a wounded buffalo bull. Apparently
his mountain ordeals had hardened him more than they

---

21 Elliott, "Ogden Journals."

had weakened him, for he survived to become a partner in the company before his retirement the following year.

THE KUTENAI TRAPPERS

At Flathead House in the winter of 1825-26 Work and McDonald had traded as much with Pend d'Oreilles and "Collespellums" as with the upriver Flatheads. They also traded with Kutenais, though at first reluctantly, for William Kittson had now established seasonal trading headquarters for these people on the Kootenai River.[22] It turned out that Kittson that season had been unable to navigate the river. When the Kutenai chief arrived at Work's post, he expected to be treated to drinks; all he got was a dram of rum mixed with water. Even this, along with the smoking, made him tipsy, and apparently made him happy. He returned later in December with some seventy of his people and a brisk trade resulted when nearly six hundred beaver plews changed hands. The Kutenais were very glad to do business, and grateful for the gift of tobacco to the chief "for his people to smoke in the night," and some ammunition and beads for himself and his leading men.[23]

The Kutenais left again December 16 to hunt in their own land, apparently well pleased except that the Pend d'Oreilles or somebody had stolen some of their horses. In farewell they renewed their plea for a real post of their own. Both this year and the following, some of them traveled to Colville, where in 1826 they met

---

[22] Ross mentions Kittson's arrival at Flathead House "from the Kootenais" in December 1824. The earlier Kootenai River post (see herein pp. 217-18), had not been regularly manned in recent years.

[23] See Elliott, "Journals of John Work."

enemies of theirs, Chief Little Wolf of the Okanogans and his people. "War was instantly declared by the Wolf," but in a few days "peace was restored, when a feast was given which took several days." [24]

At this stage of affairs, the Kutenai plea for a post on their home grounds assumed new importance because the Hudson's Bay men were afraid that American traders were on their way into these Kootenai and Flathead River valleys; and because the supply of beaver in the Snake region showed signs of abating. "It is not certain how many furs the Americans got," Work wrote in 1826, "but the Hudson's Bay party obtained only 267 beaver and a few muskrats from the Flatheads. From the Kootenais, however, who had not traded with the Americans, they traded 392 beaver and 500 rats besides other furs." [25] Kittson that summer (he later wrote to John McLeod), "visited the McGillivray's River [Kootenai] which was found navigable. In the fall I came by water to this post and I am happy to say that the trade will exceed all former years. Mr. Dease has taken the Flathead Post for the winter and to his sorrow will not turn out more than one-third of last year's return. The Americans met the Flatheads on the heads of the Missouri and traded all their furs." [26]

This dispatch was headed "Kootenais House" which at that date was located somewhere opposite the mouth of the Fisher; the Columbia Lake location had been abandoned. The Kutenai fur harvest that year was reported as 1024 beaver pelts, 274 elk skins and 473 deer

---

[24] Douglas, *Journal*, 206-7.

[25] Lewis, *John Work*, 56 fn. Gov. Simpson was to note in 1841 that the beaver had been protected from waste by "the comparatively thrifty and provident Kootenays." (*Overland Journey*, I, p. 134.)

[26] McLeod, *op. cit.*, letter of March, 1827.

skins. In 1828 or 1829 Kittson is believed to have built at the mouth of Rainy Creek, between the mouth of the Fisher and the present town of Libby. For the next thirty years the company fur collection depot or winter post known as Fort Kootenay was situated in this general locality. On the way out to the coast, furs would be picked up also at Bonners Ferry.

That fall (1826) John Work hastened back to the Clark Fork with three boatloads of trade merchandise, word having reached the company that nosey American traders were actually on their way into the Flathead country. It may have been at this time that the Flathead post was moved upriver to near where the station of Eddy now stands, supposedly "to ward off the Americans," though the two locations are only about seven miles apart. Whatever Americans these were, they made no stay so far north. The Flathead River-Kootenai River country was never much penetrated by American fur men. Jedediah Smith came through the country again in 1829 from Vancouver, and met his partners David Jackson and William Sublette somewhere in the Kootenai country, but they did not come back another year. Joshua Pilcher was then in the area, having spent the winter at Flathead Lake, in a last-ditch effort to recover the regional trade for the Missouri Fur Company. But his experience there, culminating in a visit to Colville in the spring, convinced him that the Britishers were so firmly entrenched in these mountains that it was no use trying to buck them.

The only other recorded American effort to establish in the Flathead Valley was made in the early 1830s by Warren Ferris of the American Fur Company and his party of six engaged men with packhorses, and five armed Indians. The Ferris people joined Montour of Hudson's Bay, and in a spirit of international cooperation helped him build a cabin, and spent Christmas and New Years in his company. This camp may have been on Camas Prairie or along the Little Bitterroot. Ferris wrote that from here he "passed across the Plains several miles to Flathead House." His mention of "seven buildings" at this post has been quoted as describing the layout at the original location, but probably, at this date, applied to the later site. It appears that Montour was supposed to be with the Kutenais at Rainy Creek, but didn't go in to the Kootenai River until later. Ferris and his men left in the spring for the Yellowstone, not to return.[27]

MOUNTAIN TRIBES DIVIDE THEIR FAVORS

Through the 1820s the great beaver population in the Snake River region was ruthlessly depleted. No trader knew this terrible country better than Peter Skene Ogden, whose high-pitched, squeaky voice – startling in combination with his round head and his short and rotund body – led him to turn to fur trading instead of becoming an orating barrister in Quebec, where his father was a judge in the Admiralty Court. His mother was American. By the time he first crossed the Rockies in 1819, he had been for a number of years in the service of North West Company, and he continued with Hudson's Bay after the merger.

Ogden probably traded with the Flatheads and Kutenais during his first season west of the mountains. In 1822 he began his series of Snake expeditions, and was chief trader for the whole region. Sturdy, energetic,

---

[27] Ferris, *Life in the Rocky Mountains,* 247.

persuasive, Ogden nevertheless had plenty of personnel problems during his Snake River years. His trappers deserted from fear of the Blackfeet, or from discontent with the larder, or because of allurements of Indian women, or temptation by American traders. Ogden learned as he endured. At the close of his second expedition, Ogden noted that "Of all the men who first came to the Snake country, there remains now only one alive. All the others have been killed except two, who died a natural death." [28]

Flathead tribesmen, if not Kutenai, wandered in these years as far as the mouth of the Columbia. "The Flathead Chief has just had a cloathing," McLoughlin wrote from Vancouver to the trader at Colville. "But it ought to be a rule to discourage them from coming here, as our prices are so much lower than yours, their report must give you trouble." [29] (Trade goods canoed and packed into the interior naturally were higher-priced than the same goods at the coast.)

After the Kutenais had left Work at Flathead House in the winter of 1825-26, they were replaced by an equally large party of Flatheads, who came in with a flag flying. The weather was so bad that they were accepted into the post buildings for sleeping, the highest-ranking in the gentlemen's house, all others in the Indian house. They traded next day for all the furs they had, which was not as many as expected; they said they had been obliged to spend too much time hunting. Work recompensed those who had assisted with the Snake expedition, and allowed the leaders the usual gifts of tobacco.

---

[28] Laut, *op. cit.*, 299.   [29] Barker, *Letters of Dr. John McLoughlin*, 199.

By 1827 the beaver population in the Snake country was alarmingly thin. Under pressure of international competition, all parties concerned were but opportunists. In present-day Idaho the British now operated Fort Boise and Fort Hall, the latter once the post of the American Nathaniel Wyeth, whose far-western trading ventures had come to nought. Ogden's "Snake River" expeditions were extended into southern Oregon and far into California, where Tom McKay led him along the route he and Finan McDonald had earlier taken, and beyond; and to Great Salt Lake, where Ogden was probably the first to explore the western and northern shores.[30] His Snake years over, he served in New Caledonia (later British Columbia) and the Pacific Coast area, and became a chief trader.

Work during most of Ogden's five years on the Snake was at Colville, while the Flatheads were served at their post by John Dease. When Dease became ill in 1829, Work took his place temporarily, before turning over the post to Kittson in order to succeed Ogden on the Snake. Dease died at The Dalles early in 1830, of an internal disturbance. Kittson then returned for several years to the Kootenai River, where other traders during this period were Francis Payette and Nicholas Montour. Dr. McLoughlin, who personally was a stranger to the Kutenais and their corner of his empire, wrote in 1832, "Indeed I think that Montour is even too indolent for the Kootenais."[31] It was evidently Montour who was located for a few years at the mouth of Rainy Creek, then moved upstream to the mouth of the Fisher. This upper house, John Campbell wrote,

---

[30] Elliott, "Peter Skene Ogden," 249, 251.
[31] Barker, *Letters of McLoughlin,* 280.

was called by the Indians *A hk-ie-yie*. It was a long, low building with a peaked roof of poles covered with cedar bark and earth on top, with a fireplace in one corner, built by a Mr. Montour. He traded there for two years and after him a man by the name of Paget [Payette?] who traded there for several years and after him came one by the name of Thomas Flett a Scotchman who did not remain long and was relieved by a man called Edward Berland a Canadian.[32]

This handy home service did not prevent the Kutenais from sometimes wandering, nor from dabbling in the regional game of playing the Bostons against the King George men. The American Captain Benjamin Bonneville in 1833 met some "Cottonais" on the Snake plateau, who "were anxious for him to proceed at once to their country, which, they assured him, abounded in beaver."[33]

In 1828, according to Chief Factor McLoughlin, the Columbia District, including New Caledonia, cleared 31,739 pounds sterling, as compared to the 75,000 pounds profit of the North West Company in 1814, its best year.[34] By 1831 John Work was complaining to John McLeod of "the exhausted condition of the Snake country." He considered the borders of the Blackfoot country "the only quarter now where there is a likelihood of making anything."[35] Archibald McDonald in February of 1833 noted that the profit figure for the west side of the mountains the past year had been 20,000 pounds, and McLoughlin in March declared his belief that "the Snake country is ruined and there are at pres-

---

[32] John F. Campbell, *Letters to C. N. Kessler.*

[33] Irving, *The Rocky Mountains . . . Bonneville,* 132, 134.

[34] McLeod, *op. cit.,* 124. Letter of Feb. 1, 1832. (The figure for North West Company may have covered some business east of the Rockies?)

[35] *Ibid.,* 143; Letter of Sept. 6, 1831.

ent 400 Americans in it and I can see nothing they can do to live except to go in a body to Peagan lands which will be the death blow to the Saskatchewan."[36] The Americans were, however, to continue their dwindling rendezvous for about seven more years.

Though in 1830 Hudson's Bay realized as much income from the Columbia district as from all the remainder of its northern department, the British trade steadily declined after 1835. Reports showed that the average annual take from 1841-45 was not much more than one tenth of that for 1826-1830.

The breezy and belligerent Francis Ermatinger in 1838 declared "that if any effort should be made by the government of the United States to remove them [the British] from the country, they would at once arm the eight hundred mixed bloods the Company controlled in different parts of Oregon, and by means of these and their knowledge of the natural fastnesses in the mountains, the Company would hold Oregon against any force it was possible to bring into the field."[37] But this would be proved idle boasting.

---

[36] *Ibid.,* 173; Letter of March 1, 1833.

[37] Thornton, Hon. J.Q., "History of the Provisional Government of Oregon," *Oregon Pioneer Transactions,* 1874, p. 43.

Families

Of the native wives of British fur men, Alexander Ross wrote: "The tenderness existing between their husbands and themselves presents one great reason for that degree of attachment which the respective classes of whites cherish for the Indian countries. The vigilence of these women has often been instrumental to the safety of the forts, when the most diabolical combinations were set on foot by the natives." The women are much attached to their children, he continued, "nor are they wanting in many other qualities necessary to a good housekeeper; they are tidy, saving and industrious."[1]

The fur annals of the Pacific Northwest are sprinkled with stories of traders and trappers stricken with grief over the death of Indian wives, and with occasional stories of injury or death dealt to their wives' seducers — either White-skinned or Red-skinned. There were of course some White men who were contemptuous and brutal with their native women, as there were many native husbands who were unfailingly thoughtful and devoted. Most fathers of marriageable daughters were glad to attach a White son-in-law; but the young men of the tribes could not be expected to rejoice as the intruders lured to their lodges some of the most desirable

---

[1] Ross, *Fur Hunters,* I, p. 296.

girls in camp. On the other hand, more than one White man was humiliated or infuriated to have his Indian wife leave him for a man of her own people.

The American artist Alfred Jacob Miller, sketching at a rendezvous of American traders, had as tentmate a young man of good family from St. Louis.

> One of the most toothsome wenches in camp was a Flathead girl who Miller says was "one of the belles of the Rocky Mountains." She could have been no more than fifteen or she would not have been desirable and probably not a belle. [Miller's friend] fell for her but could make no time with her. She would accept his presents and flirt with him in the presence of the gang but would not stroll in the evening. It was mortifying for [his] way with white ladies was one of the reasons why his father had sent him west, and his companions grew ribald as his sustained pursuit went on failing. Then one day the whole camp roared for a free trapper struck his tent, packed his mules, and rode off toward the hills, taking the girl with him.[2]

When the pair returned from the honeymoon, Miller immortalized them in his painting, "The Trapper's Bride."

On the whole, the men of the American fur camps were more often casual adventurers of doubtful character than were the engagés of the British companies; their relations with the Indian women were correspondingly more transitory. Usually the greatest cruelty of a White man toward his Indian woman, be the White man Boston or King George, was desertion. British traders of position nearly always left their Indian wives in the wilderness when they retired to Canada and the comforts and social refinements of Montreal, Ottawa and Quebec. "When a trader wishes to separate from his Indian wife, he generally allows her an annuity, or

---

[2] De Voto, *Across the Wide Missouri,* 325.

PETER SKENE OGDEN
Courtesy of British Columbia Archives.

MARY ERMATINGER ASHLEY IN OLD AGE
Courtesy of Frances Morais.

RED RIVER CARTS WERE USED BY THE SINCLAIR EXPEDITIONS
One may be seen in the historical museum at Banff, Alberta.
These are of a later day; the originals had broad wooden wheels. See text p. 249.
Photo courtesy of Canadian Pacific Railway.

CANAL FLAT LOCALE, AND UPPER (SOUTHERN) COLUMBIA LAKE
An old canal, dug in the 1880s by the English entrepreneur W. A. Baillie-Grohman
(see his *Life and Sport in British Columbia*), runs across the foreground. It was
to divert the spring flood water of the Kootenay into the Columbia, and protect
the lowlands above Kootenay Lake (Bonners Ferry-Creston area) for farming. Lower
Columbia Lake, site of Thompson's Kootenay House, is now known as Windermere Lake.
Photo courtesy of British Columbia Travel Bureau.

gets her comfortably married to one of the *voyageurs*.
. . . A retired partner, thus disembarrased, arrives in
Canada determined to enjoy the pleasures of matrimony
with an educated female," a resolve easy of satisfaction, for the townswomen were all aflutter at the appearance of each bronzed and hardy westerner with
retirement funds to his credit.[3]

DAVID THOMPSON AND ASSISTANTS

But not so David Thompson. He took his Charlotte
east to Quebec and continued devoted to her and their
ten children through all the years of his retirement,
which ended in heartbreak. His maps were published
by Arrowsmith without credit to their originator; his
achievements as an explorer were ignored; and no pub-
lisher could be found for his "Narrative."

There is no official record of any attachment Thompson may have conducted with a native woman in the
Kutenai-Flathead country, where he several times
wintered far from his family. However, a relative of
Archibald McDonald stated in her reminiscences that
"David Thompson had a daughter by a Pend d'Oreille
woman;" and this informant's brother remarked to an
interviewer that "David Thompson lived among my
people. He had a woman among the Selish. His descendants still live on the reservation."[4] Tradition con-
nects his blood with some prominent Montana families
today.

When Thompson died, in extreme poverty, the Montreal papers did not consider it news. He had been
criticized for not reaching the Pacific before the Amer-

---

[3] Cox, *op. cit.,* 312.
[4] Lewis, "The Daughter of Angus McDonald"; C. White, *op. cit.,* 244 fn. 2.

icans, although vindicating explanations may be cited for his delay. A Canadian who met Thompson in his later years wrote that he "has a powerful mind, and a singular faculty of picture-making. He can create a wilderness and people it with warring savages, or climb the Rocky Mountains with you in a snowstorm, so clearly and palpably, that only shut your eyes and you hear the crack of the rifle, or feel the snowflakes melt on your cheeks as he talks." [5] Thompson's Indian friends called him *Koo-Koo-Sint,* the Star Gazer.

Big Finan McDonald when he left the Columbia district also took his native wife and their children with him to Canada. They settled on a farm in Glengarry County, Ontario, where McDonald became prominent in regional affairs. The eldest daughter, Helen, however, remained to marry in the West.

Jocko Finlay died at old Spokane House in 1828 and was buried beneath one of its bastions. His blood, his name (in later generations usually spelled Finley), were well seeded into the whole region through his descendants – part of whose vitality came from the Indian blood of their unchronicled mothers and their paternal grandmother.

DIVERSION

Indian wives, like wives of any race, did not always fit the pattern, as the Indians and Whites who met Madam Boisverde in the first quarter of the nineteenth century realized with a shock. To her own people, this Kutenai wife of one of Thompson's men (there were several Boisverts or Boisverdes in the fur service at this

---

[5] Quoted by Catherine White, *ibid.,* cxl, from John Bigsbee's *The Shoe and Canoe.*

period) was known as *Ko-com-ne Pe-ca,* and she was a noisy, aggressive, heretical person who preferred to dress as a man. *Ko-com-ne Pe-ca* (Manlike Woman) was out of character not only as a female but as a member of her tribe. The Kutenais, though tolerant of sex variants, didn't like to have her around their camps, unless a battle were in the offing; then they welcomed her, for she apparently couldn't be buffaloed under any circumstances, and soon showed herself not only a smart warrior but also a persuasive leader of warriors.

This Kutenai man-woman, also known as Bundash, claimed to be in communication with special spirits, who enabled her to change her sex at will, and granted her fascinating powers. Her followers, both men and women, were spellbound by her daring and her weird rites and prophecies. At times the ceremonials she led seem to have been mild orgies. In her home country, David Thompson found her conduct "so loose" that he required her man Boisverde to send her away.

In 1811 *Ko-com-ne Pe-ca* turned up at Spokane House, and volunteered to carry a message for Finan McDonald to John Stuart at Fort Fraser, although no one else would attempt the journey and she had no idea where the fort was. McDonald allowed her to take the dispatch, and she started off dressed as a man, taking along as "wife" a well-dressed young girl "of whom she pretended to be very jealous." Her current prophecies about a race of dangerous giants soon to appear in her wake bewitched the native peoples who flocked around the two as they traveled.

Hearing of White men at the mouth of the Columbia, Bundash took this river west and showed up at Astoria, where Alexander Ross classed her as an exceptionally astute and intelligent man. The Astorians suspected the two of being spies for the British. They decided to send an expedition into the interior to verify the stories given by the two strangers concerning British traders in their homeland and of all the beaver they were taking. Then, just as they were ready to take off, a large canoe slid in from upriver with the British flag flying – David Thompson of North West Company had arrived.

Keeping out of Thompson's sight, Madam Boisverde got her bearings and prepared to go north up the coast to the Fraser River country; but now she ran into trouble. The coast natives, who knew nothing of her except her lurid prognostications about approaching giants and impending epidemics, plotted to kill her. (Perhaps it was at this time that she received the wound in the breast mentioned by one historian.) In spite of Thompson's previous censure, she now appealed to him for protection, and he tolerantly helped her make a safe get-away for the north. Her own shrewdness contrived her subsequent success: she now changed the tenor of her "religion," and prophesied only pleasant fortunes. Her followers multiplied and she arrived at Fort Fraser with a string of twenty-six horses heavily loaded with furs and other gifts.

Back in the Kutenai-Flathead country, John Work on December 12, 1825, told how "a woman who goes in men's clothes, the famous Ko-come-no Pe-ca, and is a leading Character among them [the Kutenais] was also tipsy with three-fourths of mixed liquor and became noisy." And the next day: "a present was also given to Bundash, a woman who assumes a masculine character, and is of some note among them; she acted as interpreter; she speaks Flathead very well."

Madame Boisverde's career continued to prosper. White men sought her advice about interior travel while Indians held her in awe. She became the leader of a cult that numbered thousands of Indians, and some historians believe that her weird religion was one of the sources of the ghost dances held by Indians of the Northwest many years later. Alas for Bundash, her spiritual magic could not stop a bullet. When last seen by the traders, according to Sir John Franklin, she was collecting volunteers for another war excursion; in the subsequent campaign she received a mortal wound.[6]

WIVES FOR CHIEF TRADERS

Alexander Ross, like Thompson and McDonald, took his Okanogan wife with him on leaving Columbia district. At least two of their sons made good records as college students; several daughters were active in church work. Italian-Swiss Francois Ermatinger, who began his career in the Columbia country about the time Work was leaving, married a granddaughter of Mrs. John McLoughlin, Catherine the sister of James Sinclair; but he left a daughter, Mary, in the Flathead country, whose Pend d'Oreille mother, Mary the elder, thought herself to be Ermatinger's wife. Peter Skene

---

[6] References for this section: Lewis, *Journal of John Work,* 190; Ross, *First Settlers,* 92-3, 111, 156-8; Franchere, *op. cit.,* 118, 122; Franklin, Sir John, *Narrative of a Second Expedition to the Shores of the Polar Sea,* London, 1828; Walter Taylor, "Madam Boisverde," *Kalispell Times,* undated copy in Johns *Collection,* I, p. 110; Thompson, *Narrative,* 512. Thompson earlier tells of a "Lady Conjuress," then twenty-five years of age, whom he met in 1810 at Rainy Lake House; she had been married to one of his men six years before, and he (Thompson) had banished her for misbehavior (*Narrative,* 431). This conflicts with his 1811 account of having had to send Bundash away "three years before;" but the Lady Conjuress must have been the same person as *Ko-come-ne Pe-ca,* who was certainly adventurous enough to have traveled eastward as well as westward from the Kootenay country.

Ogden's Flathead wife, Julia, and their children eventually lived at Oregon City, only Michel returning to the Flathead Valley.

Dr. John McLoughlin's wife, the mixed-blood widow of Alexander McKay, bore him three children who grew up at Fort Vancouver. Of these, David, after education in Europe and business experience at Oregon City, was to settle in the 'sixties along the Kootenai.

Seeds of Settlement

GARDENS

"I would not give them even a spade to till the soil!" declared Governor Simpson,[1] intent on keeping his trappers trappers, be they White, Red or mixed. But even Simpson could scarcely regulate the course of human nature with the rest of nature. He insisted that his traders raise gardens and crops at every post, for economy's sake; yet no engagé must be tempted to settle down and farm.

At the mouth of "Fine Meadow Creek," the Tobacco River of Tobacco Plains, David Thompson and his men in 1809 sowed some crop seeds, perhaps reasoning that because the Kutenais grew tobacco on the Plains it must be a garden spot. Passing this way again in August, two of the men were sent "to look how the garden seeds had thriven. They found nothing of the Peas, the turnips only in leaves and their very small roots worm-eaten; five or six grains of barley that were sowed have thrived well, but not yet ripe."[2] This first White man "garden" of the Columbia country didn't, of course, have much chance.

---

[1] Greenbie, *op. cit.*, 292.

[2] C. White, *op. cit.*, Aug. 24, 1809. Here a hundred years later homesteader William Parcels set out to develop garden, orchard, and fields of hay and grain (including barley) – and made a living. Here thirty years later still, the writer of this story lived for ten years with her late husband, and sowed her own vegetable and flower seeds with pleasant results. The spot will be inundated upon completion of the Libby Dam downstream.

Ross Cox, spending an enjoyable summer at Spokane House in 1815, with McMillan, Montour and several other Northwesters, related:

> Our kitchen-garden now began to assume a thriving appearance, and, in addition to a fine crop of potatoes, we reared a quantity of other excellent esculents. The soil was deep and rich; and a few melons and cucumbers which we had put down throve admirably. The Indians, who at first would not touch any thing which we planted, began at length to have such a relish for the produce of the garden, that we were obliged to have sentinels on the watch to prevent their continual trespasses. We offered some of them potatoes to plant, and pointed out the good effects that would result from their cultivation, but . . . they replied, that it would interfere with their hunting and fishing, and prevent their women from collecting their own country fruits and roots in the autumn, and thereby render them lazy.[3]

Spokane House in 1822 had increased its garden two times over the previous year. Archibald McDonald, urging the establishment of Fort Colville, noted that John Work already had a garden there. "It is truly pleasing," wrote the missionary Rev. Elkanah Walker when visiting Fort Colville in 1837, "to see the large and numerous stacks of grain, with cattle and swine feeding on the plain in large numbers. Mr. McDonald raises great crops."[4]

At Fort Vancouver, and south across the Columbia in the Willamette Valley, agriculture began to flourish so bountifully before mid-century that people in the eastern states, hearing about the land from stray travelers and the early missionaries, began to tramp out the Oregon Trail in the late 1830s. Almost no farm-seeking

3 Cox, *op. cit.*, 189-90.

4 Lewis, "Archibald McDonald." Corn was raised at Walla Walla by 1829 – with only a hoe to till the soil.

emigrants, however, stopped in the Rocky Mountains during the next several decades.

The threat of American occupation at the mouth of the Columbia forced Governor Simpson to ease his restrictions on agriculture, and to accede to expansion of the company farms at Vancouver and at Nisqually on Puget Sound. Growing unrest among the mixed bloods who were farming in the Hudson's Bay-controlled Red River Valley of Canada, persuaded him in 1854 to allow the company clerk James Sinclair to lead to the Pacific Coast a second emigration of Red River people, Sinclair having headed an earlier such party in 1841. Privately, Simpson had agreed to grant Sinclair the tradership at Walla Walla, and assistance in building up his own herd of livestock there. The company posts in the United States were in process of abandonment; since the boundary settlement (see page 253), many Company men were settling in Washington Territory.

Among the sixty or seventy members of the second Sinclair expedition, many of whom traveled on visions of California gold, were Sinclair's second wife and seven of his children, including Colin and several others by the first wife, reportedly a Scotswoman. Also of the party were two sisters of the second Mrs. Sinclair: Mrs. William Mohr, with her family, and Miss Margaret Campbell. It was their engaging and adventuresome brother, young Johnny Campbell, whose account of this journey permits readers of later generations to go along.

It is believed that all the members of the party had Indian blood in their veins except the Scotch woman, Mrs. Thomas Brown, whose husband although blond was part Indian. The party halted at Canal Flat (later so named) and again on Tobacco Plains, where Scotty Linklater, the trader, and the Kutenai Indians were most hospitable. The Indians, however, were awed and alarmed by an incident that occurred during the unpacking:

Mr. Sinclair's mount took fright at something and started to run around among the other animals; the saddle got loose and under his body. There was a Colt's revolver in the holster tied to the saddle, that somehow started to shoot, and it was fortunate that none was hit. . . There were a lot of Kootenay Indians standing around and wondering what kind of a gun that was that could shoot so often, they having never seen one of those six shooters before that time. It was a sight to see them standing around open-mouthed when they saw the pistol and Mr. Linklater showed them how it was handled. At that time the only kind of guns that they used or ever saw were those flint-lock guns.[5]

Mrs. Brown by her "rest stop" on Tobacco Plains was evidently the first White woman ever to camp, or even to set foot, on the soil of what is now Montana. According to Joe Eastland, a friend of Campbell's in his later life:

Mr. Campbell said the young fellows went all over Tobacco Plains and that it was a beautiful country, with an abundance of bunch grass. He said the Hudson's Bay Company would bring their horses to Tobacco Plains for many miles; the horses would be poor and their backs sore after a summer's hard work; in the spring they would find them in such fine shape and spirits, they would have to break them over again. They ran into a large herd of elk near Sophie's Lake. Mr. Campbell always seemed to like Tobacco Plains. He went away many times but always came back [until he left for the last time when he was old].[6]

---

[5] Campbell, "The Sinclair Party, An Emigration Overland etc."
[6] O. Johnson, *op. cit.,* 27.

After reaching the Spokane country, the expedition members scattered out, most of them going on to the coast, though Johnny Campbell remained in the Spokane country for a time. On Tobacco Plains, Sinclair's people had left a number of cows for the Kutenais, but the tribesmen didn't therefore turn at once into stockmen and farmers; in fact, they neither milked nor butchered the White men's cows for their own use.

SEEDS OF DEGENERACY

Sir George Simpson, during his journey around the world in 1841, described a group of Kutenais whom he met in the upper Columbia country as "miserable beings, small, decrepit and dirty. Though of the men there were two that might be called handsome, yet of the women there were none." [7] Yet Cox had written of the Kutenais some eighteen years earlier that "The greatest cleanliness and neatness are observable about their persons and lodges. They are rather handsome, above the middle size. . ." [8] These early reports of course varied in part because different explorers met different small groups of traveling families and friends, and under different circumstances, including the critical circumstance of the current season's food supply.

Canadian government explorer John Palliser in 1858 told how his party ate so much fish at a Kootenay Lake Indian camp that the guides were unable to stir. His associate Dr. James Hector, exploring at the head of the Columbia in salmon season during the same period, found that the Kutenais there had ample food on hand, including dried berries and fish, moose and buffalo

[7] Simpson, *op. cit.*, I, p. 130. [8] Cox, *op. cit.*, 234.

meat. But the Kutenais met by Simpson in 1841 said they were starving, "and if their tongues had been silent, their emaciated bodies would have told the same melancholy tale." The plight of this party wasn't however to be blamed entirely upon an unfavorable season. The men explained boastfully that they had just lost all their possessions in a fine reckless round of stick games.

Gambling had always been a weakness with these nomadic mountain people, for whom life was often bleak and excess property a burden anyhow. With the new wealth in horseflesh, and more recently all the alluring new articles of property-in-hand brought by the traders, betting on horse races and stick games flourished with a new profuseness.

The two contestants in a stick game, which resembles "Button, Button, Who's Got the Button?" may be acting for a whole line of allies, squatted facing the line of opponents; the betting may be between individuals, or among the players and spectators who contribute to the "pot." Unlike a White man's card game, the stick game session is no desultory or tensely business-like interval of disjointed movements and sounds. It is a swift, rhythmic program of chanting voices, swaying bodies, flowing gestures and lifted mood. To the Kutenais at the time of Simpson's visit, gambling was more available than firewater as an escape from growing bewilderments due to the White invasion. The Flatheads were nearer to the American trappers and traders; many of them experienced the abandonment of the rendezvous; stray Whites from trap line and emigrant trail began to filter into the Bitterroot Valley. Liquor, venereal disease, contempt for conventional morals both White and Red, hit the Flatheads sooner and harder than it hit the Kutenais; yet many of the Flatheads remained surprisingly clean of spirit.

Smallpox made its ghastly way into the mountains well before the White men got there in person. The Piegans and the Flatheads may have had it from the Snakes about 1780, the Plateau Kutenais from the Piegans by way of the Tunaha. Other epidemics occurred about 1808, 1847 and 1870. During the 1808 epidemic, said to have come from the Crows, all the Flathead groups suffered severely, the Spokans most of all. "Some of the long lodges were quite full of dead and dying people. So many people died that they could not be buried, and the dogs ate the bodies."[9] This sickness was utterly strange to the shamans, who knew no medicine to make against it. Pain the Indians could withstand, but the degrading horrors of this particular White man's gift filled them with a fear deadly destructive in itself.

By 1846 the American emigration into Oregon Territory had encouraged the United States government to demand that the Canadian-United States boundary line should run along the fortieth parallel, thus excluding the whole Columbia country, and even Puget Sound, from British dominion. However, there was still nothing that could be called White settlement in the Flathead-Kutenai country, where for some time yet agricultural activity would be restricted to small plots around regional missions, and casual stockraising in the southwestern valleys of what was to become Montana Territory.

The Oregon Trail by 1846 was deep in dust or mud,

---

[9] Teit, *Salishan Tribes,* 316, quoting Michel Revais.

and strewn with the skeletons of buffaloes, human beings and discarded equipment. Yet so many ardent travelers got through that the populace of the Willamette Valley was feeling the need of local government, and the mid-Columbia natives were ominously growling. Most of these newcomers of an alien race looked upon the Red men as a nuisance. Among the Whites, however, were Christian missionaries Catholic and Protestant.

The Missions

NATIVE PRE-CHRISTIAN RELIGION

"The Whites ask where Kutenais come from to here," said Little Jim Eneas, past eighty and blind, but very straight-backed as he sat on his block of wood outside the cluttered cabin near Windermere. "I tell you," he offered with quiet emphasis and a tolerant half-smile for the ignorance of the Whites. "They no come here from nowhere. This is true what I tell you." In Little Jim's voice there was an echo of dignity and authority.

This is how – a big fish live in Nelson [Kootenay] Lake; grow very big; eat brother and wife of Big Chief, swallow canoe and all. Big Chief so high, when he walk up Nelson Lake – water deep there, you know, deep, deep – it only come up to his thighs. He walk all over lake, chase fish up Columbia [after, apparently, going down the lower Kootenay into the Columbia], way up into Columbia Lakes, tramp in mud to make flats – you know Canal Flat – so big fish can't get back [down the Kootenay River]. Then he throw stone, kill fish, cut him open and let out brother and wife. Then cut him up – [Jim's gestures showed the victor throwing the remains of the fish around.] Lips make cliffs at Dutch Creek and at St. Mary's River, across; back makes hill east side Canal Flat Lake, look just like fish back. Then he take [some part of fish body], work up with hands, so scatter around, make Kutenai Indians. So there Kutenais are.[1]

---

[1] The word used by Little Jim to indicate the part of the body from which the Kutenais were made could not be understood; quite possibly it means "the testes," but this is only a guess.

"Now I have told you." Was the indulgent twinkle partly a realization of fantasy in his own "belief," or did this primitive creation story satisfy Jim and his people?

The big fish or water monster – in Kutenai, *Ya-woo-nik,* the Deep Water Dweller – does his dirty work in the legends of many native North American tribes. Little Jim's story is a version of one continuity of the "War on the Sky" series told to Boas. The Water Monster is the villain also of widespread northern Deluge tales, less distinctively Kutenaian than the War on the Sky tales. The Kutenai Deluge story as recorded by Curtis overlaps the goings-on usually belonging to the War on the Sky. In the Flathead range, a monster or dragon killed in the Valley of the Jocko, originally "The Valley of the Great Snake," was a dweller not in water but among rocks. His jaws were the bluffs between Dixon and Ravalli, his belly the Jocko Valley, his tail the Coriacan Defile.[2]

Little Jim's Great Chief is *Nalmuqtse* or *Nahlmokchi,* who sometimes is spoken of as the forefather of the Kutenais. He can't stand up or he will bump his head on the sky, or at least knock off his headdress; he crawls about on his hands and knees naming the mountains, and the river and lakes that appear on his back trail in the depressions he makes as he goes. The story of the making of Canal Flat in Boas is very much like Little Jim's version, except in its conclusion. Boas was told

---

2 Stone, *Following Old Trails,* 179, 186; Hollensteiner, *Letters:* "Legends Told by Two Feathers." The Coriacan Defile, the pass between the Jocko and Missoula Valleys, was named for two Kanaka (Hawaiian) employees of Hudson's Bay, who were killed here by Blackfeet raiders. Neighboring tribes tell similar legendary tales accounting for familiar natural features in their own provinces.

above left:
FATHER ANTHONY RAVALLI, S.J.

above right:
FATHER JOSEPH MENETREY, S.J.

lower left:
FATHER ADRIAN HOECKEN, S.J.

These portraits courtesy of
Gonzaga University Archives.

St. Ignatius Mission and Town, Lower Flathead Valley, 1954

See text page 282.

that the meat of the monster was all given to other tribes for food, before the Kutenais were remembered; only the blood was left to nourish the Kutenais, therefore they would always be few. Granville Stuart gives a similar account, except that it is the Nez Perces who were nearly forgotten. But as Jim Eneas tells it, the story becomes a creation myth.

A deluge story recounted by Baptiste Mathias, aged Kutenai leader at Flathead Lake until his recent death, also involves canoeing spirits – "a few Nupeeka" – who "knew that the canoe was going to tip over. They knew, too, that this place was going to be taken over by people later." This is as much as Mathias told of the appearance or creation of man; he did say that the Nupeeka left picture messages on the rocks offering to help people as guardian spirits.[3]

The creation of the sun and moon in regional legends involves the ever-present animal spirits, who take turns trying to serve as these luminaries; none are satisfactory until the two sons of Lynx come along, and shine just right.

Turney-High wrote that "The Flathead world was made by a Creator named *Amótkan,* a spirit almost if not actually personalized into a diety. At the bottom of the world lived a goddess called *Emtép.* The whole question of the Creator is anything but clear. Flatheads claim that the *Amótkan-Emtép* theology was not part

---

[3] Griswold, *op. cit.* The pictographs, pectographs and rock paintings in various parts of the Flathead Valley are apparently simple records or messages, scarcely qualifying as works of art. Of recently-discovered pectographs near Moyie Lake in Kutenai country, Bayard Iverson wrote: "It appears that in idle moments the Indians have with any sort of pointed rock chipped out to a depth of a quarter of an inch or so, deer tracks, moose tracks, bear tracks, a few designs, and even a butterfly eight or ten inches across," (correspondence). See note on rock paintings at Kila, Montana, in O. Johnson, *op. cit.,* 12.

of their ancient religion, but is a diffusion from the West. Most think the Creator was the benevolent sun." [4] Angus McDonald commented that "the name *A mot Kain* may be coeval with the first conceptions of man regarding a Head Power Chief or Cause." He said that Christians had nothing to do with the making of this word. [5]

An interrogator was told by Kutenai leaders at Bonners Ferry in 1931 that their people believed in "a Supreme Creator which they called the Great High Spirit, who created everything. Since He created the sun, moon and stars before He created humans, the Indians believed these three bodies to be more important to Him than man. The Kutenai also thought the Great Spirit was so powerful and awesome that no human was worthy of addressing it directly even in prayer. For this reason they talked with the Great Spirit through the sun, moon and stars, and that is why they held the Sun Dance." [6]

Possible symbolism in the geneology of the two Lynx who became the sun and the moon, like the possible symbolism in other goings-on of the myths, is only vaguely apparent to strangers from the translations. Even with this allowance, the pre-Christian Kutenai and Flathead creation legends of course seem primitive compared to Genesis, or to the latest scientific treatises on the evolution of the universe and of organic life. Yet do the most established or the most highly-researched attempts to rend the veil provide any explicit and incontrovertible picture of the origin of either planets or personalities?

[4] Turney-High, *Flatheads*, 22.   [5] Angus McDonald, *Letters*.
[6] Causton, *op. cit.*, Apr. 6.

MORALITY IN THE MYTHS

The animals, persons and spirits in the legends of the Mountain peoples were forever getting into trouble because they didn't do as they were advised by their elders, superiors or guardian spirits. This is the plain and only moral to many stories as they appear to us in the translations. The "superiors" might be relatives or chiefs; but just as often they were unrelated, non-official persons especially gifted with intelligence, insight or spiritual powers. Social consciousness or responsibility to the group appears most often in concern for the village or tribal food supply.

The Flathead tale, "Bobcat and Magpie," gives a description of a large encampment of various kinds of people – bears, dogs, cats, birds, and all sorts of animals. The men of the camp wanted to marry the one daughter of the chief, but she would have none of them. After they all had been rejected, Bobcat climbed to the top of the chief's tepee one night and looked down the smoke hole. Below he saw the lovely daughter asleep, snoring with her mouth open. Bobcat urinated down the smoke hole into the girl's mouth. She had a baby because of this. In a test, the baby only stopped crying when Bobcat picked him up, and so he was identified as the father.

> The people were jealous of Bobcat and did not want him for the Chief's son-in-law. They decided to kill and burn him. Bobcat, aware of their intentions, ordered his new wife to wait around the camp until everyone had left, and then to search in the ashes where they burned him until she found one of his bones, which she was to place under a burl from a tree. The people killed and burned Bobcat. When they abandoned camp, they took all of Bobcat's possessions, leaving only his wife and the child.

Bobcat's wife did as he had ordered, and she waited over the burl with the bone in it. Suddenly she heard her name called, and looking over her shoulder she saw a large fine tepee with furnishings inside it, and Bobcat was in there.

She went into the tepee. Bobcat told her not to look at him as he was not entirely healed. At the end of three days, however, her curiosity got the best of her and she looked at him and saw that his face was shrunken (the Indian name for Bobcat, *Senk'asu,* is translated "Shrunk-up"). After his wife had seen him, Bobcat started hunting. He had such good luck that soon they had more than they could eat and all sorts of robes and furs.

The tribe of people that had burned Bobcat were less fortunate and they were starving. Magpie thought of the Chief's daughter and baby and wondered whether they were still alive. One day she went back to the old encampment. . . Mrs. Bobcat invited Magpie in to eat all she wanted. She asked about how things were in the main camp and about her father. When Magpie told how they were all starving, Mrs. Bobcat gave her all the food she could carry and ordered her to go home, but to say nothing. [But Raven found out about the good food in Magpie's lodge, and when the Chief heard the news, he decided to] move over there, as his camp was hungry. When the tribe arrived, Bobcat went to each lodge and portioned out different parts of meat. At Raven's he left eyes, at Dog's he left bones, at Magpie's he left grease, at Wolf's he left lean meat, and so on. That is why all these animals prefer certain animals or particular parts of animals to eat.

The story then relates the kidnapping of the son of Bobcat and the chief's daughter by three spinster frogs, and tells how the parents found and rescued him after he had grown to be a young man. "Bobcat took his wife and son back to the main camp, and he was made the Chief." [7]

Instead of harping on hard-and-fast rules of behavior, these stories express tolerance, a sense of the incompre-

[7] Weisel, "Ten Animal Myths of the Flatheads," pp. 3 et al.

hensible richness of reality, and a corresponding sense of humor. The villains are seldom all bad or the heroes all good. Coyote is the supreme example: sometimes infinitely wise and successful, he is at other times ludicrously inept and unlucky; sometimes he endures great sacrifices for the good of the spirits or people; nevertheless he has bags and bags of tricks to pull, and they run the scale from merely mischievous to gruesome and mean.

Yauke'kam, the Kutenai spirit leader, born of Young Doe, daughter of Frog, and Doe's husband White Stone of the water, is definitely benevolent; he goes to great risk and trouble to originate for the people their supply of arrow wood, bow wood, flint and other necessities, and with Coyote's help he kills the destructive parent Thunderbirds. Yet at times the stories confuse him with Coyote or Chicken Hawk; and when he tries to become the sun, he is too red, and has to be rejected. The people fear him because of his great powers, and finally kill him and throw him into the water. But he is resurrected by the fish who are the friends of his father, White Stone; he then goes off to explore the lands of the sunrise and the sunset. Parts of the *Yauke' kam* story are included also in the legends of Plateau Salish.[8]

The Kutenais and Flatheads, like most non-literate people, felt deeply and humbly the unity and mystery of all life, animate and inanimate, and accepted with both reverence and humor their inability to understand it. To live with this bewildering ignorance and the inscrutability of fate, they adopted beliefs as to controls, which often "worked" because of the strengthening effect of faith.

[8] See Boas and Chamberlain, *Kutenai Tales.*

But these tribal beliefs were tolerant of individual interpretations and inspirations, and of the beliefs of other groups, honoring them all according to their evident usefulness. It is impossible to imagine Flatheads or Kutenais as missionaries, or as righteous zealots torturing people for not conforming to their own religion.

PILGRIMAGES TO ST. LOUIS

Traditionally the Flatheads and Kutenais first heard of the medicine of the Christian shamans from the converted Iroquois who came among them. Some of the fur traders were also devout men; how much informal missionary work they effected is little known. Any tidbit or more of news about the White men flew fast and far among the natives. Speeches made by Governor Simpson to members of one tribe were repeated to him word for word when later he visited tribes far distant. Though he was apparently not a religious man himself, Simpson sometimes talked to the Indians about Christianity. As a matter of company policy, he conferred at Spokane House in 1825 with eight chiefs of the Flatheads, Spokans and other tribes, about sending some of their young men to Canada to be educated. When the natives consented to send two of their boys to an Anglican school at Red River, Alexander Ross chose Coutenais Pelly and Spokane Garry, named for two Hudson's Bay officials. During a visit back home, Pelly and Garry stirred up considerable religious excitement in their region. In 1830 they returned to Red River, with a number of companions, for further training. Pelly died at Red River, and Kootenay Collins soon after returning home, but Garry and the Nez Perce Ellice became influential among their people.

The group of twenty-four Iroquois credited by the missionary Father L. B. Palladino with introducing the Flatheads to Christian ideology arrived in the mountains "between 1812 and 1830" from "the Catholic Mission of Caughnawaga, near Sault St. Louis on the St. Lawrence. We do not know what motives led them to undertake this journey, but unconsciously they were fulfilling the designs of Divine Providence."[9] Teit says this group came in the early twenties as employees of Hudson's Bay, and that their leader was Ignace La Mousse or Big Ignace. Among the Kutenais baptised by De Smet in 1842 was "the wife of an Iroquois who had resided for thirty years in this tribe. The Iroquois and a Canadian [evidently the Catholic Edward Berland] occupied themselves in the absence of a priest in instructing them."[10] A few Iroquois had been in the region even before Thompson's time.

The Jesuit Father Palladino believed it was Ignace La Mousse who inspired the Flatheads to send an official delegation to St. Louis in 1831, the so-called First Pilgrimage; others have repeated this explanation. Although Ignace was not a member of the four-man group, and although three of the four "delegates" are now known to have been Nez Perces, it is possible that these three had married among the Flatheads, and that they had been given a more or less definite assignment by the Flatheads to look for a Christian leader as described by the Iroquois.

Another historian, however, suggests that the Nez Perces were jealous of the influence of Spokane Garry, and wanted to outclass him by bringing in an American

---

9 Palladino, "Historical Notes on the Flatheads," 8.
10 De Smet, *Life, Letters and Travels,* 371.

medicine man – hence their journey to St. Louis. Actually the western Indians at that time could have had no idea of the contrasting divisions among the Christians. There is some support for the premise that these first four "emissaries" traveled eastward out of mere curiosity, and were befriended in St. Louis by Christians who reinterpreted their purpose until the trip became in the religious press a "romantic hegira," "a Macedonian cry," and eventually was compared to the search for the Holy Grail. Other writers suggest that the Indians were looking for a "Book" like the Bible Spokane Garry had been reading aloud to the Spokans and to visitors of other tribes, including the Nez Perce leader *Ish-hol-hol-hoats-toots,* who was called by the Whites "Lawyer," reportedly because of his astuteness. As early as the 1825 conference with Simpson, the assembled chiefs "joined in a most earnest request that a missionary or religious instructor should be placed among them." [11] Whether or not the first recorded trip of Flathead Valley Indians (if such they all were) to St. Louis was a loud and specific call for Catholic missionaries, even Protestants of the time admitted that subsequent journeys were definitely undertaken in search of Blackrobes.

The four bewildered travelers of 1831 sought out William Clark, as planned, and were befriended by him and by the Catholic priests, but they could not communicate clearly with anyone. Sickened by the unfamiliar food, climate and surroundings, the two older men, the Flathead Man of the Morning, baptised Paul, and the Nez Perce Black Eagle or *Keepellele,* baptised Narcisse, died in St. Louis. Rabit-Skin Leggings and

---

[11] Elliott, "Religion among the Flatheads," 4.

No Horns on His Head started home the following spring, only to lose their lives on the way.[12]

The death of a few Indians was seldom a matter of much note among the White men, but in this case the tragedy served an unforeseen purpose. The circumstances became known among church people, and before long "the religious press was on fire" with calls for missionaries to Oregon.[13] Through the well-meaning fabrications of an educated Midwestern half-breed who actually had never met the Nez Perce and Flathead visitors, but who knew about head-flattening among the far-western natives, these four became endowed in the Protestant press with flattened, sloping, peaked heads which seemed a symbol of their pitiful barbarism. The chronicles within a few years included a heart-breaking speech attributed to one of the younger Indians as the two turned homeward without the Christian teacher for whom his people yearned.

Some of the Flatheads first met a Protestant missionary when Methodists Jason and Daniel Lee went west with Nathaniel Wyeth in 1834. Influenced by Wyeth's advice and by the repelling experience of the rendezvous, the Lees decided to pursue their work in the Willamette Valley rather than in the Rocky Mountains. The following year, Dr. Marcus Whitman and Rev. Samuel Parker of the Board of Foreign Missions (Presbyterian, Congregational and Dutch Reformed

---

[12] The artist George Catlin painted portraits of the two on the Missouri River boat, entitling the paintings with the men's names and tribe. One of the two lived long enough to meet some of his people in the buffalo country, but was there killed by Blackfeet.

[13] De Voto, *op. cit.*, 8. The half-breed, William Walker, part Wyandotte (he later became the first governor of Kansas), sketched a picture of the poor flat-headed ones which was printed in the *Christian Advocate and Herald* in 1883; see Drury, *Spalding and Smith,* 73.

churches) arrived on Green River for the rendezvous,
and conferred with a large camp of Nez Perces and
Flatheads. Whitman then turned back to recruit assistance in the East, while Parker went on to the Coast.

When Whitman returned in 1836, with his wife,
Rev. and Mrs. Henry Spalding, and William Henry
Gray, they passed on through the country of the hostile
Blackfeet and the shocking rendezvous, past the rough
country of the wandering Bannacks and Flatheads, to
build their mission among the Cayuses and Nez Perces
at Waiilatpu near Walla Walla, and at Lapwai on the
Clearwater near today's Lewiston, Idaho. Two years
later, Rev. Elkanah Walker and Rev. Cushing Eells,
with their wives, also came west for the board. After
a trying journey, including a stop at the rendezvous
where wild and gruesome "entertainments" were staged
in their honor, they set up their mission at Tshimakain,
"a place of springs," about twenty-five miles northeast
of Spokane.

Neither the Flatheads, apparently the most eager for
a new religious leader, nor their neighbors the Kutenais, had yet any priest or pastor to serve them. In 1835
Ignace La Mousse had taken his young sons Charles
and Francis (Saxa) all the way to St. Louis to have
them baptised. The priest who officiated wrote that the
boys "were of handsome figure and very intelligent.
They understood a little French. They received the
sacrament of regeneration with much devotion, their
father on his knees in tears." [14] This time the emissaries
returned safely, with a promise from Bishop Rosati
that a Blackrobe would be sent soon to the Bitterroot.

But the Flatheads and their neighbors waited month

---

[14] Garraghan, *The Jesuits of the Middle U.S.*, I, p. 247.

after month in vain. A new year began and still they had no White teacher and no new medicine to help them. Their eyes and thoughts kept turning toward the East. Some of them that year must have turned their feet eastward also, unless the group spoken of in a Catholic report had left home earlier. These people were of mixed blood, French, Kutenai, Flathead and Iroquois, and were found living on the lower Missouri, where they were baptised in July by the Rev. Van Quickenborne at Kickapoo Village (near Fort Leavenworth, Kansas). "They came with the intention of not returning and of looking to the salvation of their souls." Rev. Quickenborne wrote that on his second visit to the settlement near Kickapoo Mission, he found them all sick, in despair of being able to live there, and talking of going back to their mountains.[15]

In the spring of 1837 Ignace La Mousse himself set his course again toward the city of the White men. This time he was accompanied by three Flathead men and one Nez Perce. At the American rendezvous they joined William Gray, who had been encouraged by Spokane Garry to establish among Garry's people, and was headed East to seek the support of his board. Always bent on reaching heaven in his own headlong way, Gray would not wait for the main body of the Missouri brigade. With him, besides the Indians, were several others, including a mixed-blood son of Francis Ermatinger enroute to school at Montreal. In Nebraska the price of Gray's recklessness was paid – but not by Gray. The travelers were surrounded by a large party of Sioux, who forced the Flathead-Nez Perce delegates

---

[15] *Ibid.,* I, p. 259 fn. 61. From a letter by Rev. Van Quickenborne dated at Kickapoo Village, Oct. 4, 1836.

to shoot it out with them — until Ignace and his men were past all fighting forever. Ignace, dressed as a White man, could have stood with Gray and saved his skin, but he would not. Gray later displayed to Flathead Indian Agent Peter Ronan the scar of a slight bullet wound which he said he had suffered when he tried to defend the Flatheads, and told him that young Ermatinger also resisted, and that the Sioux only released the White-blooded men from captivity some days later.[16] A present-day historian, however, claims that "in the mountains men always believed that William Gray, would-be servant of God, swapped his Indians' lives to the Sioux in exchange for his own."[17]

The death of Ignace La Mousse was undoubtedly a great sadness to the Flatheads, who had all admired him as a man, no matter what they thought of his Christian teachings. But no Flatheads went along two years later when Little Ignace (or Aneas or Eneas, no relative, or at least not a close relative, of Ignace La Mousse) and Peter Goucher, both Iroquois, made the journey to St. Louis, and this time had the good fortune to meet the Jesuit, Father Pierre-Jean De Smet. A native Belgian already working among American Indians, De Smet had heard of the petitions from the Rocky Mountains even before he met Ignace and Goucher; after consulting with his bishop, he promised at once to go west. Ignace remained to guide him, while Goucher returned to the Bitterroot to tell the good news to the people in the mountains.[18]

---

[16] Ronan, *op. cit.*, 25-26. See also Drury, *First White Women over the Rockies*, I, p. 237.   [17] Lavender, *Land of Giants*, 195.

[18] Compare with the accepted accounts of the pilgrimage, an account by a Flathead as given to Curtis, *op. cit.*, VII, p. 47.

ARRIVAL OF DE SMET

When Father De Smet arrived at Pierre's Hole in western Wyoming in 1840, he was overwhelmed by his welcome: eight hundred Flatheads, including Pend d'Oreilles and Kalispels, together with hundreds of Nez Perces and members of other tribes, were on hand to meet him. Big Face or *Tjolizhatzay,* chief of the Southern Flatheads, asked in the name of his people: " 'Show us the road we have to follow to come to the place where the Great Spirit resides.' Then he resigned his authority to me; but I replied that I had no other object in view than their spiritual welfare." That evening the Father wept for joy as about two thousand gathered before his lodge to recite prayers.[19]

After hundreds of baptisms, De Smet returned to St. Louis to look for helpers. By fall of the following year he was in the Bitterroot Valley, accompanied by Father Nicholas Point and Gregory Mengarini and three lay brothers, all Europeans. Near present-day Stevensville, the Indians constructed a large cross of cottonwood for the first Mass at St. Mary's Mission. "That roughly hewn cross," Father Palladino later wrote, "was the symbol of the missionaries' hopes, as it must have been the terror of the infernal hosts who for ages had lorded it over these regions as sole and absolute masters." [20]

Buildings for the mission were begun at once. The news spread and representatives of twenty-four tribes were said to have visited St. Mary's that first fall. Father De Smet spent November along the Clark Fork among the Kalispels and Pend d'Oreilles, returning by

---

[19] De Smet, *Letters and Sketches,* 142.   [20] Palladino, *Indian and White,* 41.

Christmas to find the chapel ready for services at St. Mary's. At the end of the year the Jesuit summarized the work in the mountains: "The whole Flat Head nation converted – four hundred Kalispels baptised – eighty Nez Perces, several Couers de Aliene, many Kootenays, Black Feet, Serpents [Snakes] and Banocs." [21] By spring the Flatheads were building fences and cultivating the land around the mission with tools brought by Father De Smet from Fort Colville.

Setting off for the mouth of the Columbia in the spring, De Smet made a detour from Camas Prairie toward Thompson Lakes to meet a group of the Kutenais.

> We arrived about three o'clock in sight of the Kootenai camp. When I was about twenty yards from them the warriors presented their arms, which they had hidden until then under their buffalo robes. They fired a great salute, which frightened my mule and made her rear and prance, to the great amusement of the savages. They unanimously declared themselves in favor of my religion, and adopted the beautiful custom of their neighbors the Flat Heads, to meet night and morning for prayers in common.

On their way back to the Clark Fork on April 16, De Smet and his four companions stopped at the Hot Springs where the Indians told the Father that "after the fatigues of a long journey they find that bathing in this water greatly refreshes them." [22]

Father De Smet, a record traveler of his time, now went down to Vancouver and the Willamette Valley, en route promising priests to the Coeur d'Alenes and Kalispels, and returned overland to St. Louis, with a stop at St. Mary's before the end of October. The next year (1843) he crossed to Europe and returned with

---

[21] De Smet, *Letters and Sketches,* 319.   [22] *Ibid.,* 358-60.

Father Joseph Joset and others, who came with him to St. Mary's in 1844. The Jesuits by 1846 had established the parent mission of today's St. Ignatius at "The Bay of the Kalispels" on the Pend d'Oreille River near Cusick, Washington, and Sacred Heart *(Skoto-Tomish* or *Skoot-loty)* for the Coeur d'Alenes on the Coeur d'Alene River ten miles above the lake, preceded in 1842 by a church on the St. Joe River. St. Francis Borgia at Swan Lake for the "Upper Kalispels" was only a station for services where no church was ever built.[23]

To these Europeans, the states of mind and habits of living of the Rocky Mountain natives must have seemed as strange a wilderness as the very mountains; they must have had great faith in their mission in order to carry on. Father Nicholas Point, Father Anthony Ravalli, and above all Father Joset, were responsible for the development of the Coeur d'Alene Mission, where the old church is now known for Father Joseph Cataldo, who in 1866 left Sacred Heart to establish St. Michaels on Peon's Prairie nearer to the present city of Spokane. At the Bay of the Kalispels the Indians put up fourteen log buildings under the direction of Fathers Adrian Hoecken and Ravalli, and broke the soil for nearly three hundred acres of grain in the surrounding lowlands.

AMONG THE KUTENAIS

Father De Smet in 1843 went for the first time to visit the Kutenais at their home villages. He arrived first among the *Arcs-a-Plats* at Bonners Ferry, of whom he wrote: "They know neither industry, art nor science;

[23] See especially Wm. L. Davis, *St. Ignatius Mission;* and Schoenberg, *Jesuit Mission Presses.*

the words *mine* and *thine* are scarcely known among
them." Here he was a guest at the annual Fish Festival,
and prepared to establish the station of the Assumption
of the Virgin. "Thanks to the instructions and counsels
of a brave Canadian, Mr. Berland, who for a long time
had remained among them in the quality of a trader, I
found the little tribe docile, and in the best disposition
to embrace the faith. They sang canticles in the French
and the English tongues." The Cross of the Assumption was erected "on the shore of a lake." [24] Leaving the
Arcs-a-Plats, De Smet with two companions started up
the Kootenai River, evidently on foot.

> After a few days journey we arrived at the Prairie du Tubac, the
> usual abode of the Kootenais. Their camp is situated in an im-
> mense and delightful valley, bounded by two eminences. I found
> about thirty lodges of Kootenais; hunger had forced many fam-
> ilies to cross the great mountain. I was received with every
> demonstration of joy and filial affection. [A cross was erected
> and] the chiefs advanced and prostrated themselves before that
> sacred ensign, which speaks so eloquently of the love of a Man-
> God, who came to redeem a fallen race. On the feast of the Holy
> Heart of Mary I sang high mass, thus taking spiritual possession
> of this land. I administered the sacrament of baptism to 105
> persons, among whom were twenty adults.[25]

The Jesuit traveler was delighted and amazed with
the landscape and the wild life as he went north up the
Kootenay to Windermere Lake, where the feast of the
Nativity of the Blessed Virgin was solemnly celebrated
for Francois Morigeau, a Frenchman, his Scotch-
Indian second wife and ten Morigeau children, and
several families of Shuswaps camped with them.

---

[24] De Smet, *Oregon Missions,* 127-9. This spot is said to be on what is now
an abrupt little "island" rising above the broad cultivated flats which have
been drained for farming, west of the town of Bonners Ferry.

[25] *Ibid.,* 203. This station may have been located on today's "69" Ranch,
north of Eureka, an old Kutenai camp site.

Descendants of Edward Berland believe that he came west with Francois Morigeau, which would be about 1818. Two years before Father De Smet found Berland at Bonners Ferry, Governor Simpson after crossing the Continental Divide westward during his journey around the world was met by Berland, with twenty-seven horses, at Columbia Lake. Later the augmented Simpson party came upon some of the Lower Kutenais under their chief, known as Grande Queue from the length of his braid. Simpson wrote:

> Many years ago I had taken a son of this chief, naming him Kootenay Pelly. The youngster, a fine, clever, docile lad, died [of injuries after he fell from a horse] – a blow from which the father never recovered, and though the mention of the deceased would have been utterly repugnant to savage etiquette, yet I was pretty sure that the Grande Queue, as well as myself, was thinking rather of the poor boy than of anything else.[26]

Berland and Morigeau had come west for North West Company, Francois at least from Saint-Martine. Berland transferred to Hudson's Bay after the amalgamation, but Francois turned free trapper, and moved into the Upper Columbia country, via Canoe River, with Chief *Ken-pe-skut* and his followers, traveling by canoe. Called by the Whites Peter Kinbaskit, this well-known North Thompson chief was highly spoken of by early explorers. He and his fifty or sixty people of mixed tribal blood allied themselves with the Stonies, Assiniboine people who often came to the Lakes country to fish.

Father De Smet wrote eloquently of the independent life led by Morigeau, the "monarch who rules at the source of the Columbia." [27] Morigeau and his wife accompanied by some at least of the children, later moved

---

[26] Simpson, *op. cit.*, I, p. 130.　　[27] De Smet, *Oregon Missions*, 209-10.

to the Colville Valley. Frank, the namesake son, one of the children by the earlier wife, and Baptiste, the youngest son, in 1843 took active part in the development of the Windermere country. The enterprising Sophie Morigeau is a story unto herself.[28] Scores of contemporary residents of the Flathead Valley claim descent from Rosalie Morigeau who married Edward Berland's son John, and her brother Alexander who married Rosalie Finley, a granddaughter of Jocko.

PROGRESS AND PAUSE AT ST. MARY'S

Anthony Ravalli, S.J., sent from among the Colville Indians to assist Father Mengarini at St. Mary's in the Bitterroot Valley, found the mission a stimulating challenge to his talents as a doctor, mechanic, musician and artist. "Father Ravalli can do anything," people said. By 1846 there were at St. Mary's twelve houses, a church, a flour mill, a saw mill, and various farm buildings. The cattle numbered forty head. There were horses, hogs, chickens and an annual harvest which yielded several thousand bushels of wheat, potatoes, and other grains and vegetables. In spite of periodic abundance, the mission personnel often came close to starving during the winter when most of the Indians were away on the hunt.

By now the Oregon Trail at times and in places was a crowded thoroughfare. The fears and resentments of the natives all along the middle and lower Columbia broke out in 1847 among the Cayuses, who murdered Dr. Marcus Whitman and his wife and twelve other Whites at the little settlement of Waiilatpu. Special forces operating in this case were an epidemic of

---

[28] See O. Johnson, *op. cit.,* 41 *et al.*

measles; the influence of Tom Hill, a Delaware Indian who was spreading word of what White men had done in the East to his family and his tribe; and the presence among the Cayuses of a half-breed malcontent named Joe Lewis, one of whose cronies, an admirer of Hill, was Nicholas Finley.[29] Another factor was the character of the Whitmans, who in spite of their dedication to the Christian cause, didn't really feel drawn to the Indians, and came to believe that the paramount need of the region was settlement by the Whites.

The Protestants did not like to admit that the ritualism and pageantry of the Catholic services, the simple dogmatism of the beliefs as offered to illiterates, and the aura of holiness about the priests, was especially suited to appeal to the Indians. Nor did they like to admit that the foreign priests gave a more undivided attention to their charges than most of the early Protestant missionaries did. The Jesuits, besides being consecrated and well trained, had no families to support and no particular interest in settlement by Whites from the United States.

A few of the westward bound emigrants of the time, along with assorted trappers and traders, White and mixed-blood, wandered into the Bitterroot Valley,

---

[29] Duncan McDonald referred to Lewis as "A Mexican named Jo." (*New Northwest,* IX, no. 43, p. 3.) Nicholas or Nicoli Finley, son of Jocko, was sometimes with two of his brothers and their half-breed friend Dumont, who had settled near what is now Chewelah, Wash. Four of Nicholas' brothers, Francois and Zavier, Patrick and Koostah (evidently Augustus, also referred to as Yoosta), are mentioned in various accounts as residing in the Spokane country during this period. A Finley descendant, Mrs. Arnold Trahen, writes that Nicholas was employed in 1846 at Tshimakain, where he pitched his lodge. Mrs. Walker in her diary does mention his visiting there, and also his part in the disturbances among the Cayuses. He continued to try to stir up trouble even after the Whitman massacre. Consult Drury, *First White Women,* and *Spalding and Smith;* also Lavender, *op. cit.*

where they commonly camped near the mission. Some of these men "led notoriously licentious lives, to the scandal of the whole tribe. When they did not receive all they wanted, and when their immorality was rebuked and checked, they took their revenge by poisoning the simple minds of the Indians." [30]

The Flatheads had swallowed whole the Jesuits' religious claims and rites, but they could not assimilate Christianity complete in a few years. Such restrictions as monogamy seemed to them unrealistic, nor could they give up their ancient sumesh as one would scratch out a phrase in a written law.

As peoples go, the Kutenais and Flatheads were naturally devout and good of heart. They honored integrity of character and recognized that there were spiritual qualities in nature and men. But as with all people, their deepest need was to survive, and if possible proudly. To the majority of them, the single most impressive attribute of the White men was their killing power. Since the Blackfeet now had guns also, it would require some further strong medicine to defeat them – and who, they reasoned, must possess greater medicine power than the makers of guns? Such was their anticipatory faith that when they were on their way to meet Father De Smet for the first time, under the leadership of Chief Chalax of the Pend d'Oreilles, they won a battle against an overwhelming force of astonished Blackfeet, killing fifty of the enemy (according to the account of the Mountainaires) and losing not a single man themselves.

[30] Palladino, *Indian and White,* 65. See also Diocese of Helena, *Register,* Helena, Mont., Aug. 3, 1941; Ronan, *op. cit.,* 35; Mullan, "A Military Road from Fort Benton to Walla Walla"; and Weisel, *Men and Trade on the Northwest Frontier.*

In the early days of St. Mary's, several of the priests at different times accompanied the Flatheads on their hunting and fighting forays across the mountains. With luck and their new-born confidence, the Flatheads were successful against the Blackfeet in these first years of their conversion. Father Mengarini told of a battle when only four Flatheads were killed, although the Blackfeet were said to have lost twenty-four men. Father De Smet himself ascribed various Flathead victories to the protection of the Christian God, and gladly reported to his superiors that the Flatheads considered "the medicine of the Blackrobes the strongest of all."[31] The Blackfeet were so impressed by the power of the Christian prayers used by the Flathead warriors practically as battle cries, that in 1846 they took advantage of an opportunity to ally themselves with the Flatheads and Nez Perces against a common enemy – the Crows – and to petition Father De Smet, then on his way east for the last time, to put their people also under the protection of his Great Spirit. Father De Smet then contrived in the camp what he considered a great peace among the traditional enemies of the mountains and the Plains, through the Nez Perces in particular were not as sanguine and eager as they might have been in accepting it.[32]

The Blackfeet, it turned out, had not been effectively tranquilized. The old conflicts continued, the Piegans at times taking horses and scalps at the very gate of the mission in the Bitterroot. Flathead prayers for victory and security of life were not always answered, and

---

[31] De Smet, *Oregon Missions,* 326. As De Smet repeated in his letters the story of the earlier Flathead victory under Chief Chalax, the number of Blackfeet dead increased with each account!   [32] *Ibid.,* 354.

doubtless the tribesmen found that other chronic difficulties also failed to disappear like magic with baptism. The words of scoffers and tempters both Red and White began to have more telling effect.

Beset by these many difficulties, the Jesuits in 1850 leased their improvements at St. Mary's to "Major" John Owen, a former sutler with an advance American military party in the area, for use as a trading post. The mission priests were assigned to California and elsewhere; St. Mary's remained closed for sixteen years.

PROTESTANT MISSION

For nine years the Walkers and the Eells labored with the Spokans at Tshimakain, holding religious services daily when the Indians were about, teaching the children in their homes and in school, encouraging the planting of crops. Yet not one Indian joined the church in all that time. Father De Smet with partisan sarcasm reported in 1842 that these missionaries had "baptised several of their own children" and were raising only enough crops for their own use, lest some of the savages might linger in the neighborhood.[33] The Calvinist missionaries, Protestants explained, did not feel that infants must be baptised to save them from hell; and they did not believe in granting church membership until the petitioners had undergone personal experience of conversion.

It is true that Indian converts, both Catholic and Protestant, were more often women and children than men; and that not all the men who held back, or backslid, were incorrigibles. Some of them were no doubt sincere skeptics.

---

[33] *Ibid.*, 368.

Rev. Spalding at Lapwai worked away at learning the Nez Perce language, and printed a booklet for his Indian children on the mission hand press; the same press was used to turn out a "Flathead Primer" prepared by Rev. Walker. Rev. Walker and Rev. Eells took turns going to preach among the Pend d'Oreilles and Coeur d'Alenes, and reluctantly gave up the idea of going to the Southern Flatheads.

Spokane Garry had become discouraged and wasn't much help. His own people ridiculed his alien ways; his training in the more ritualistic Anglican church had not prepared him for the emphasis these missionaries placed upon conversion, nor for their stern strictures against gambling, drinking and smoking. Sir George Simpson's statement that Garry had "relapsed into his original barbarism, taking as many wives as he could get,"[34] has been discounted by other historians; but at any rate he was a disappointment to the church people at Tshimakain.

"Apparently the truth has produced little deep or permanent effect," the missionaries wrote. "Among those who are most attentive to religious instruction, the opinion has been quite general that to understand the book, abstain from gross vice, and perform some externals of religion, constitute all that is required to fit a person for the enjoyment of God."[35] How strangely this reads as though written not particularly of newly-contacted Indians, but of so many White Christians of that time and this. Nor were these Indians the only ones who did not always welcome the doctrine of original sin. "As a general thing the people consider themselves

---

[34] Simpson, *op. cit.,* I, pp. 44-5.
[35] Drury, *Spalding and Smith,* 185; report of Walker and Eells.

to be good," Asa Smith wrote of the Nez Perces in despair.

It would take time for the preachers and the natives to begin to understand each other. After the Whitman massacre, both Lapwai and Tshimakain were closed. The Spokans tried repeatedly to bring the Walkers and the Eells back from western Oregon to the old mission. At last, in the early 1870s, Rev. Spalding returned at the request of Spokane Garry, and inspired among the Nez Perces and Spokans a religious awakening that resulted in hundreds of new church memberships. Among the leaders of the regenerated church was an Indian who had been taught in the Walker home as a child.

ST. IGNATIUS

The beautiful meadows at Cusik which the Fathers had anticipated would make fine farmlands for the Kalispels, were so often flooded that the mission was moved to higher ground. Even here, the snow piled up so early and so deep, and lay so late, that the Indians went hungry much of the time. In the autumn of 1854, Chief Alexander of the Pend d'Oreilles, a brilliant leader with some admixture of Snake and Tunaha blood in his veins, led the Fathers far upriver to the Lower Flathead Valley. One of the priests during the summer had made five small barges and a great many boxes to pack the things; after harvest the Pend d'Oreilles came with about a hundred pack horses to help carry everything. Father Hoecken sold the cattle for two thousand dollars and so had the means to build up the new place.

Father Hoecken reported that he found the new site lonely, but beautiful, and the region rich in fish and game. Within a few weeks the workers had erected several frame buildings, a chapel, two houses, a carpenter shop and blacksmith shop. As Easter approached the following year, over a thousand Indians, Upper Kutenais and Flat-Bows, Pend d'Oreilles, Flatheads and "Mountain Kalispels," had arrived at the mission, planning to make it the site of their home camps. Some 18,000 rails had gone into fences, and a large field had been placed under cultivation. "Besides a large number of children baptised," Father Hoecken wrote, "I have had the happiness to baptise upwards of 150 adults of the Kutenai tribe, men of great docility and artlessness of character." [36]

Among the White men who lent assistance during the establishment of St. Ignatius in the Mission Valley was Lt. John Mullan, who had come out from Washington, D.C. to Washington Territory – separated from Oregon Territory in 1853 – with its first governor, Isaac Stevens. To occupy his leisure time as head of a territory that included not only the present state of Washington, but also what is now Idaho, western Montana and part of Wyoming, Stevens was to serve as Superintendent of Indian Affairs for the territory, and director of the northwestern railroad surveys just ordered by Congress.

The three jobs were closely related. The railroad surveys were to be carried out under the direction of the Secretary of War. The settlers were afraid that the natives in Washington and Oregon territories might rise, any day now, in bloody rebellion.

[36] Garraghan, *op. cit.*, II, p. 312.

Armed Orders

DEVELOPMENTS ON THE MID-COLUMBIA

The second Sinclair Expedition, arriving in the Columbia country late in 1854, entered a sort of dispersed hornet's nest, though for the present most of the activity was restricted to passionate buzzing. Ignoring threats against his life, Governor Stevens got busy trying to round up the tribes for a treaty council; to support him, Oregon volunteers were joining the small number of United States troops in Washington Territory. The Oregon Donation Law of 1850 granted 640 acres in the territories to family men who would improve the land, a smaller amount to single men; bold newcomers were searching out likely locations all over this invitingly vast and varied land.

James Sinclair evidently left his own family, and his sister-in-law Margaret Campbell, at Walla Walla while he went on with most of the others to Vancouver. The people of the expedition scattered; many tried out California, but most of these returned to Oregon.

Stevens, a short-statured man with compensatory self assurance and drive, that summer persuaded the representatives of some two to five thousand assembled mid-Columbia natives to sign away their freedom at Walla Walla – though as he left, the Indian women were dancing with men around the campfires: an ominous sign, warned Scout Billy McKay, grandson of Dr.

McLoughlin's wife Margaret, for in pre-campaign dances women were lures to enlistment.

After concluding treaties with the Flatheads and Kutenais at Council Grove near Missoula, and with the Blackfeet on Judith River, Stevens in October was on his way east when near Fort Benton an exhausted rider overtook him, to report that the Indians were on the warpath all over the Pacific Northwest. The governor hurried westward again across the Rockies, and first of all met the Spokans and Coeur d'Alenes at Antoine Plant's place just south of the present-day city of Spokane.[1] Chief Kamiakin of the Yakimas had been among them and they were sullen. But Stevens, with the assistance of regional priests and perhaps of Spokane Garry, transformed their mood to friendship and went on to Lapwai, where the Nez Perces assured him of their loyalty to the Whites and gave the group escort as far as Walla Walla. Here they were met by Oregon militia who had killed the Walla Walla chief, Peu-peu-mox-mox, defeating his followers. The Indian wars were on.

James Sinclair was caught in the midst of hostilities at The Dalles, and lost his life during the Indian siege of Bradford and Company's store building in March of 1856. Martial law was declared in Washington, and the sporadic conflict on the Columbia and northwards and southwards continued. Fresh mineral discoveries in the region were attracting gold-hungry hordes. To the Indians of the Pacific Northwest, long accustomed to fur traders who for their own good took a certain interest in the persons and welfare of the Indians, often

---

[1] See Peltier, "The Council on the Spokane"; and William Compton Brown, *The Indian Side of the Story,* published by the author, Okanogan, Wash., 1961.

marrying among them, these heedless settlers and even more heedless miners were a plague to be bitterly resisted. Yet their very numbers and their very contempt suggested to the Indians the hopelessness of their own cause.

There were intermittent triumphs for the Red men, but White reinforcements armed with cannon and long-range rifles soon put a virtual end to the defense – or the rebellion, as the Whites saw it.

Both Johnny Campbell and his sister Margaret weathered narrow escapes during the hostilities, but in 1859 Johnny was able to go down to Oregon City to visit their widowed sister, Mrs. James Sinclair. Margaret was by then three years married to Billy McKay, better known as Dr. William. Both Campbell and Colin Sinclair were eventually to return to the Rockies.

COUNCIL GROVE

After the clashing tumult and sharp danger of the Walla Walla council in 1855, the meeting with the Flatheads and Kutenais at Council Grove in July must have seemed to Isaac Stevens and his associates a quiet and friendly interval. The great Pend d'Oreille warrior Big Canoe spoke the feelings of the assembled peoples when he asked reproachfully why they were being asked to sign a peace treaty: "I never saw your blood."[2] It was the boast of these tribes that they had never slain a White man. A few of the Kalispels, led by the warrior *Xane'wa,* joined the rebelling Spokans in the Steptoe Butte campaign, where *Xane'wa* lost his life; but many more of the Kalispels went north or east to avoid the conflict. The Pend d'Oreille Spotted Coyote, who was

2 Stevens, Isaac, "Flathead Treaty Council," 292.

said to be bullet-proof, fought with the Spokans and was unhurt; but when he saw his comrades slaughtered by cannon balls, he said, "We must give up fighting and make peace or leave the country."[3]

Among the Kutenais and Flatheads were quite a number of conscientious Christians. Among them also were many persons who already bore in their veins the blood of White trappers and traders. Both peoples were disciplined and willing to listen to the White man's idea of reason. And of course they were not so strong in numbers as the tribal populations of the mid-Columbia. It was estimated without a formal census that there were four hundred Flatheads, six hundred Pend d'Oreilles and four hundred Kutenais to be considered. About three hundred Kalispels were not represented at the council.

The assembled tribesmen, nearly a thousand strong and festively outfitted, had heard from the interim agent, Thomas Adams, that the Blackfeet had promised to sign a treaty restricting their residence, and setting aside a buffalo grounds to be held peaceably in common with the trans-mountain tribes. This if true was a real inducement to cooperate with the Whites. But although they knew that the Blackfeet had been hard hit by smallpox, the mountain people were skeptical; recently the Plainsmen had stepped up their raiding, reasoning that this might be their last chance to make legal war.

Some thoughtful elders could not believe that perpetual peace, even if achieved, would be a healthful state of existence. The picture the White men held of the Indians settling down as farmers and wage-earners simply could not be transferred to the minds of natives

---

[3] Teit, *Salishan Tribes,* 371.

who had so little past experience from which to imagine such an existence. Naturally the Flatheads did
not like the idea of giving away their lands, but they
had as yet seen few settlers. The majority of them did
not distinctly realize that by this proffered treaty the
heroic extent of their ancient range was to be shrunken
almost to a single valley, where they would be expected
to settle and live according to White man ways and
laws.

The issue was confused by the yet unsurveyed international boundary which cut across the range of the
Kutenais, and by the shifting and overlapping land use
by the different groups in recent times. Arbitrarily, in
their ignorance and self-absorption, the Whites had
decreed that the three tribes(or four, if the Kalispels
are considered separately), should be settled upon a
single reservation. Stevens suggested the Bitterroot Valley as the home for all these people, who should then
recognize the Flathead chief Victor as the chief of the
confederated tribes. And he expected his treaty to be
signed within a few days! "I am confused," said one of
the delegates, in effect. "I thought we were three tribes,
not one. We'll have to talk this over." [4]

Although the Bitterroot was apparently not an ancient place of residence for the Upper Flatheads, they
had made it their home valley for some generations. It
was the more precious to them for having provided a
refuge as the Blackfeet drove them off the buffalo lands
where they had once pitched their lodges freely at any
season. Its climate was mild for the region; it was well
supplied with bitterroot and camas, fish and game; its
guardian mountains had a lofty yet intimate grandeur.

[4] Stevens, *op. cit.,* 290.

Traditions already enveloped the valley's familiar features. At Ram's Head Encampment on the East Fork was a famous tree with the horns of a mountain ram embedded in the trunk; the sheep who once wore the horns, the Flathead said, was attacking one of the first Flathead hunters ever to come this way, when he rammed into the tree and left his horns there. And this valley was the place where the Flatheads had lately learned something about Christianity, about farming and accumulating possessions, about holding a bit of earth as a continuous family home. Sixteen log cabins inhabited by Flathead families, as well as many skin lodges, were clustered about the old mission, now Fort Owen; each had its small garden. Around the Flathead village a few White settlers, mostly onetime trappers, traders or prospectors, were cutting down trees, building cabins, putting up corrals for the issue of Oregon Trail livestock, planting crops and finding the soil good.

In the Lower Flathead Valley, the mission of St. Ignatius had now attracted as more or less permanent residents many Pend d'Oreilles and some Kalispels and Kutenais, with stray Spokans, Coeur d'Alenes and mixed-blood descendants of traders and trappers. Under guidance of the priests, the residents were raising grain, gardens and livestock on a modest scale.

Kutenaian groups, usually excepting the Lower Kutenais, had always passed through and camped in the Upper Flathead Valley north of the lake; in recent times some of them had been staying here for longer and longer periods. By 1849 White men married to Kutenai women evidently had some influence in the shift south. At the head of the lake by the mid- or late

forties lived Joe Ashley and his friend Francois Gravelle, Frenchmen who had come to the Flathead-Kutenai country from Quebec, to marry sisters of Kutenai
blood. Here by 1848 were Jocko Finlay's sons Mich-
quam, called Nequam or Jocko, and Francois or Frank,
known as Penatzu or Penache or Benetsee,[5] and a number of other wanderers, most of whom had married
Kutenai Indian women. Ashley's cabin along Ashley
Creek between the lake and the later town of Kalispell,
back against the western hills, has been described, perhaps mistakenly, as a Hudson's Bay post.[6]

The fur business wasn't what it used to be, either for
demand or price, though Hudson's Bay was still doing
fairly well in Kutenai country. Here in the Flathead
Valley the bunch grass grew richly; visions of fattening
livestock flickered in and out of the fireside talk above
Flathead Lake, competing for attention with rumors of
gold-pan fortunes.

Then came the news from Sutter's Mill, and the
White men, husbands or bachelors, took off for California – though most of them were to return no richer.

WHICH VALLEY?

Heading the Upper Flathead delegation was the
Christian chief, Victor, said to have been partly of
Tunaha descent, and no relation, or very distantly re-
lated, to any of his predecessors in office. The last of

---

[5] Duncan McDonald mistakenly identified Penatzu as "Antoine" Finley;
Duncan's father Angus, like most historians, and like Penatzu's own descendants, said he was Francois.

[6] It is of course possible that Ashley or one of his neighbors may have kept
trading stock on hand for dealing with the Indians. On the theory that Howse
or some other Hudson's Bay trader built here, see pp. 213-14; also consult
Stone, *op. cit.;* articles in the Johns *Collection;* MSU thesis by Montana Isch on
"Development of the Flathead Valley."

these predecessors, according to Peter Ronan, was *Estowish Semmegee-itshin* or Grizzly Bear Erect, baptised Lyola by Father De Smet.[7] Victor's Salish name, as given by Teit, meant Plenty of Horses; his christened name "Victor" the Flatheads could only pronounce "Mit-to." Lt. John Mullan described Victor as "mild and gentle as a woman, and innocent of wrong as a child," yet "brave in battle."[8] Heading the Pend d'Oreilles was the respected Chief Alexander. Chief Michelle (Shot-Head or *Kisklamakl*) led the Kutenai delegation; mostly he followed the lead of Alexander; the interpreters spoke Salish.

Stevens flattered the chiefs, praising their prowess, and assuring them that the government agent would fully respect their authority. They would be given good cabins and farms, he promised, and salaries of several hundred dollars a year. He spoke chiefly through the interpreters Gustav Sohon and Michael Revais. The latter was of mixed White and Pend d'Oreille blood, and could speak some Kutenai, but it is doubtful

---

[7] Ronan, *op. cit.,* 44; De Smet, *Letters and Sketches,* 284, and *Oregon Missions,* 174; Teit, *Salishan Tribes,* 377. De Smet's Big Face, apparently the same as his "Bravest of the Brave," the first Flathead baptised by the Jesuit, was praised by him as a loyal Christian as well as a great man to his people. He is given by Palladino as the predecessor of Victor and is apparently the same man as Standing Grizzly Bear, listed by Teit as a chief for both the Kalispels and the Flatheads; both Big Face and Standing Grizzly Bear were said to have died about 1839. Yet Ronan's Grizzly Bear Erect (having a Salish name corresponding to that of Teit's Kalispel chief Standing Grizzly Bear), had only died, according to Ronan, in 1854. It is possible that one of the dates is incorrect, or that a father and son are concerned here.

Ronan gave Joseph *Celp-stop* or Crazy Country as the predecessor of Alexander. The Pend d'Oreille chief during Thompson's time was Red Eagle. Sometimes of course, the war chief or camp chief is confused with the head chief.

[8] "Noted Indians and Founders of the Flathead Mission," in *Indian Sentinel,* Bureau of Catholic Indian Affairs, Wash., D.C., Oct. 1919, p. 21.

whether Michelle and his fellow-Kutenais understood very clearly what was going on.

In spite of the rosy picture painted by Stevens of the life of a reservation chief, none of them could make up their minds to come all together in one valley. Victor claimed he was the head of the Salish and that both the Bitterroot and the Mission valleys belonged to him; at one point he tentatively agreed to live in either place. And Alexander at one time said he was willing to move to the Bitterroot if assured that he would go to hell if he didn't. But neither chief could be held to these positions. Alexander thought it would be a good idea for the people of the three tribes to live together, but he did not see the Kalispels and Kutenais moving all that way to the Bitterroot, and didn't think his own people would want to leave their St. Ignatius Mission. Victor at last said simply, "I am content in my own valley," and remained immovable.[9]

As the days passed, Stevens (though in a report of the previous year he had called the Flatheads "the best Indians of the mountains or plains") lost patience and accused the chiefs of not talking straight; they counter-accused him of talking sharp like a Blackfeet. The transcript of the exchange bares the pathetic attempt of the Indians to keep green their pride and hope, while at the same time propitiating the imponderable power of the White race, and indulging their desire to be friends with its obviously human members. The meetings had several times to be adjourned to give the confused tribal members more time to consult. Father

---

[9] Stevens, *op. cit.* See also Stone, *op. cit.;* W. L. Davis, *op. cit.;* Ronan, *op. cit.;* Burlingame and Toole, *op. cit.*

Adrian Hoecken came from St. Ignatius to use his influence for a settlement. Stevens at last proposed a reservation bounded on the east by the ridge of the Mission Range, on the south by the divide between Jocko Valley and Missoula Valley, on the west by a line crossing the Clark Fork between Horse Plains and Camas Prairie, and on the north by an east-west line cutting Flathead Lake in half.

Victor shook his head. He insisted that the Bitterroot Valley must also be included. Stevens was finally obliged to add to the treaty Article Eleven:

> It is, moreover, provided that the Bitter Root Valley, above the Loo-lo Fork, shall be carefully surveyed and examined and if it shall prove, in the judgment of the President, to be better adapted to the wants of the Flathead tribe than the general reservation provided for in this treaty, then such portions of it as may be necessary shall be set apart as a separate reserve for the said tribe. No portion of the Bitter Root Valley, above the Loo-lo Fork, shall be opened to settlement until such examination is had and the decision of the President is known.[10]

With this evasive provision Victor had to be satisfied. Together with the other two chiefs and fifteen of the leading men of all three tribes, he now signed the agreement. The Flathead sub-chief Moses turned away when the paper was set before him. "You have pulled my wings off and let me down," he said.[11]

Stevens and his party now left for the Judith Basin to meet the Blackfeet. Accompanying him were many of

---

[10] Kappler, "Treaty with the Flatheads."

[11] Stevens, *op. cit.,* 311. The Moses who did sign is listed as a Kutenai, and was probably the same Moses who later became an Upper Kutenai chief, the second of that name (See Graham, *op. cit.,* 172; this story confirmed by Peter Andrew, interview).

the Indians with whom he had been conferring at
Council Grove, together with Father Hoecken, who
built a church in the Judith Valley during the delay
before the Blackfeet and the large delegation of Nez
Perces and other traditional enemies of the Plainsmen,
could be assembled for the signing of the treaty. By
this agreement, the Blackfeet were to be confined to a
reservation in north central Montana (of today), while
the headwaters of the Missouri and Yellowstone rivers
were set aside as a dreamland where hunters of all
tribes would shoot at the bison but never at each other,
and presumably would never try to steal each other's
horses. The historians who marvel at Stevens' achievement in persuading the Plains marauders to keep the
peace, did not live in the valleys of western Montana
during the next twenty-five years.

As for the Kutenais, the government said to them in
effect: either get inside the reservation line, or get north
of the United States-Canadian boundary and let the
British authorities worry about you. Michelle's ambi-
tion was "to have one great Kutenai reserve for all the
bands, wherein the whole people could live and practice their old life as nearly as possible." [12] Instead, there
was a scattering and confusion among all the bands.

In about 1840 a group of *Akiyeniks* from the Fisher
River country, after their young chief Tamar or Red
Sky [13] had been killed by the Blackfeet, had migrated
to Tobacco Plains, joining an Upper Kutenai band

[12] Turney-High, *Kutenai,* 17.

[13] According to Hollensteiner, Frank Linderman got some of his stories
from the Kutenai "Old Tom (Tomah or Red Sky)" at Flathead Lake. This
Old Tom was doubtless a namesake of the Middle Kutenai chief killed around
1830.

there under Not Grizzly Bear, predecessor of Michelle.[14] The Kutenai Sallad, enumerating the bands of the tribe in the 1860s, referred to the *Ac-Ke-Ye-Nicks* as "The men of Tobacco Plains." Members of both this migrant group and the original Tobacco Plains band were with Michelle at the treaty conference. Edward or Edwald, at this time chief of the original Tobacco Plains people, did not attend, though he was considered head of all the Kutenais. After the council, some of the Middle Kutenais lingered in, or returned to, the Upper Flathead Valley (or perhaps these were mostly Kutenais who had been camping here more or less regularly even before the council).[15] They now moved south along the west lake shore to the vicinity of today's Elmo and Dayton, to be within the reservation; but they continued to hunt and camp also in the Upper Valley, even into the 1890s after the Whites had established Kalispell.

Edward is said to have been the son of Unknown Bear, the last non-Christian chief of the Tobacco Plains Kutenais.[16] He and his people, not knowing the where-

[14] See Curtis' portrait of Not Grizzly Bear the younger, son of the chief. A peak to the east of Tobacco Plains is "Not Grizzly Bear Mountain" on the Kootenai National Forest map.

[15] Teit, *Salishan Tribes,* 319. Mose Mathias, son of Baptiste Mathias who until his death in the early 1960s was considered leader of the Flathead Lake Kutenais, confirmed that his father came from the area of "Jennings" (a town built later at the mouth of the Fisher River); he said that the father of Baptiste's first wife, Catherine Andrew (whose mother was Bitterroot Salish), was also a Jennings Kutenai. There are Andrews today at Cranbrook and Windermere.

[16] It seems likely that Chief Not Grizzly Bear was the same person as Chief Unknown Grizzly Bear, and that the migrant Middle Kutenais at first lived under this Upper Kutenai leader (note wording in Malouf and White, "Early Kutenai History") before choosing Michelle as a chief from among their own people. Curtis, however, understood that Not Grizzly Bear was a Middle Kutenai of Tunaha ancestry.

abouts of the forty-ninth parallel, nor understanding how it could be of importance, continued their usual wanderings and their old camps on both sides of the unsurveyed boundary. Michelle, disillusioned by what he considered broken promises of White officials, took his followers to Windermere, leaving Baptiste or *Ka-kulua* (Rose Hips) in charge of the Flathead Lake Kutenais.

It appears that the ancestors of all or nearly all the people now on St. Mary's Reserve near Cranbrook were Middle Kutenais, particularly perhaps from the Libby locality, who went north around the time of the Stevens treaty; while the Windermere people are descendants of the Jennings branch of the Middle Kutenais, led at Tobacco Plains by Michelle. These people insist even today, however, that "there were always Kutenais at St. Mary's and Windermere." The older stock either has disappeared or has merged with that of the newcomers. Sallad's contemporary, Su-Su, referred to the Cranbrook Kutenais not as *Adamneks* or *Akámneks,* the older band name for residents here, but as *Get-a-Mook-Ke-Nicks*. Turney-High was told that the *Akámneks* were extinct. Peter Andrew at St. Mary's says his grandfather used to go back and forth between Libby and Cranbrook. In late times, at least, there seems to have been a separate line of chiefs at each of the three Upper Kutenai localities: Ft. Steele (St. Mary's Reserve, site of St. Eugene Mission), Windermere (Kutenai and Shuswap Reserves), and Tobacco Plains (Canadian portion). Succeeding Edwald was David Paul, chosen at the time of the establishment of the Tobacco Plains Reserve in British Columbia in 1887. His successor was Paul David.

The Bonners Ferry people under Chief Abraham claimed that Michelle had not represented their band; they continued as non-treaty Indians. Frustrated by conflicting promises of various Whites, the majority of them refused to move either to the Salish-Kutenai Reservation in the United States, or to the Canadian reserve established at Creston.[17]

The Flathead and Kutenai elders and their proud warriors might brood unto heartbreak at the prospect of their people corralled and under orders from an alien and indifferent race, but as in time beyond record the world around, the absorbing consideration was "How do we eat?" For the present this meant little change from the usual scrounging for game, berries and roots, though the treaty had promised that the United States would pay the signatory tribes $120,000 over a period of years, to be expended under the direction of the President for the removal of outlying groups to the reservation, for building houses and barns and fences, and for breaking up the land for farming. A school was to be immediately provided for the young people.

FORT CONNAH AND FORT OWEN

It is often hard to determine who was the number one man on the young Indian reservations of the Northwest – the agent or the trader. In the Flathead-Kutenai country in 1855, the only distribution posts for government supplies were Fort Connah in the Mission Valley and Fort Owen in the Bitterroot, neither of which was a "Fort" by anything but generalization, though John

---

[17] Rose Causton was told that Abraham was the grandson of Three Moons through his father Timar or Big Gunner, later known as Thomas Blind (baptised Thomas by De Smet; he later became blind).

Owen had strengthened the old mission barricade, and Fort Connah had a bastion fourteen feet square. "Fort" Kootenay, no fortress at all, had recently been moved upriver to Tobacco Plains, was not in business the year around, and was difficult to reach.

The Mission Valley post had been planned by Hudson's Bay as a successor to Flathead House, partly because so many Indians now gathered about St. Ignatius Mission, partly to thwart threatened American competition. Neil McArthur, a clerk formerly at Fort Hall and Flathead House, began the buildings at the new location in 1846, but left the next year when Angus McDonald took over. McArthur subsequently engaged in private business enterprises at Hell Gate and at Colville. McDonald, who once wrote, "I believe that on the last day when you hear the sound of a trumpet that you shall also hear the sound of the Scotch bagpipe as it is longer and louder," [18] decided to name the new post after a familiar and scenic river valley in Scotland, the Connen; but when Francois Finlay who was with him had difficulty pronouncing the Scotch, he indulgently contracted the name to Connah, sometimes written Conna or Konah.

In a lowland not far away from the post was a natural brush corral; some have said this feature led to naming the locality *Sinyalemin (Sin-a-jail-men, Se ni el em)*, "The Surround," because elk were surrounded here; others had it that the wildlife surrounded consisted of Blackfeet raiders; others thought of the whole valley as Sinyalemin, because of the all-surrounding mountains. The site of the post itself, Angus wrote, was called by the natives *Kootel-tzin-ape (Colin-toze-naps)*, "from

---

[18] Angus McDonald, *Letters to Judge Deady,* Jan. 31, 1877.

an alley formed by birch and willow groves on the left of the stream [Post Creek]. Each of the tributaries [of the Flathead River] has stories enough for a hundred Othellos and McBeths." [19]

> [As Fort Connah] provided the Colville district with certain products obtained only from buffalo country, it was an important link in a chain of posts. Though the main exportation was furs, it also carried on a trade in dried buffalo meat, pemmican, buffalo fat, apishamores [saddle blankets usually of buffalo skin with the hair on], raw-hide cords and hair cords – all necessary for the transportation of the Company's goods on horseback. These materials could not be obtained in sufficiently large quantities at any other post on the west side of the Rocky Mountains. [20]

Angus McDonald, first assigned to the Flathead country as an apprentice clerk in 1839, had been stationed as trader at widely scattered posts of the Columbia Department. His wife Catherine, whom he married at Fort Hall, was one-half Nez Perce through her mother, one-fourth Mohawk, one-fourth White. Although Angus in his travels carried a full set of Shakespeare along with his provisions for the stomach, he felt enough at home among the natives to take part in a *San-ka-ha,* a farewell to warriors on the eve of battle, held on Camas Prairie in 1850. As the women wept and the dancers performed to "that staid, insisting strain, I stripped with the leading men, painted with vermillion my upper body, and mounted on my black buffalo

---

[19] Angus McDonald, "A Few Items of the Old West." In the text of the treaty, Post Creek is evidently referred to as Prune Creek, Mission Creek as Se ni el em Creek.

[20] Hearings, *British-American Joint Boundary Settlement Commission,* II, p. 66, Aug. 1856. This was the testimony of Neil McArthur regarding the earlier Flathead post on the Clark Fork, but is quoted by both Partoll, "Fort Connah," and Weisel, *Men and Trade on the Northwest Frontier,* as applicable equally to the successor post, Fort Connah. Note Barker, *Letters of Dr. John McLoughlin,* 44, 89.

charger with full eagle feather bonnet, cantered round and round with them, keeping time to the song." [21]

Angus McDonald, after seeing the post well established, returned in 1853 to Fort Colville as chief factor, although he had become more and more attached to the Flathead Valley. Left in charge at Fort Connah was Michel Ogden, whose wife Angelina was a half-sister to Angus's wife. The post included several small log buildings, the bastion, a log corral and a few acres indifferently cultivated.

Although the United States was tolerating Hudson's Bay posts within its territory until the boundary could be surveyed, Stevens in 1855 ordered Fort Connah closed because it came within a United States Indian reservation. This left Fort Owen as the agency supply depot. But since Stevens could not stay to check, Ogden continued to do business with the natives for Hudson's Bay, sometimes crossing the mountains with them to hunt bison himself. He became the best of friends with his trade rival John Owen, who was shrewd, sociable and a lover of literature, but addicted to drink.

AGENCY AND MISSIONS

The first agent on the reservation for the Confederated Salish and Kootenai tribes was Richard Lansdale, a Maryland-born mid-westerner with some medical and military training. He set up modest headquarters at the mouth of the Jocko River. Stevens sent $1,775 for the agency that summer (1856), of which $500 was turned over to Owen for supplies. Asked in the fall to take over as agent himself, Owen did so reluctantly and set out to better the situation if possible.

---

[21] Angus McDonald, "A Few Items of the Old West," 192.

He ordered tools, plows, wagons and mill machinery, and was sent hard bread, rice, sugar, moldy coffee, shawls, flimsy flannel and other nearly useless goods. Finding it impossible to serve both groups of Indians, he closed the Jocko station in the summer of 1857. Two years later, it was reopened with a sub-agent in charge, but the new man did not last long on the job. Owen, who ran accounts headed "Flat Head Tribe" and "Indian Department," as well as the "Agency" account, complained that wages and bills for goods went long unpaid.

Congress had still not ratified the Council Grove Treaty. In the fall of 1858, Father De Smet persuaded a group of Indian leaders to go to Vancouver for a conference, supposedly with a regional Indian agent. Among those making the trip were Old Melkin, chief of the Lower Kalispells; Victor and Andrew Seltice of the Coeur d'Alenes; Adolph of the Kutenais, Arlee of the Flatheads, and Alexander of the Pend d'Oreilles. In 1859 the treaty was finally ratified. That year Owen brought two agricultural assistants to Jocko, and in 1860 the reservation people received their first annuity payment, and were able to break up a little ground for farming.

"Other provisions of the treaty were forgotten in the throes of the Civil War and Reconstruction." [22] Owen in 1860 moved the agency headquarters further up the Jocko to a site several miles southeast of the present town of Arlee. He became so frustrated by the erratic policies of the Indian Service that in 1862 he resigned in disgust. John Mullan was pleading with the govern-

---

[22] Garfield, "Diary of a Trip to Montana," 159. A good deal of information on Owen's term as agent is taken from Weisel, *Men and Trade on the Northwest Frontier.*

ment for better treatment of the Nez Perces and Flatheads who were noted by all travelers, he said, as "two
bright shining points in a long and weary pilgrimage."
And Edward P. Geary, Indian Affairs superintendent
headquartered at Portland, noted that "the Flatheads
and cognate tribes are a noble race, magnanimous and
brave." [23] But such appeals had little effect in Washington.

The agent who succeeded Owen reported that among
the three tribes there were about eight hundred acres
under cultivation, the tribespeople still depending upon
buffalo meat as their economic mainstay. During the
years that followed before appointment of Peter Ronan
in 1873, different agents succeeded each other so thick
and fast that no one of them could accomplish much –
even if he happened more or less by political accident to
be somewhat qualified for his job.

By 1864, Father Urban Grassi and his associates at
St. Ignatius saw the fulfillment of their ardent desire
for an Indian school. Dormitory and classroom buildings went up, and four Sisters of Providence made the
frightening journey from Montreal to serve as teachers.
The Indians Joseph and his wife Adelaide were sent to
meet them on their way from the Coeur d'Alene Mission where they had arrived from the coast after a
month of travel by horse. En route to the Flathead
country, "they prayed, they sang, they chatted as they
went along, and had many a hearty laugh over the
incidents of the road." At Jocko, according to Palladino, "the surly agent treated both fathers and sisters
with even worse than cold indifference." [24]

---

[23] *Commissioner of Indian Affairs,* 1858, p. 383; 1860, p. 181.
[24] Palladino, *Indian and White,* 142-43.

Once at their posts, the Sisters sturdily personified the dignity of manual labor as they swept, cleaned, washed and scrubbed to get the new school in order. The Indian and part-Indian girls who came to them to be mothered and scolded, learned scrubbing in their turn, along with sewing, cooking, sanitation, the three R's, manners and prayers – all quite happily, to hear some of the later pupils tell it when they were older. The Indian students, like older members of the congregation, were especially apt at music. Palladino reported that the women had "a correct ear" and voices of plaintive charm; when the male voices joined in, the hymn became more strongly wild in flavor. A visiting bishop declared that "it sounded as if a dozen at least of harmonious wolves were scattered among the congregation." [25] Early attempts to teach native boys in day-school classes were not a success. Book learning and routine labor were not these youngsters' idea of man's estate.

Agent Alvis Galbreath in 1869 testified that "the missionary labors of the Rev. Fathers at St. Ignatius have not been in vain, for many of [the Indians] are exemplary Christians. I may remark that the labors of the Rev. Fathers have been very arduous and difficult. Some compensation should be given them by the government." [26]

SAME OLD BLOODY STORY

Colonel George Wright during the Indian wars on the Columbia, anxious to learn how the Blackfeet were behaving since they had promised to keep the peace, sent Dr. William McKay's brother Alex, along with

---

[25] *Ibid.*, 176.
[26] *Commissioner of Indian Affairs*, 1869, p. 294.

another experienced scout, William (Billy) Hamilton, to reconnoiter. Hamilton had a brave reputation among the Whites; he was as ruthless an Indian fighter as any on the fur frontier.

The two scouts were at St. Mary's Lake in present-day Glacier Park, near a camp of buffalo-hunting Kutenais, when, as Hamilton told it later[27] they were obliged to kill three Blackfeet intent on taking their scalps (or at least their horses). The Kutenais, who were short of powder and lead, and who had also clashed with the Blackfeet, then welcomed the two White men as allies. Hamilton made Chief Black Bear a present of a ten-pound keg of powder and a sack of trade balls.

Before they could even break camp, they killed five Blackfeet who were attempting to run off their horses. Fifteen miles along their course toward the Divide, two hundred fifty of the enemy had to be driven off, with casualties on both sides. Alex McKay, always out in the forefront when a scrap developed, was among the injured. The Kutenais now made haste westward across the mountains toward their own country (probably by what is now Logan Pass), where they could round up the scattered bands of braves, and mass their warriors for the fight that was certain to come.

Next day, having crossed the North Fork of the Flathead and climbed to the pass at the head of Grave Creek, they saw from the trail four hundred fifty mounted Blackfeet only three hundred yards away.

Others were on foot. They charged; one made off with a white mule, Hamilton's favorite service mount. Hamilton went after him, disregarding danger on all sides. In an almost hand-to-hand

[27] From Hamilton, *A Trading Expedition among the Indians in 1858.* Quoted is an abstract appearing in *Montana: Its Story and Biography,* by Tom Stout, 1921.

encounter, he made a "good" Indian and regained his mule. Forty Kootenai reinforcements arrived [from Tobacco Plains]; the yell they turned loose made the Blackfeet think their numbers were legion, and they retreated into the timber, taking their dead and wounded.

McKay had been hit a second time; Hamilton again dressed his wounds. The Kutenais were now calling him and Hamilton "chiefs." The Kutenai wounded, including six women, made their own medicine men stand back and requested that Hamilton dress their injuries. The party moved on down through Grave Creek Canyon, and across the Plains to the Kootenai River, evidently to the site of the old tobacco garden and the mission cabin. Here the women dug rifle pits and made ready for a siege. Hamilton and the chief's son went up to the Hudson's Bay post – Fort Kootenay – for provisions, and brought back the trader, Scotty Linklater (or Linklighter), who added to their outfit, on his own account, provisions for a feast.

Several days later, a hundred Blackfeet appeared whooping and were met in open battle by a like number of Kutenai warriors accompanied by Hamilton, McKay and Linklater. The Blackfeet were driven into the timber, but Hamilton could not prevail upon the Kutenais – who were uncertain how many warriors were hidden among the trees – to follow up their advantage. He did persuade them to start a brush fire and smoke the enemy into the open, where a few were killed before they could make their escape. A number of the defenders were killed; others were wounded. Among the latter was Scotty Linklater, who seemed quite proud to have an arrow removed from his thigh. The Indian women rigged up a travois to carry him north to his

CHIEF VICTOR
of the Bitterroot Valley Flatheads.
From De Smet's *Oregon Missions and Travels.*

UPPER FLATHEAD SUB-CHIEF MOIESE (MOSES)
Kal up Squal che or Crane Necklace. Elk mane headdress.
Photo courtesy of Fred E. Peeso.

PIAL (BASIL) FINLEY
Courtesy of Emerence Marengo.

ANGUS MCDONALD
Courtesy of British Columbia Archives

post. "I am acquainted with fifty trappers," Hamilton later wrote, "and know if they had been in this skirmish, that fully half the Blackfeet would never have returned to their country."

SETTLERS

By 1860, soldiers stationed along the route of westward migration had eased one of its most horrifying hazards; the Oregon Trail thereafter frayed into many wandering strands. Inside what was to become Montana Territory in 1861, the Bitterroot Valley proved to be one of the first and most inviting locations the emigrants discovered. Since the late forties, a few enterprising White men had been buying worn-out livestock on the trail for wintering in the Beaverhead, Deerlodge and Bitterroot valleys. The stockmen and traders found the Indian men good fellows and often helpful. They hunted together, raced their horses, gambled and drank; they sorted and branded their livestock in communal roundups, a process early perfected by the Nez Perces and their neighbors. The White men also found Indian women available as wives or obliging housekeepers. It was no longer unheard-of for a Flathead woman to sell her favors. Neither was it unusual for her sister or cousin to live in dignity and virtue, perhaps to become deeply devoted to the Catholic religion.

Some of the earliest settlers of the Bitterroot and of Hellgate, forerunner of Missoula, came in over the mountains from Fort Hall, where Richard or "Captain Johnny" Grant was in charge for Hudson's Bay from 1842 until 1851. Grant, a widower when he arrived in the West from Canada, had married the widow of William Kittson, Finan McDonald's daughter Helene.

Washington territorial elections in 1863 drew seventy-four voters to the polls at Hellgate, Fort Owen and Jocko Agency. Among the county commissioners elected was Christopher P. Higgins, who married a daughter of Captain Grant and Helene and became an associate of Frances L. Worden in Missoula's pioneer business enterprise, Worden and Company, Merchandise; another was Granville Stuart, rancher and miner south of Hellgate, who as he prospered gave up his Indian woman in favor of a White wife. Chosen justice of the peace was Henry Brooks, father of mixed-blood Sophie Brooks who married Jocko Finlay's grandson Pial (Basil).

So was the Indian blood of fur-trader wives spreading dilutedly through the new population, glowing forth time and again in a sparkle of dark eyes, a rich gleam of skin and hair, in hearty vitality often coupled with dogged endurance, wild impatience of routine and restraint, clinging superstitions. But to cool-headed observers it was evident, here as in all mixed populations, that there were all kinds of Indians and all kinds of half-breeds, as there were all kinds of Whites.

Johnny Campbell told how in 1866 "the valley at the head of Flathead Lake was pretty well settled by the whites, stock-raisers and farmers, and from there all along down the valley to the Reservation, and on down to Hellgate and Bitterroot Valleys."[28] At this period, however, "pretty well settled" could mean an occasional cabin as the traveler rode along. There were almost no White women in the region. Duncan McDonald said the settlers all left the Upper Flathead Valley in the late sixties because of raiding Blackfeet. Nor did the

---

[28] Campbell, *Letter to T. C. Elliott.*

Blackfeet confine their forays to the Upper Valley. Emerence Marengo, daughter of Pial Finley, says her grandfather Patrick Finley (sometimes known as Jocko Patrick) one year put in a crop of grain east of what is now Polson, but the Blackfeet came over, and the family had to leave. When they returned the geese had eaten all the grain. Finley Point in Flathead Lake near Polson was named for Pial who continued to ranch here. According to census listings, Abraham, Augustin and Dominic Finley were in the Bitterroot in 1860. Three years earlier an "Abram Finley" brought a government express dispatch from Olympia to the Salish-Kutenai Agency.

The withdrawal from the Upper Valley was only temporary, although the influx of Whites into the region slowed down in the seventies – between the placer boom of the sixties and the hard-rock boom of the eighties.

Pick and Pan

EARLY GOLD

West of the Flathead-Kutenai country, glitters in gold pans drew men to new locations each year. Northern California, the Fraser River country north of the border, the mountains of central Idaho – many a prospector shook up color successively in all these localities during the fifties and sixties. Among them was David McLoughlin, son of Dr. John McLoughlin, who was involved in the "McLoughlin Canyon fight" between Indians and miners in the Okanogan country.[1]

Francois Finley, better known as Benetsee, lived as many a man of today lives only in his runaway dreams. One record refers to him as a Red River man; evidently he was one of Jocko's sons born in Canada; Cree blood is indicated in the tribal records of some Finley descendants. Benetsee began his career as a trapper, but by this time he was ranging about the Pacific Northwest with a few pack-horse loads of trinkets, ammunition and other goods, trading anything from beads to horses, hunting and fishing as he went, staying where he liked, at Indian camps or White settlements, as long as he liked but no longer; now and then he changed his women.

---

[1] See full account in William Brown, *Pilgrimage to Fort Okanagon*, pamphlet, Okanogan, Wash., 1951. Copy in private library of Jerome Peltier, Spokane, Wash.

In California, Francois watched the gold panning and the doings at the gold camps with easy-going interest, but soon returned to his home of sorts in the Deerlodge Valley – with the first wagon ever brought north out of California, his descendants claim. Francois' mobility at this point was somewhat hampered by his growing family. In his home valley, Finley was

> impressed with the remarkable resemblance of the country to the district in California where he had seen gold washed, and particularly by the resemblance of the gravel bars and sand of Gold Creek [first known as Benetsee Creek] to the streams he had seen worked for the yellow metal in the West. He therefore in 1850 or 1852 set to work panning the gravel. After many efforts he found some fine particles that resembled gold, and accumulated a teaspoonful which he took to the Hudson's Bay Post and showed to Angus McDonald. McDonald sent it to another of the Company's posts and it was pronounced gold.

So goes one account of the first discovery of gold in what is now Montana. In other versions, Benetsee found the gold on Flint Creek, brought it to the post for trade, and so the news spread to Granville Stuart; or Angus McDonald told Finley to keep the discovery quiet because Hudson's Bay didn't want miners in the area; or McDonald grub-staked him for further work, but Francois soon got tired of so much hard labor for such uncertain returns.[2]

No one printed the intimate little story of the actual discovery as told by Benetsee's daughter Sophie to her children. One day as her father lay sick at the family's camp, Sophie used to confide, he sent her off on an errand. Tired and hot as she returned, she stopped at a little creek to wash her face in the cool water; noticing

---

[2] Quoted portion from "Angus McDonald," in *Whitefish Pilot*. For round-up on Finley and the discovery of gold, see Stuart, *op. cit.,* I, p. 137 fn. I.

the pretty black sand with glittering flecks, she took some of it to Benetsee, wrapped in her headscarf.[3]

Whatever the exact truth of the matter, it was not Finley nor McDonald, but Granville Stuart and his brother James who in 1862 began to develop Montana's first placers in the Deerlodge Valley near their American Forks ranch. Lt. John Mullan was now pushing his delayed road project from Fort Benton to Walla Walla, and the Stuart ranch was a way station at the crossroads with the north-south travel route. The sensational strikes around 1863 at Bannack (later Dillon), at Last Chance Gulch (Helena) and Virginia City swamped for the time being all interest in the sites first located by Francois Finley. Within five years after the discoveries, the new placers had attracted some ten thousand Whites to the area, where they washed out thirty to forty million dollars worth of gold.

There were home seekers pure and simple among the first emigrants into the Flathead-Kutenai country, but there were also drifters dodging military duty in the Civil War, from the North and from the South; refugees from criminal prosecution or social disapproval or economic failure in the East — and now this plague of avid prospectors. Men disappointed in the first camps of the West struck out in all directions hoping tomorrow would be their lucky day; in the mountains of the Flathead-Kutenai country there seemed to be at least one creek for every prospector; but a man had to get a hustle on or somebody else might find the right creek first.

Among the natives here, the mountain spirits were especially featured in myth and legend. Their "Old

[3] McElderry, interview.

Man" sang: "Since the world first grew I have lived until now. The manitous of the mountain peaks, the manitous of the canyons, the manitous of the wind, the manitous of the trees and water are all in me. I am strong, I am everlasting." [4] Not only sacred traditions, but crowding memories of human incident, invested the natural features of the ancient range. Now the Indians watched as the White men hacked at their earth, with eyes and hearts for nothing but the yellow metal which they worshipped, but did not cherish except to squander it in carousing, or hoard it to gain excessive possessions and ascendancy over their fellows. The mixed-bloods were of many minds in the circumstances, but the attraction tended to be stronger toward the White man ways, increasingly predominant.

WILD HORSE

In 1863 "a half-breed named Findlay and two companions were passing through the [Upper Kootenay] country. Leaving the creek which has since been named for Findlay, they came to Wild Horse Creek. Here they cleaned up about $700 in pumpkin seed gold. On their way out to Frenchtown [near Missoula], they sold this gold to a man named Linklighter, a Hudson's Bay factor at Tobacco Plains, and the only White resident in the valley at that time." [5] This Findlay seems to have been Benetsee Finley, who according to Gravelle also found gold at one time in what is now Glacier Park. Other accounts put "two Finlay brothers, sons of Jaco Finlay," on the scene; while others credit the discovery to Joe Ashley, Jack Fisher and an unnamed third man –

4 Barbeau, *op. cit.*, 29; see also Chamberlain, "Kootenay Indians," *op. cit.*
5 *Fort Steele Prospector*, Mar. 18, 1896.

who was doubtless this "Findlay."[6] Before 1864 had passed, there were reported to be one to five thousand miners, shopkeepers and laborers in the new camp on the Upper Kootenay. Most of the supplies came in by pack train from Walla Walla. Beef on the hoof arrived from Salt Lake City via Tobacco Plains.

Fortunes were made and lost, here as elsewhere in the region. The presence of mining populations was forcing political changes. In July 1871, after some hesitation, British Columbia (named as a colony in 1858) joined the young Dominion of Canada. South of the forty-ninth parallel, Washington territory in 1865 was split on the line now dividing Idaho from Washington and Oregon, but the territory of Idaho thus created was sliced the following year to make the territories of Idaho, Montana and Wyoming. The surveyors assigned to run the line along the Continental Divide understandably strayed into the Bitterroots on their way north – thus decreeing the Idaho panhandle, and placing the Salish-Kutenai Reservation in Montana.

The boom at Wild Horse deflated after the first few years, and David McLoughlin who had been trying his luck there, left the mining game for good when he took over a small Hudson's Bay post near present-day Creston, B.C., known as Fort Flatbow. Soon afterwards he moved south just into Idaho, where he operated his own ranch and store at the site known to the Whites today as Porthill. In 1866 he took for his wife the Kutenai woman Annie, daughter of Grizzly Bear and Mary. According to David's daughter Amelia King, Grizzly Bear was a Montana Kutenai.

Before 1860, the only White men who had seen the

---

[6] Graham, *op. cit.; Fort Steele Prospector, ibid.*

Upper or East Kutenai country were a few fur traders and occasional explorers. During the Wild Horse excitement, innumerable Whites streamed in by way of Tobacco Plains and by way of Bonners Ferry, Idaho, where Walla Walla business man Edwin L. Bonner, a native of New York state who later invested at Missoula, saw the Kutenais canoeing miners across the river, and astutely decided that a ferry here would be surer money than prospecting.

LIBBY CREEK TRAGEDY

Prospectors also blundered in from the Clark Fork to the mazing courses of the Fisher River and Libby Creek and their tributaries. What happened in 1866 at the mouth of Libby Creek, where Middle Kutenai hunters watched the comings and goings of the miners, was recorded by Martin Fry, a brother of Dick Fry who later bought out the Bonner ferry; by Colonel George Hunter, son-in-law of Steven Allen, one of the prospectors involved; and by M. R. Cowley, who was assisting Bonner's partner John W. Walton at the ferry when the trouble occurred. Cowley, who was closer to the incidents than the other two, also gave with his own narrative a version by Joe Herring (sometimes written Herron or Heron), one of the miners, and a third version by Sallad, one of the Indian hunters. Cowley's rendering of the Indian talk is obviously no literal interpretation, but it is nevertheless revealing.[7]

Among the twelve miners of the party, according to Cowley, were "Joe Herring, Anthony Cavanaugh, Mr. Allen, Captain Jack Fisher, Pat Miller and a person

---

[7] Cowley, "A Libby Creek Tragedy"; Fry, "Indians in the Kootenay Country"; Hunter, "Reminiscences of an Old Timer."

who went by the peculiar alias of Carribou Jack."
Hunter tells how Allen struck a prospect "in the mountains north of Pend d'Oreille Lake, and named the
creek 'Libby' for his daughter [Hunter's wife, Elizabeth, nicknamed Libby]." Four of the miners, Herring,
Allen, Cavanaugh and a man named Lacking,[8] were
delegated to go down to Spokane Bridge for supplies.
When they returned with their loaded pack horses to
the spot where they had to cross the Kootenai near the
mouth of Libby Creek, some of the Kutenai hunters
canoed men and supplies to the south bank and swam
the horses across. In payment, the Indians were given
some sugar and flour which turned out to be a curious
bait.

Six of the young Kutenais (not including Sallad)
camped with their families near the White men, who
expected to go on up the creek next day to join the main
party. Fry's story has it that the Indian women could
not get their minds off these tempting boxes and bundles
and cans. They hounded the men to throw a scare into
the Whites, and then make off with their supplies.

The Kutenai men consented to try. Visiting around
the miners' campfire, they warned the Whites in anxious
tones that Blackfeet were headed this way and might
arrive at any moment. When the miners showed no
signs of alarm, the Indians in the night fired shots over
the other camp and set up a war-whooping that would
have frightened greenhorns into hiding. But these four
believed the local Indians to be harmless, and just
wouldn't risk the whole enterprise by deserting their
supplies. As for the Kutenais, frustration grew to sense-

---

[8] Still a fourth source gives one of the names as John Moore.

less anger, or to desperate calculation. The next morning they made a surprise attack reported by Herring:

> At daybreak, we put the saddles on our horses and were preparing to put packs on them when, as Mr. Allen and myself were standing nearly opposite each other, I heard the report of a gun, the yell of an Indian and felt the sting of a bullet in my shoulder, which after hitting me passed through Mr. Allen's heart, when we both fell to the ground. The Indians then charged into the camp. I called to the two men that were left to grab our shotguns and break for cover.

The Indians followed the two into the brush, and although they were both armed, they were killed, as was Allen. Herring escaped into the creek and up into the mountains, where after seventeen days of pain, delirium and near-starvation, he was found by fellow-prospecttors of another party, who took him to Missoula when he was stronger. Here, Herring related, "I recovered and resumed the burden of life anew. I lost all the taste I ever had for prospecting and settled down to a humdrum mode of making a living."

Three of the guilty young Kutenais took off for British Columbia; Antoine, who had killed two of the three dead miners, went with the other two hunters to the Lower Kutenais. Cowley wrote:

> About ten days after the supply party had returned up the river, the eight men who had remained at Libby Creek came down to Bonner's Ferry and told us Joe Herring and his party were killed by the Kootenai Indians, and they were going out to Spokane and Montana to raise a war party of miners, and come back and sweep the river of every Kootenai Indian on it.
>
> We asked them why they did not hunt for their friends and find them, dead or alive, and they replied they had heard the shooting and did not want to be killed too. Their story sounded altogether too thin, for we knew the Kootenai Indians as kindly,

inoffensive people, who had never moltested a white man, much less killed one.

Not many days after this, as David McLaughlin was sitting in his dooryard near Flat Bow Lake, three strange Indians sauntered into the place, stood around a few minutes and then walked away. He asked some of the other Indians why they did not shake hands with the strangers, and they replied, because they have killed some white men up the river, and we have no wish to shake hands with such people. David then sent a letter to Bonners Ferry telling what he had heard.

[Cowley consulted with Chief Abraham who promised to] go to Flat Bow Lake and bring all his people up to their winter home, about three miles from Bonner's Ferry, and hold a general council, and asked the writer to be present. I went and found about eighty warriors assembled in a large tent. Abraham arose and addressed them in substance as follows: "Warriors. We are gathered together for the purpose of discussing a very momentous question – nothing less than to decide whether we will fight or give up our kinsmen who were concerned in the killing of some white men at Libby Creek to the whites who will hang them. I am informed by my white friend that the law of the white man is, that if only one of six did the killing and the other five were present and did not try to prevent it, they were all equally guilty, and if surrendered, all will suffer death. Shall we give up our three brothers to the whites to be hanged, or shall we fight for, and defend them to the bitter end. Abraham, your chief, the son of Timar, has spoken."

Whereupon an Indian whom the writer knew for about as worthless a wretch as ever lived, arose and opened the discussion. He said: "My name is Su-Su, and I am opposed to giving up our brothers to the whites to be strangled. I am in favor of fighting to the bitter end and driving the whites out of our country now and forevermore. First, I have nothing to lose but my life, and that is comparatively worthless. I am forty years old, have a wife and five children, and ever since I can remember I have had to rustle from year's end to year's end for a bare living.

What business have the whites in our country, anyhow? If there is any truth in what we hear about them, they are the destroyers of every other race they came across. We did not invite them here. Did not one of their people kill our brother Ki-Kin, on the hill near by? [9] Again, who killed Shu-Wa, our brother once removed, of the Get-a-Mook-Ke-Nicks on Wild Horse Creek. A white man. [The White Men!] Curses on them and the shadows they make. They are all liars and the truth is not in them. Oh, my brothers, we have a beautiful country. It was given us by God for us and our children for an inheritance forever. But give in to the demand of these white men once and we are slaves forever. I say, away with them. Let us fight them now, tomorrow, at once. War to the knife – and to the death. And no matter what comes of it, the die is cast and I am content. Enough; Su-Su, the son of the great chief Buffalo Heart, has spoken."

Several speakers followed in the same general line. Then an old Indian whom I knew to be the best man of the tribe, in fact one of the best Indians I ever met, by name Humpfoot, arose and said: "I have listened to the silly, vicious twaddle of Su-Su and the warriors, who have so far spoken until I tire, and am sick at heart. Su-Su the warrior, forsooth, says he has nothing to lose except his life, and says that is not worth much. Well, I agree with him there. But is he not talking [only] for himself? No other man here can entertain any such sentiments, unless his mind is unsettled.

"Su-Su says let us fight. How many rounds of ammunition has he got to commence war with? Do I hazard the truth if I say he has not five? I am better off than he and always have been and I have not ten. Fight the whites? Why should we fight them? Su-Su maintains that our brothers had a right to kill them. Bah! They did not kill them. They murdered them. Do you hear? They murdered them and their blood is calling to God now. Does Su-Su justify in his brother what he condemns in the white men? We have no war with the whites as a race, as a whole. They have always treated us well. Are we all to be condemned for the action of those of our people who have murdered the white men at Libby? I say no. Did they kill the men because

---

[9] A White man who had recently shot a Kutenai on Huckleberry Hill near Bonners Ferry was said to have explained that he did it "for luck."

they were white? They do not say so. They killed them for what
they had. They might do the same thing to me if I had anything.
Leaving aside the justice of the demands of the whites for the
surrender of those men, our brothers, how long would we last if
we concluded to fight the whites? A week if we would hide; not
a day if we would stand our ground. Why? Because the whites,
every one of them, have repeating guns that shoot sixteen times
without reloading, pistols that shoot six times. Ah, what have we
got? One gun each, hardly that. A flint lock shoots once and that
not certainly on a rainy day. One white man is equal to twenty-
two Indians.

"Again, how about food? I have as much as any of you, but
not enough to last four days, and the whites all have plenty.
Every one I ever saw had more than all of us. We must think of
our defenseless children and our old people. The whites are as
numerous as the sands of the river. If any of you think you can
fight the whites with all the advantages against you, try it, and
that will be the end of you. Enough. Humpfoot, the son of All
Eyes, has spoken."

There was a visible change in the looks and demeanor of the
members of the council when Humpfoot had finished. An utter
silence prevailed for some minutes, and then, in quick succession,
one after the other five or six of the bravest and best men of the
tribe made short but stirring speeches, taking the same ground
as Humpfoot.

Abraham then dissolved the council, saying he would
take the action that seemed to be indicated. A few days
later he sent the men of the murder party who were in
his camp to Bonner's Ferry with the horses, pistols,
guns and saddles taken from the White miners, having
led the guilty ones to believe that if they gave these up
freely and told the White men where the rest of the
plunder was cached, they would be forgiven. Cowley
recognized the chief's strategy, and with the help of
Walton, and Bonner (who had recently come in), and
a passing miner, captured and bound the three, and held

them for a posse of miners that arrived next day. Cowley's story continues:

> Next morning they started with the prisoners tied securely on horses, with the calculation of taking them up there [to the scene of the crime] and giving them a trial. Fate ordained otherwise. They had only traveled about fifteen miles when one of the prisoners got his feet loose and made a break for liberty. Two pistol shots were fired at him as he ran, both of which took effect. [Fry's story has it that the Indian jumped into the river at the Moyie crossing, and swam out into the Kootenai before he was shot.] The boys then concluded that two Indians were more than they could watch, so they hanged one and buried the two on the spot, and kept the other to show them where they hid the plunder at Libby Creek, and when they found it all, they hanged him too.
>
> Of the three that escaped to British Columbia, the Chief of the Upper Kootenais gave two up to the British Magistrate at Wild Horse Creek, who in turn handed them over to a party of Americans, the murders having been committed on the American side of the line. They were hanged a little distance away from Wild Horse Creek. The sixth Indian went out to the buffalo country and was never apprehended.

Although Sallad in reporting how he discovered the three dead miners after the shooting said, "What I saw there I have sorrowed for ever since," he concluded his story with these words:

> In some way or other the three Indians were by some species of treachery given up to the whites, who shot Antoine and hung the other two, the vilest manner of killing known, disgraceful and humiliating to any man calling himself a warrior. Then, though the whites murdered our brothers, they made no provision for their families, three women and ten children. My people are poor and it fell mainly on me to support those widows and children. And so in my grief for the death of my people and in my poverty, an additional burden is added to the weight of years. I approach the gloomy portal of the hereafter with a broken heart.

FORT STEELE, AT THE MOUTH OF WILD HORSE CREEK

During the second mining boom in the area, which began in the 1880s.

Photo courtesy of C. F. Dement

THE CONFLUENCE OF LIBBY CREEK AND THE KOOTENAI RIVER

A view to the northeast, during the flood year of 1954. The murder of the miners probably took place a mile or so up Libby Creek; the bodies when found were buried on a hillside in that vicinity. Photo by Robert Gilchrist.

Only a short time before the sixties, it was said of the Kutenais that if they found even the smallest things, such as a pocket knife or a piece of tobacco, they would bring it to the camp of the probable loser and cry it up and down until they contacted the owner. Even as late as the 1880s, Colonel Samuel Steele of the Northwest Mounted Police reported that during the year he spent in the neighborhood of the Wild Horse mines, not one case of theft or drunkenness among the Kutenais was brought before him, though these Indians packed large quantities of liquor for White merchants. But temptation to steal increased with the increasing knowledge of White-man possessions, and observation of White-man morality concerning possessions, and with resentment bred of the White men's contempt for Indians. The old pride in traditional accomplishments and integrity crumbled. After all, the old ways had not saved the Red men from defeat by the White men – and had never brought them all the alluring things the White men had. Some of the more irresponsible Red men, and some of the prouder, keener or more patriotic, became embittered or actively renegade.

CHANGING TIMES

There is no record of what profits may have been realized by Francois Finley or any of his brothers in all this mineral discovery and production; none of them got rich. Finley blood entered many Flathead family lines; Finleys intermarried with Flathead Lake Kutenais through several generations.

Michel Ogden, his mind unsettled by a head injury suffered when he fell from a horse, relinquished Fort Connah to Lachlan McLauren in 1861. McLauren soon left to take a claim not far up the Bitterroot River from Missoula, leaving the post to the management of Napoleon Fitzstubbs, who according to John Campbell was "an Englishman who did not remain long, and who was subsequently on the police force in the Yukon."[10] The reservation agent of the period, A. H. Chapman, obtained permission from Washington to eject Fitzstubbs, but did not make the move. Succeeding Fitzstubbs was James McKenzie, husband of Angus McDonald's daughter Christina, who served about two years before relinquishing to Christina's brother, Duncan McDonald, the last trader. In 1871 after the boundary survey, Duncan was ordered to close the post. The next year, Fort Colville too being closed, Angus McDonald left Hudson's Bay Company and came to the Flathead Valley where the reservation Indians by common consent allowed him to take up land at old Fort Connah.

New mineral strikes in Montana were drawing outsiders to Butte, Helena and Marysville; by 1870 the territorial population was 20,595. Cattle driven from Texas provided beef for miners, or ancestored native herds. Granville Stuart, although the placers on Gold Creek yielded rich profits in the early seventies, turned to stock raising. Here was one form of agriculture in which the Indian men, as cowboys, could take a certain natural interest – though their instincts sometimes ran more to rustling this tame game than to rearing it. The Flatheads, however, frequently returned to the owners stock stolen from the Whites by the Bannacks or Shoshones.

With the aid of small government allowances, the

---

10 John Campbell, letter to *Kootenai Times*.

staff of St. Ignatius, augmented in 1884 by the arrival of Ursuline Nuns, was able to operate a kindergarten and boarding school for boys as well as for girls. The struggle to master the native languages continued at the regional missions. On two small printing presses, one at St. Ignatius and one at Sacred Heart (relocated in 1877 at De Smet, Idaho) leaflets, programs, broadsides and booklets were printed in Salish, Kutenai, Coeur d'Alene, Nez Perce, Blackfeet and Crow, as well as in English. Included were a "Kalispel-English Dictionary," and a "Kootenai Catechism" by Philip Canestrelli,S.J., who later wrote his "Kootenai Grammar." [11]

The future would not fulfill all the hopes of Palladino and his associates; but the selfless work of the priests and nuns and incoming Protestant ministers, and of frontier teachers and doctors and selected editors, was at least as useful as the ardent enterprise of leaders in the hardrock mining business, soon to become a colossal financial-political game in which the individual miner would be no more his own sweet boss.

---

[11] Wilfred P. Schoenberg, s.j., *Jesuit Presses.*

Across the Line

CHRISTIAN KUTENAIS

With good reason the Kutenais were proud of their rich language, but it was an isolating factor in their relationship with the Whites. Quite a few of the priests and preachers at the regional missions had mastered Salishan, but Father Grassi from Washington, after visiting the Flathead Lake Kutenais, pronounced Kutenaian the most difficult of all the Indian tongues he had known. Most of the priests were obliged to work through interpreters.

Father De Smet, when he last spoke with Upper Kutenais at St. Ignatius in 1859, renewed his promises that priests would visit them. Records of any visits before the 1870s are scanty, though Father Menetrey did make trips to Tobacco Plains during the 1850s. In December 1861, De Smet reported that "the Kootenais have built a little log church of round logs on the great Tobacco Prairie," carrying the logs themselves for more than a quarter of a mile, and later attaching two rooms for the use of visiting priests. Here baptisms and marriages were celebrated. This was apparently the church that stood near the old tobacco gardens along the Kootenai River, where early settlers observed the ruins some thirty years later, and where Hudson's Bay had a fur collection depot in the 1860s.[1] The Canadian

---

[1] See De Smet, *Life and Letters*, 962; O. Johnson, *op. cit.*, 13, 17.

John Palliser, writing of his visit to Tobacco Plains in 1858, mentions a church cabin here, recently built by the Kutenais.

Father Tosi from one of the Washington missions visited the Lower Kutenais intermittently from 1868 to 1871, and returned to them with Father Joset in 1886. In 1871 Father Urban Grassi, S.J., formerly at St. Ignatius but then at Yakima, Washington, visited the "Upper Kootenys" in October, and told of instructing them to build a chapel, which they completed before his second visit the following year. It is hard to say whether Father Grassi's "Upper Kootenys" were the Tobacco Plains or the Windermere people; he noted that though the older people remembered the visit of De Smet, the children up to the age of twenty years had never seen a "Blackgown," adding that "he had the happiness of baptising 260 adults and blessing forty marriages." [2]

LAST YEARS OF FORT KOOTENAY

Edward Berland in about 1846, after the United States-Canadian boundary treaty, moved Fort Kootenay upriver to Tobacco Plains, where it was located first on the east side of the river about five miles south of the actual border (the line was yet unmarked – probably this location was at the pond later known as Lake Livermore, near the mission cabin built for De Smet).

---

[2] *Woodstock Letters,* II, pp. 157-60. Father Grassi was here four and a half days above the "Middle Kootenys" under Michelle; but Michelle during this period might have been camping anywhere from Jennings to Windermere. If the church of which Father Grassi spoke was on Tobacco Plains, it probably was the one noted by the pioneer settlers, on Johnny Campbell's homestead, several miles north of the earlier church mentioned by De Smet.

Because this site was exposed to raiding Blackfeet, the post was soon shifted to the west side of the river at the mouth of Dodge or Dirge Creek, and later to the mouth of Young Creek farther north. This "fort" was also called Tobacco House, and by the Indians *Oos-nik-takoothl-yam*. After Berland's death about 1852, John Linklater, known to his associates as Scotty, and to the Kootenais as *Lov-yapie-na-na* or "Little White Man," came to take charge of Fort Kootenai.[3]

The current trader when he came upriver in the fall seems to have chosen for the winter whatever site took his fancy. There is some indication that one or more of the traders sometimes set up business ten miles farther east, near what is now Eureka – a traditional village site of the Kutenais.

Captain John Palliser of an official Canadian exploration party found a camp of Kutenai Indians on lower Tobacco Plains and reported them "the most wretched-looking fellows I ever met; men, women and children, all living on berries, the men naked and the women nearly so." They were, however, hospitable and friendly; willingly they shared their supply of saskatoons and choke cherries, fresh and dried meat.[4]

Dr. Augustus Thiebodo, Canadian explorer, in 1850 watched Linklater trading with the Indians, and thought this valley

one of the most beautiful I ever saw, the Indians are a fine handsome-looking lot of people, unusually clean. There are 300 Kootenais at the site of the Mission, where they raise fine wheat and other crops. They brought in about 200 pounds of meat to trade for powder, lead, salt and soap. They had five or six hundred head of horses, many of them very fine. Services are held in the chapel morning and evening, and three times on Sundays. It

[3] O. Johnson, *op. cit.*, 14.   [4] Palliser, *Reports*, 1859, p. 33.

is quite a beautiful sight to be in our tent and watch the little
Indian village among the trees and see the strangely painted
savages wandering about and staring at us and every now and
then laughing at any little thing that happens. I never saw any
people so quiet and apparently so contented.[5]

All this was before either the boundary surveyors or
the miners had invaded the Tobacco Plains country.
In 1860 and 1861 the official United States boundary
survey party with a corresponding British party
marked the forty-ninth parallel from the Columbia
River to the summit of the Rockies. One of the men
who worked on the survey was John Campbell. He had
been packing supplies to miners in gold camps of
several territories and British Columbia, until 1860
when he took a ranch in the Colville Valley – and
Edward Berland's daughter Lucille or Lucy for his
wife. Even then he could not stay put.

Scotty Linklater remained a bachelor among all his
Indian associates, and did not marry until after he
retired to Scotland in 1864. Johnny Campbell was sent
up from Colville by Angus McDonald to carry on
Linklater's work until his official successor, young
Michael Phillips, not long out of England, could take
over. When Phillips arrived from Fort Shepherd,
Canadian successor to Fort Colville, he sent Campbell
north to Wild Horse to trade at the Indian camps.
Phillips soon moved up to Wild Horse himself, and
first established near what is now the Mounted Police
monument just out of Fort Steele. He later told how he
once carried out to Fort Hope $45,000 worth of gold on
one of the 150 horses of his brigade string; the other
pack animals carried about $7,000 worth of furs. The

5 Thiebodo, "Diary," 327-8.

trail Phillips used on these trips, planned to serve the mining camps from the west, had been cut out four feet wide by the Canadian government, and was known as the Dewdney Trail for Edward Dewdney of the Royal Engineers.

The customs office set up at Wild Horse to check on gold taken out by American miners was moved west in the early seventies to Joseph's Prairie, named for the Kutenai chief who resided here with his band. The new customs officer, Henry E. Seelye, moved into the first building ever constructed on the site of Cranbrook, a log house with chimney of baked clay that had belonged to Michael Phillips. Whether Phillips traded out of this Joseph's Prairie house or only lived in it is not certainly known. The location of the post at Fort Steele is given as "where the highway reaches the north branch of Wild Horse Creek. A garden was made on the flat below but this is now covered by twenty feet of gravel from the mining up on the creek." [6]

Both Clara Graham and Bayard Iverson name Phillips as Fort Kootenay's last trader; Johnny Campbell, however, wrote that Phillips gave over in 1869 to one Joseph Hardisty. Phillips, who after his trader years took up ranching, told his friend Charley Edwards that "he often had to leave his ranch after high water as the Piegans were often raiding the country for horses and frequent fights took place with the Kootenai." [7] The Kutenais continued to hunt buffalo across the mountains until about 1880.

Phillips' wife was Rowena, daughter of Chief David

---

[6] Iverson, *op. cit.,* 48.

[7] O. Johnson, *op. cit.,* 56. See Graham, *op. cit.,* 168 et al, for a story of one of the last incidents of Kutenai-Blackfeet enmity.

of the Tobacco Plains band. The children grew up on the Phillips Creek ranch, at the foot of the eastern mountains and just north of the international border. Their fearless father took active part in developing the country.

Johnny Campbell, who in later life remarried, wandered from Colville to the valleys of western Montana, serving as trader, school teacher, interpreter, finally homesteaded on the third of three claims he located on Tobacco Plains. His last years were spent rather lonesomely at Lillooet, B.C. From there he wrote most of his valuable letters to enquiring historians. The two educated and respected sons of his first marriage, Duncan and Victor Lewis Campbell, grew up on the Flathead Reservation with their mother, and are not known to have married.

Surround

CHARLO THE ROCK

Out of a sky comparatively clear for the Bitterroot Flatheads in 1872 came the shocking order from Washington: You are to remove to Jocko.

Victor, the Flathead chief at Council Grove, had died the previous year, leaving as widow his second wife Agnes or Agate, *Slem-Hah-Kah,* whose "manners manifested the gifted woman she really was, dignified, sensible, tactful and remarkably refined. 'Lo, there goes the queen!' whispered the young people."[1] The new Chief, Charlo, usually spoken of as the son of Victor and Agnes, was said by Palladino to be Victor's son by his first wife. His Indian name was *Slum-qui-i-kie* or Little Claw of a Grizzly Bear. He inherited not only the chieftainship — through tribal consent — but also his father's unshakable resolve never to give up the ancestral home of his tribe in the Bitterroot Valley. Special Agent W. J. McCormick wrote in 1868:

> It was the duty of the government to have prevented the influx of white settlers until the government either had declared the region an Indian reservation or formally opened it to settlement. But not so; the whites were permitted to occupy the most eligible portion of the valley for agricultural purposes, fields were enclosed, houses and barns built, until now the valley presents a spectacle of agricultural prosperity rarely equalled in any of the

---

[1] Palladino, "Historical Notes on the Flatheads," 21.

new States or Territories. I am fully persuaded that the Flathead Indians would not have concluded a treaty with the government if they had not been induced to believe that they were to
enjoy and possess the portion of the Bitter Root valley designated
in the treaty as a permanent reservation.[2]

But the White settlers were clamoring for titles to
their land, and for roads, bridges, and schools. An 1872
manifesto by President Grant declared that the Bitterroot Valley had been surveyed (when, and by whom?)
and found less suitable for the Flatheads than the Jocko
Valley, and that the removal was therefore ordered.
Congress in June 1872, appropriated $5,000 for the
expense of moving, and a $50,000 allowance for the
improvements the Flatheads would be leaving behind.
General James A. Garfield was sent to reason with the
stubborn chief.

Meanwhile a Virginia City newspaper printed
alarmist warnings that a large body of Nez Perce,
Colville and Spokan Indians stood ready to join the
Flatheads in revolt, and demanded organization of a
volunteer company to drive all the "surly vagabonds"
from the valley. Garfield, however, reported that "from
the conversation of citizens it soon became apparent
that the chief anxiety of the settlers was to secure the
establishment of a military post, and that the market
which would thus be afforded for their home products
was really a matter of greater consideration than protection against hostile Indians."[3]

Garfield persuaded Charlo and a group of his leading men to go with the government party to Jocko
Valley on reconnaissance. The chief was not impressed;

---

[2] *Commissioner of Indian Affairs,* 1868, p. 208.

[3] *Ibid.,* 1872, p. 109. The Nez Perces were peaceably camped in the vicinity,
en route to buffalo.

but Garfield noted with calculation the growing rift between the leader and his sub-chiefs Adolph and Arlee (Red Night or Henry, called by the Flatheads A'lee).[4] Scorned by Charlo as a "renegade Nez Perce," Arlee had spent his life among the Flatheads and had led them in battle, though his father, and perhaps his mother also, was Nez Perce. Persuasively Garfield offered homes and farm implements as promised by the treaty but never delivered to this group, plus six hundred bushels of wheat, and cash payments provided by Congress, to be allowed over a period of ten years. No one, he stated, would be forced to move against his will. Charlo turned his back in disbelief; his decision to remain in the Bitterroot endured.

When the ratified agreement was published in Washington, it bore Charlo's "X" for signature, along with the marks of Arlee and Adolph; witnesses included Montana's Governor B. F. Potts. But as Garfield's own reports testified, Charlo had never signed. His mark had been added in the printed version by government officials who were convinced it was far better for Charlo and his people to be near the agency headquarters (and out of the way of pressing settlers in the Bitterroot) and that the chief would accede once the move got under way. The chief was being treated as a child and as a trifling nuisance; how could White officials, if they were men, expect this to render him cooperative?

Arlee and a small group of the Southern Flatheads in 1873 trekked to Jocko; a few more families followed in the next several years. But Charlo and the majority

---

[4] Teit was given to understand that Arlee's followers were more closely related by marriage to the Pend d'Oreilles, while Charlo's group said that "if they had to share a reserve with other tribes they preferred to go with the Shoshoni." (*Salishan Tribes,* 325.)

of his people, numbering about 360, refused to go. On
the reservation proper, Agent D. Shanahan testified in
1873 that the agency property was almost worthless
and the Indians without any confidence in the government. According to his report, he immediately went to
work to improve conditions, completed the homes
promised Arlee's people, and put more land into production.

St. Mary's Mission had been re-activated in 1866, but
the position of the Bitterroot people became more and
more trying. Charlo, a devout Christian in spite of his
treatment by the Christian Whites, yearly grew more
bitter and glum. Yet when Looking Glass of the rebelling Nez Perces came into the Bitterroot during
the campaign of 1877, Charlo, risking scorn, refused to
shake hands with him because, as he put it, the hands
of Looking Glass were bloody. "When the warring Nez
Perces made their appearance on the Lolo Trail," a
later-day historian wrote, "the alarmed citizens came
to the Salish Chief with the promise, 'You help us
against Chief Joseph, and you shall have your Bitterroot Valley secured to you.' Charlo, responding with
alacrity, sent his white-turbaned warriors to join the
forces at Fort Fizzle." [5] Teit was told that all the
Flatheads remained neutral except that a few scouts
helped the White soldiers.

PETER RONAN

Naturally the presence of the Nez Perces tended to
feed White resentment against Indians as a race. The
Flatheads were subjected to both general and specific
vituperations.[6] In this atmosphere, in 1877, Scotch-Irish

[5] McWhorter, *Hear Me, My Chiefs!*, 358 fn. 4.

Peter Ronan, ex-rancher, ex-miner, ex-editor, became
the Indian agent on the Salish-Kutenai Reservation.[7]
The people in his charge were referred to by some of
the Whites as "Ronan's Pets," but no one who knew
Ronan and his honorable position in the state would
criticize him seriously.

Ronan believed that Charlo would be better off in the
upper valley on the accepted reservation; when he
could not persuade him to come, he tried with little
success to see that government aid reached the chief and
his people where they were. Hopefully in 1883 he took
Charlo and a group of his leading men to Washington;
but no change of mind nor heart was effected in either
Charlo or Uncle Sam. The agent's concern went out
even to the stranded Kutenais at Bonners Ferry and the
restless Kutenais of Tobacco Plains (United States
portion). He tried in vain to have the northern boundary of the reservation extended to the Canadian line.
He tried desperately to persuade the Bonners Ferry
people to come to the Flathead Valley; only a few individuals and families responded.

Nor was Ronan able to restore the western line of the
reservation to its original treaty designation. Prospective settlers had found the land near present-day Paradise too good for Indians; political influence in the
young territory prevailed, and Washington upheld the
theft. As to the northern boundary, the reservation Kutenais, no surveyors, had assumed the line at the west
shore of the Lake to follow a natural ridge just north
of a sizeable area of good meadow land where they

<hr>

[6] See corresp., *New Northwest,* Aug. 30, et al., 1878. Also Duncan McDonald's defense of the Nez Perces and Flatheads in the Nez Perce War, series of
1878 in this publication.

[7] See Howard, *Northwest Trail Blazers,* for biography of Ronan.

grazed their stock and cut hay. After a survey showed the actual half-way point up the lake to be four miles south of the line as understood by the Indians, White and mixed-blood stockmen took over the choice ranch-land, and allowed their stock to range even further south on land legally belonging to the reservation.[8] According to one record, by 1884 nearly half of the total reservation acreage was owned or controlled by Whites. (This probably included mixed-bloods who held rights through their Indian wives.)

But Ronan kept very busy with what rights and resources he was allowed. He pleaded for plows and seed in preference to blankets and food doles. By 1877 he could report that even the Kutenais were beginning to improve their lot. He managed to bring a limited amount of government school money to St. Ignatius Mission; many of the young people, both boys and girls, now received an elementary education in the mission boarding schools.

By rights, as a progressive American citizen Peter Ronan should have been elated at news of projected transcontinental railroads. But as a friend of the western Indians he feared the colonizing propaganda which the railroad companies used to gain support. Though he and his Indians protested, a right-of-way was granted across the reservation for the Northern Pacific route through Jocko Valley and hence down the Clark Fork toward Spokane. Trains were running by 1883, and steamboats on Flathead Lake made access easier to the Upper Valley. (The branch line to the foot of Flathead Lake was not built until nearly forty years later.) Many would-be ranchers who came into western

---

[8] See Biggar, *op. cit.,* and *Commissioner of Indian Affairs,* various.

Montana "on the cushions" raised funds to improve their places by working in the copper mines at booming Butte. Flathead Valley beef could now be shipped by rail to Missoula, Butte, and Chicago.

The wail of the railroad engine whistles on the prairies announced, if without specific intention, the end of the buffalo. Now the Flatheads and Kutenais must kill local game, or raise or buy beef, or petition for doles, or go hungry. Money for buying came only from selling hides, cured buckskin products, furs or fuel wood, or from taking employment; jobs were scarce and unpopular. Lumbering and mining had no appeal for the full-bloods; one early lumberman has said that the Indians were afraid of the hazards of woods work – as well they might be. The larger stock ranchers were centers of comparative prosperity for a certain share of the people on the reservations, especially the mixed-bloods.

CAPITULATION

North of the border, the Kutenais had a few more years of freedom than the Montana Indians, to live and travel where they would; the miners monopolized only limited land areas. But the Canadian Pacific Railroad crossed the Rockies almost neck-and-neck with the United States' lines, and grants of land to British settlers in the 1880s squeezed the protesting Kutenais onto their several small reserves. Chief Isadore of Joseph's Prairie was only quieted by the intervention of Father Nicholas Coccola, O.M.I., of St. Eugene's Mission on the St. Mary River near Cranbrook, and by the arrival of Col. Samuel B. Steele and his contingent of Northwest Mounted Police in 1887.

St. Eugene's had been established in 1873 by Father
Fouquet and Brother Burns, who first of all erected a
log building to serve as living quarters, hospital and
church. Soon after the arrival of the Mounties, Father
Coccola came to take charge, and by his firmness and
fairness won the respect of both the Kutenais and the
Whites. In order to support a school, and persuade the
Indians to settle, the Fathers encouraged stockraising,
introduced farming, and built a grist mill.

At Tobacco Plains, when Judge Peter O'Reilly met
with the Kutenais there in 1884, and asked Chief David
to choose his land, David at first said, "Good, I will tell
you what land I want for the Indians. I want all the
country from the Coast in the far South to the Arctic
on the North, and from the Atlantic on the East to the
Pacific on the West." "Talk sensible and choose your
land," reproved Judge O'Reilly. So David outlined the
ancient range of the Kutenais, extending across the
Rockies and across the Canadian-United States boundary line. "We cannot talk about United States land,"
protested Judge O'Reilly; "it is on the other side of the
boundary."

"What is the meaning of this boundary line?" asked
Chief David. "It runs through the middle of my house.
Why should you without asking me or considering me,
divide my property and also divide my children?" But
at last the chief, his back to the wall, outlined his final
request: "I will choose my land from the American
Boundary line from where it crosses the top of the
mountains west of me, thence North to the mouth of
Elk River, thence up the river to the top of the South
Fork of same, thence along the Eastern mountains as
far as I can see, and south to the American line again."

O'Reilly, according to the Tobacco Plains people, then said they would meet again the following day; but when the Kutenais assembled, they were told that O'Reily had packed up and left. Some time later, when the Indians were away from their village, government surveyors came and outlined a small reserve of 10,531 acres along the Kootenay just north of the border, much of the land rocky and poorly watered. "Thus our lands have been stolen," claim the Kutenis.[9] Other Kutenai reserves in British Columbia include St. Mary's near Cranbrook, 18,425 acres; Lower Kootenay south of Kootenay Lake, 5,961 acres; and the Columbia Lake Reserve of 8,401 acres, close by the 2,733-acre Shuswap Reserve.

The rapid settling of the Upper Flathead Valley brought further discontentment among the Flathead Lake Kutenais, of whom a small vagabond group camped mostly near Kalispell, outside the reservation. Chief Baptiste, killed by the Blackfeet in 1876 near the site of present-day Hungry Horse dam on the South Fork of the Flathead, was succeeded by half-Iroquois Eneas Paul, whose title Big Knife, inherited from his father, had been given the elder Big Knife by the Pend d'Oreilles. The first Big Knife was the Iroquois Ignace (synonymous with Eneas or Aneas or Inneas) hired by David Thompson in Middle Kutenai country in 1811. De Smet in 1842 mentioned an Iroquois living among the Kutenais who must have been the same man; he had come into the country soon after 1800. The birth of

---

[9] From signed statements by Francis Plasway, Swasa Wakum and Joseph David; copies now at MHS; see abstract in O. Johnson, *Tobacco Plains Country*, 54-55.

Chief Eneas Paul in 1828 was recorded on the Mathias family calendar string.[10]

Chief Eneas was no lover of the Whites and on one recorded occasion treated White men with contempt, but he was respected by all responsible citizens for his devotion to his people, and his ability to keep his own band members and the Kalispell country vagabonds pretty well in hand. Stockmen by the late 1880s were establishing also on Tobacco Plains among the Kutenais who still camped and hunted on the United States side of the line, even after the designation of the British Columbia Reserves. The several "Indian scares" in the Flathead and Tobacco valleys led to no bloody uprisings, though Negro troops were sent up from Fort Missoula on one occasion as a precaution. Four Indian renegades of assorted tribal affiliation were rounded up in the Flathead and hung at Missoula on the last day of 1890, to the delight of newswriters who condemned these and all the other "dirty, stealthy creatures, the serpent in this Garden of Eden." It was years later before Will Cave, Montana state historian, reviewing these events, openly condemned also the Whites of the times, who killed Indians on the sly, sold them liquor which sometimes resulted in their killing each other,

---

10 Malouf and White, "A Kutenai Calendar Record." Teit was told that Chief Big Knife was the one who "made treaty with the United States and obtained a share of the Flathead Reserve." (*Salishan Tribes,* 378.) There was no "Aeneas" nor "Big Knife" listed among the Kutenai treaty signers; perhaps one of his Kutenai names was Paul See, or Gun Flint (the fifth Kutenai signer, with Michelle and Moses, was Little Michelle.); or perhaps because of his Iroquois blood he was not eligible to sign, even though he had used his influence in the negotiations.

Chief Eneas Paul, Big Knife II, or Koostata I, was to be succeeded after his death in the early 1900s by his son Eneas Paul Koostata II. This Kutenai family line had considerable intermixture of White blood: Finley, Ashley, Gravelle, etc.

and were often guilty of "the rape of Indian girls of tender age."[11]

The White settlers of the Bitterroot now renewed their urgings that the Flatheads be removed, presenting "a petition signed by the very man who had solemnly pledged to them the perpetuity of their homes" at the time of the Nez Perce campaign.[12] Chief Arlee, Charlo's old rival and enemy, was dead at Jocko. In 1891 the Bitterroot chief, his families wretchedly poor, his purposeless young men addicted to gambling and drink, gave in. "For their sake I will go. All I want for myself is enough ground for my grave. We will go over there."[13]

The substance of Charlo's desperation is exampled in a narrative describing family life of a Flathead male alcoholic in the Bitterroot a few years before the move. Characterized by Dr. Malouf, the recorder, as an extreme yet not uncommon instance, the story is told by a daughter of the Flathead man, when she was older:

> My father hunted when he could, but usually all we could do was fish through the ice [in winter]. When we had caught enough of them my father took them to a farmer or to a store. He was supposed to get groceries with them, but often he got himself some liquor. Sometimes my father shot goats in the Bitterroot Mountains, and then he sold the fat to the missionaries at St. Mary's in Stevensville, where they made it into candles. Moccasins made by mother, intended for exchange for groceries, were also taken by him and exchanged for liquor, or he would gamble them away. Sometimes we had no blankets, no horses, no nothin'.

---

[11] *Daily Interlake,* Kalispell, Mont., Dec. 19, 1890; Cave, "Missoula Hangings," *Daily Missoulian* (Mont.), May 9, 1937. See Johns *Collection* for various articles on the renegades, their crimes, their roundup and punishment.

[12] McWhorter, *op. cit.,* 358.   [13] Stone, *op. cit.,* 88-9.

One day the drunken father fired a gun at his hungry wife as she rode horseback with her twin infants, the shot severing one of her braids and causing her and the babies in their cradleboards to fall to the ground. There her husband beat her mercilessly until a small boy (of another family) got a rope looped around the man's foot, mounted a horse with the rope, and dragged him off. Later in camp the obsessed Indian again beat his wife to the ground, sat on her when she attempted to rise, threatened her with a knife until the narrator, then about eight years old, cried:

> "Don't, don't, don't kill her; wait until my sister and brother get nursed. They are crying already, and they have been crying a long time. Wait until they are through nursing and then kill my mother!" Then he left mother alone. It seemed a long time before mother was breathing again. Her breasts were black and blue from the terrible beating that she had received. I propped up the twins so that they could nurse. Afterwards we sat by the fire and father built it up a little. He even made mother a little more comfortable. Evidently he was feeling much better after his orgy. He even fixed us a little supper.[14]

The move to Jocko Valley was made in installments. A few houses were provided for the emigrants, but not enough to go around. The first winters at the new location were bitter ordeals. Elizabeth Heidelman, wife of an agency doctor, speaking of the years around the turn of the century, remembered how "Charlo was just broken-hearted. He showed it in every line of his face. He was a fine man, but anybody who didn't know him would say he was an old crank. You would be too, wouldn't you?"

In spite of the depths of the difficulties facing them, Agent Ronan and the Jesuits and Sisters of St. Ignatius

---

[14] Malouf, "Louis Pierre's Affair," excerpted.

helped to usher in a comparative Golden Age in the Flathead country – as old-timers later viewed it. Ronan reported in 1888 that "a large majority of the Indians have advanced greatly in the arts of peace and are owners of herds of cattle and horses and take as good care of them and as much pride in the ownership as the average white stockmen." [15] At about this time, a group of sixty-two Kalispel Pend d'Oreilles from near Sandpoint, Idaho, under their Chief Michel, came to the reservation, and proved themselves "willing workers of good character," although repeatedly disappointed by the failure of the government to provide for them as promised. Most of the Spokans and Kalispels went to the Kalispel Reservation on the Pend d'Oreille River in Washington, and to the Coeur d'Alene and Colville reservations. A few Bonners Ferry Kutenais were brought to the Flathead Reservation around 1900; a few others went to the Colville Reservation.

Of great economic support on the Salish-Kutenai Reservation were the sweeping miles of bunchgrass still remaining although some four thousand acres were now in cultivation; and the energy of the leading mixed-blood stockmen, including Michel Pablo, part Mexican or New Mexican Indian, and his partner Joe Allard. Pablo and Allard were raising not only cattle and horses, but also buffalo and catalo – the buffaloes ancestored by a few head brought across the Divide by Walking Coyote, a Pend d'Oreille. Angus McDonald was one of the ranchers whose herds thrived. Missoula Mercantile Company was on the reservation for profit, but at times their traders took a certain interest in the welfare of the Indians.

[15] *Commissioner of Indian Affairs,* 1885, p. 126.

On the larger ranches at least, life was good. Valley residents ate heartily, they almost literally lived in their saddles. Young and old, male and female, Red and White, they rode and roped on the range together, explored the countryside and the mountains, camped out to fish, hunt, pick berries; they raced their prize ponies and held parades; they lazed or galloped along to the neighbors to visit, to waltz or war dance (for fun or show), to play cards or the stick game, sometimes to drink and brawl, as often to flirt, gossip, sing, and toss or tease the toddlers.

As the White population of the area grew, and particularly as the portion of White women to White men increased, the color line toughened; this sometimes meant bitter frustration to mixed-bloods. Life became more complex and more enervating.

INUNDATION

As the century approached its close, the increasing herds of cattle and horses and buffalo were depleting the bunch grass in the valleys to an alarming degree. Roundups of wild horses for the canneries eased the situation temporarily (roundup of the buffalo did not take place until around 1909) but the state of the range was poor enough to be cited as one justification for the cry of the White people: we must convert the Indians to more intensive farming and to individual responsibility by placing them on small allotments; then – parenthetically – the remainder of the reservation farm land can be opened to homesteading by the Whites.

The forces Ronan had feared with the coming of the railroad were about to be activated. Ronan had reported in 1879 that there was almost no crime on the

KUTENAI CAMP AT BONNERS FERRY

In the earliest years of White settlement. Note both canvas and mat lodges.

Photo courtesy of Jim Stephenson.

FLATHEAD DELEGATION TO WASHINGTON, D.C., 1883
Standing: Hand Shot Off, Peter Ronan, Michael Revais.
Seated: Antoine Moiese, Charlo, Grizzly Bear Far Away.
Reclining: Abel
Courtesy of Montana Historical Society.

CHIEF ENEAS PAUL OR BIG ARM II
Courtesy of Montana Historical Society.
See text pages 345-346.

PAUL ENEAS OR CHIEF KOOSTATA
Last chief of the Flathead Lake Kutenais.
Photo courtesy of Fred E. Peeso.

CHIEF DAVID
Of the Tobacco Plains Kutenais.
Courtesy of National Museum of Canada.

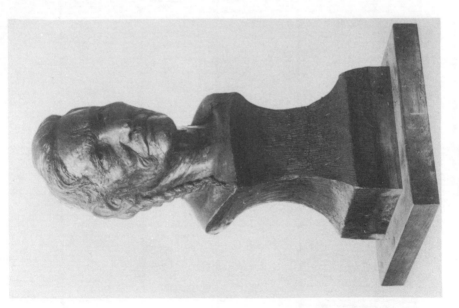

SUZETTE FINLEY KOOSTATA
First married to Eneas Koostata's brother Isaac.
Photo courtesy of Fred E. Peso.

reservation; but now, because of the lawlessness brought to the area by the railroad construction camps, the independent young Indian police of whom both Ronan and the tribes had been so proud, had to be replaced by salaried lawmen under stricter agency supervision. Mrs. Heidelman told how one young Flathead mother of good family took to hanging around the railroad workers along the line, meanwhile leaving her baby in the buggy; one day the horses ran away and the baby was killed.

"The traders skinned the Indians, and so did the Agents," according to Mrs. Heidelman's reminiscences. She added her personal version of the notorious Smead case:

W. H. Smead [agent from 1898 to 1903] was a crook when he came. He sold hay off the Reservation and kept the money, sold the Indians cheap whiskey at a big profit, charged them big fees for settling their claims when the Homesteading law went into effect, and tried to keep them off the best land. He refused to license anybody who wanted to trade on the Reservation, unless he was a Missoula Merc man and of course that was Anaconda Copper [the mining corporation that pulled the strings in Montana for many years].

The government started an investigation into Smead's behavior but it got tabled and he got reappointed. Then a former fellow-legislator who had it in for him got the matter reopened and Smead was sent to the Pen. Roosevelt said, "I never knew we had anyone so dirty in the government service." Smead died in the Pen.

Following Smead came Sam Bellew who was even worse. His son was the paid clerk though he was in the last stages of cocaine addiction and was always incapacitated. Doctor kept his cocaine bottles way up high but the son broke in and stole them and blamed the Indians. Bellew when he was charged with irregularities said, "To hell with the government; politics put me here, politics will see me through." He would take Doctor's team out at night, bring it back exhausted, wouldn't let him have another for visits to the Indians; he cared nothing for the Indians. The trader [name not specified] sold rot-gut whiskey; he and Bellew's son put on dances so rotten that the better class of breeds wouldn't go. Things got so bad, the Priests said, "This can't go on; no Indian knows who is his wife, with this sleeping promiscuously all over the Reservation." [16] Then you wonder why the Indians didn't do better. If it hadn't been for the Fathers, I don't know what the moral situation could have led to.

The next Agent was Morgan [Fred C. Morgan, 1908-1918], straight as a string but it was all new to him; he wanted to quit in three weeks, but Doctor persuaded him to stay. The trader Beckwith at St. Ignatius dealt pretty fair, and so did Sterlings at Ronan; things were beginning to straighten out.

Agent Morgan was soon to preside during the headlong influx of homesteaders onto the reservation in 1910. Forced to sell their surplus animals for lack of range, some of the mixed-bloods morosely squandered their bank rolls. Other ranchers, remembered Bill Matt, "tried to farm, bought machinery, and went broke. Eighty acres was just a garden spot. We should have got 320 acres like the Blackfeet. We didn't cry about it at the time; but when I look back now – What a wonderful country we had! – before the homesteaders." Others, like Alexander Morigeau, converted successfully to dairy farming, which became a surer proposition with the coming of irrigation.

There were still in 1960 a few people on the reservation who came there from the Bitterroot as children in the years around 1891. They included Jerome and Batiste Lumpry (doubtless descended from Joe Lompry or Lamprey or Lamphere, a Canadian married to a Snake women, who settled in the Bitterroot), Jerome

---

16 "No Indian" was not of course meant literally. Major Samuel Bellew served as Agent 1904-1908.

Vanderburg (grandson of Louis Vanderburg, who took the name of a White Man), Mary Ann Pierre Coombs and Susan Pierre Big Sam; Mr. and Mrs. Louis Nine Pipes and Andrew Nine Pipes, the two men sons of Antoine Nine Pipes and grandsons of Joseph Nine Pipes, favorably spoken of by Bitterroot pioneers; and Lucy Charlo Pellew, granddaughter of Chief Charlo through his son Martin who succeeded him as the last Flathead chief. Lucy's straight back, quietly assured bearing and serene features suggest true royalty of character. Nor is it only among the descendants of chiefs that the signs of a native dignity are yet conspicuous upon the reservation.

Dave McLoughlin, growing old at Porthill, complained that the Kutenais clung to their wild ways, criticized them for not conforming with more enthusiasm to the ways of the Whites. Yet Dave confessed how he himself liked to wander in the mountains and commune with the God who made them, and once declared that "everyone ought to use his own mind and judgment and leave others alone to follow theirs as they please, especially [as to] civilization, as that affair is a difficult problem for all." [17] The Flathead sub-chief Moses said that "after the Fathers and Whites came, we died. I think it is too much study." [18] By "study" Moses plainly had in mind the excessive concern for tomorrow that spoils the easy satisfaction of today; and all the doubt of the old ways, and the painful effort to understand the new – the inescapable purgatory of change.

Even Duncan McDonald wrote in the 1880s: "Of course no man, no matter to what extent he may be

---

[17] D. McLoughlin, "The Upper and Lower Kootenai;" and letter to "Theodore," OHS files.   [18] Stone, *op. cit.,* 94.

accused of a sentiment or other sympathy with the Red Man, is prepared to deny the fact that 'the Progress of Civilization,' 'Struggle for Existence,' 'Survival of the Fittest,' – no matter by what term we recognize the decree of Fate – has rendered inevitable the final extinction of the Indians." [19] For the Kutenais and Flatheads, as for many other North American tribes, such prophecies have been borne out only in the sense that the number of full bloods has dwindled in most groups. But the descendants of the frontier full-bloods, bearing all proportions of the Red racial strain mixed with White, have multiplied, at least in the United States. In Canada, Kutenai Indian blood has remained more pure, and the population on the reserves has gradually decreased.

Some of the people from the reservations of both nations live under lamentable conditions; others have adapted themselves comfortably to White ways; many of the young people have scattered over the United States and Canada, prospering in industries and the professions.

The claim of the Flatheads and United States Kutenais on the "Flathead Reservation for the United Salish and Kootenai Tribes," filed with the United States Court of Claims in 1951, was settled in the 1960s by a payment of $4,431,622. The tribes had asked eighteen million. According to the tribal secretary, F. J. Houle Jr., writing in March 1969:

> Over three million dollars of the judgment money was distributed to the membership – $550 per capita. Five hundred thousand was invested in our Tribal Credit Program to make home and business loans to Tribal members. Our Credit Program

---

[19] D. McDonald, *New Northwest,* Aug. 16, 1878, p. 3.

is the single most significant factor in the improved social and
economic well being of the tribes. Many used their families' $550,
according to a family improvement plan submitted as a pre-
requisite to receiving the money, and purchased new homes or
remodeled their old homes. There is over five hundred thousand
dollars remaining to be used for economic development of the
reservation. At present this money is in time saving certificates in
banks drawing excellent interest.

One source of income for the Flathead Reservation
people is a share of payments for electrical power gen-
erated at Kerr Dam on the Flathead River just below
the lake – where the outlet had cut its way through the
ancient moraine. Other regional dams, though not built
on Indian reservations, are located within the former
range of the two tribes.

To the natives here, their rivers were much more
than drainage courses leading toward the Columbia.
They were drinking fountains and swimming pools.
They were, especially for the Kutenais and the Pend
d'Oreilles (including the Kalispels), thoroughfares,
race tracks, parade grounds, and sometimes in stretches
of white water or times of flood, antagonists to be
fiercely fought. They were crop-water, the Lower Kutenai in particular depending upon fish for livelihood
at different seasons. They were true companions at
camping sites, generous with lively incidents of deer
drinking, bears fishing, birds skimming. They were
endless screen shows, art gallaries, contrived of the
interacting relationships of rock, water and light, and
the moods of the persons watching. They were libraries
of legend.

The latest and greatest dam in the Flathead-Kutenai country is still under construction in 1970 – the
Libby Dam on the Kootenai River near the old village

sites of the *Akayenik*. If by some historical hocus-pocus these ancestral Kutenais could stand above the completed dam, how would they feel to see the boiling river tamed and hushed beneath the new-born lake? What would they think of this dam monster, over four hundred feet high above bedrock, over three thousand feet long at the crest, like some shining mountain ridge dropped there?

They might understand that the dam could probably prevent disastrous flooding of the old fishing swamps of the Lower Kutenai, now diked farmland; but they could scarcely catch the connection between the mystic machinery in the dam's bowels, and the extravagence of captured firelight sprinkled into a hundred towns. Perhaps they would not be really surprised at this or any other manifestation of the power of their river.

Nobody either Indian or White wants to turn back now into the wilderness. But if as frontiersmen of the Flathead-Kutenai country we could have opened our eyes, minds, doors, hearts, we might have admired the elemental democracy in which these regional natives lived, without individual or tribal desire to dominate anybody. We might have marked that they were not embittered because the weaker ones among them died more easily and left fewer dscendants than the stronger – a merciful evolutionary provision that can only be temporarily frustrated by modern warfare, modern medicine and lots of money. We might have noted how the majority of these Red men lived in pride and dignity before their families and neighbors, because of vitality and the attainment of their simple personal intentions; yet in humility before the mysterious forces of nature. They knew well what it has taken modern science to confirm for the literate – that all forms of life are closely related. What most of us realize now only as we realize a mathematical formula, the Flatheads and Kutenais felt in their bones and blood and spirits, from living rigorously out of doors in close touch with animal, fish, bird, reptile, insect, plant, rock, water, sun, cloud, wind, stars – undistracted by books, pictures, machines, rigid institutions, and arbitrary schedules of spending time.

Understood and respected, Indians like the Flatheads and Kutenais might have helped us to adapt more profitably to accumulating knowledge and possessions. It is not too late; each frontier begets another.

Bibliography

Bibliography

Some sources only briefly quoted or referred to in the text, and not of general interest to the subject, are not included in this bibliography; instead, a full citation has been given in the footnotes.

Special abbreviations used: GUA, Gonzaga University Archives (Spokane, Wash.); MHS, Montana Historical Society (Helena); MSU, Montana State University (Missoula); OHS, Oregon Historical Society (Portland); OHQ, Oregon Historical Quarterly (Portland); PNWQ, Pacific Northwest Quarterly (Tacoma and Seattle, Wash.); WHQ, Washington Historical Quarterly (Tacoma); WSU, Washington State University (Pullman).

BOOKS AND ARTICLES

Baker, Paul E. *The Forgotten Kutenai.* Boise, Ida: Mountain States Press, 1955

Barbeau, Charles Marius. *Indian Days in the Canadian Rockies.* Toronto: Macmillan Co., 1923

Barker, Burt Brown, ed. *Letters of Dr. John McLoughlin 1829-32.* Portland, Ore: Binfords and Mort, 1948

———. *The McLoughlin Empire and its Rulers.* Glendale, Calif: Arthur H. Clark Co., 1959

Boas, Franz. "The Kootenay"; "Physical Types of the Indians of Canada"; and "Salish Tribes of the Interior of British Columbia," in *Annual Archaeological Report, 1905;* Appendix to the Report of the Minister of Education, Ontario, Canada

———, and A. F. Chamberlain. *Kutenai Tales.* Washington, D.C: Bur. of Amer. Ethnol., Bul. 59, Smithsonian Inst., 1918

———, H. K. Haeberlin, James A. Teit and Helen Roberts. "Coiled Basketry in British Columbia," in *Bureau of American Ethnology, 41st Ann. Rept.,* Washington, D.C: Smithsonian Inst., 1928

British Columbia Heritage Series, I. Vol. 8: "The Kootenay." Victoria, B.C: Dept. of Education, 1952

British Columbia Yearbook. Victoria, B.C., 1897

Burlingame, Ralph, and K. Ross Toole. *History of Montana,* 2 vols. New York: Lewis Historical Pub. Co. Inc., 1957

Campbell, John V. "The Sinclair Party – an Emigration Overland along the Old Hudson's Bay Company Route from Manitoba to the Spokane Country," William Lewis, ed. *WHQ,* VII, no. 3, July 1916, p. 187

Canestrelli, Philip. *Kootenai Grammar,* Wilfred E. Schoenberg, S.J., ed. GUA, 1959

Causton, Rose. "The Kootenai Indians," Paul Flinn, ed. *Bonners Ferry Herald,* series in successive weekly issues, 1961

Chamberlain, Alexander F. "Kootenay Indians," in *Annual Archaeological Report, 1905;* Appendix to Report of the Minister of Education, Ontario, Canada

Commissioners of Indian Affairs, Annual Reports. Washington, D.C: Govt. Printing Office

Coues, Elliott. *New Light on the Early History of the Greater Northwest, from the Journals of Alexander Henry and David Thompson,* 4 vols. (paged consecutively throughout). New York: Frances P. Harper, 1897

Cowley, M.E. "A Libby Creek Tragedy," in *Gonzaga,* official publication of Gonzaga University, v, no. 6, March 1914, p. 272

Cox, Ross. Adventures on the Columbia River. New York: J. & J. Harper, 1832

Curtis, Edward S. *The North American Indians,* Frederick Webb Hodge, ed., 20 vols. VII, 1911; IX, 1913. New York, v.d.

Davis, William L., S.J. *History of St. Ignatius Mission.* Spokane, Wash: the author, 1954

De Smet, Pierre-Jean, S.J. *Life, Letters and Travels,* Hiram Martin Chittenden and Alfred Talbot Richardson, eds., 4 vols. (paged consecutively throughout) New York: F. P. Harper, 1905

————. *Letters and Sketches,* 1841-42, Rueben Gold Thwaites, ed., in *Early Western Travels,* vol. XXVII. Cleveland: Arthur H. Clark Co., 1906

————. *Oregon Missions and Travels over the Rocky Mountains,* Thwaites, ed., in *Early Western Travels,* vol. XXIX. Cleveland: Clark, 1906

DeVoto, Bernard. *Across the Wide Missouri.* New York: Houghton Mifflin Co., 1947

Diocese of Helena (Montana) *Register,* souvenir Centenary number. Helena, Aug. 3, 1941

Douglas, David. *Journal, 1823-1827.* London: Wm. Wesley & Son, 1914 (reprint, N.Y: Antiquarian Press, 1959)

Drucker, Philip. *Indians of the Northwest Coast.* New York: McGraw Hill, for Amer. Museum of Natural History, 1955

Drury, Clifford M. *First Women over the Rockies,* 3 vols. Glendale, Calif: Arthur H. Clark Co., 1963, 1966

———. *Henry Harmon Spalding.* Caldwell, Idaho: Caxton Printers, 1936

———. *Diaries and Letters of Henry H. Spalding and Asa B. Smith relating to the Nez Perce Mission.* Glendale, Calif: Arthur H. Clark Co., 1958

Elliott, T.C. "The Discovery of the Source of the Columbia." *OHQ,* XXVI, no. 1, March 1925, p. 23

———. "In the Land of the Kootenai." *OHQ,* XXVII, no. 3, Sept. 19, 1926, p. 279

———. "Journal of Alexander Ross, Snake Country Expedition, 1824." *OHQ,* XIV, no. 4, Dec. 1913, p. 366

———. "Journals of John Work." *WHQ,* V, nos. 2, 3, 4, April, July, Oct., 1914

———. "Peter Skene Ogden, Fur Trader." *OHQ,* XI, no. 3, Sept. 1910, p. 229

———. "The Peter Skene Ogden Journals, 1827-28." *OHQ,* XI, no. 3, Sept. 1910, p. 355; *OHQ,* XI, no. 4, March 1911, p. 382

———. "Religion among the Flatheads." *OHQ,* XXXVIII, no. 1, March 1936, p. 1

Ermatinger, Edward. *York Factory Express Journal.* Ottawa, 1912

Ewers, John C. *The Blackfeet.* Norman: Univ. of Okla. Press, 1958

———. "The Horse in Blackfoot Indian Culture," in *Bureau of American Ethnology, Bull. 159.* Washington, D.C: Smithsonian Inst., 1955

Ferris, W.A. *Life in the Rocky Mountains.* Denver: Old West Pub. Co., 1940

Fort Steele (B.C.) *Prospector,* March 18, 1895. Copy in B.C. Archives, Victoria, Canada

Franchere, Gabriel. *Voyage to the Northwest Coast of America in the Years 1811, 12, 13* (translation). New York: Redfield, 1854

Garraghan, Gilbert J. *The Jesuits of the Middle United States,* 3 vols. New York: American Press, 1938

Garfield, James A. "Diary of a Trip to Montana in 1872," Oliver W. Holmes, ed., in *Frontier Magazine,* xv, no. 2, Winter 1934-35; MSU

Graham, Clara. *Fur and Gold in the Kootenays.* Vancouver, B.C: the author, 1945

Greenbie, Sidney. *Furs to Furrows.* Caldwell, Idaho: Caxton Printers, 1939

Griswold, Gillett, ed. "Archaeological Sites in the Flathead Lake Region, a Symposium," in *Anthropology and Sociology Paper No. 15.* MSU, 1956

Hamilton, William. "A Trading Expedition among the Indians in 1858 from Fort Walla Walla to the Blackfeet Country and Return," in *MHS Contributions.* Helena, 1900

Howard, Helen Addison. *Northwest Trail Blazers.* Caldwell, Idaho: Caxton Printers, 1963

Howay, R.W. "David Thompson's Account of his First Attempt to Cross the Rockies," in *Queens Quarterly* (Kingston, Ont., Canada), Aug. 1933

Hunter, Col. George. *Reminiscences of an Old Timer.* San Francisco, 1887

Irving, Washington. *Astoria.* New York and London: Putnam's Sons, undated

————. *The Rocky Mountains,* from the Journal of Captain Bonneville; Portland: Binfords and Mort, Klickitat Edition, undated

Jenness, Diamond. *Indians of Canada.* Ottawa: Nat. Museum of Canada, 1958

Johnson, Olga, with co-authors. *The Story of the Tobacco Plains Country.* Eureka, Mont: Pioneers of the Tobacco Plains Country, 1950

Kappler, Chas. J., compiler. "Treaty with the Flatheads," in *Indian Affairs, Laws and Treaties,* 2 vols. Wash., D.C: Govt. Pntg. Office, 1904. II, pp. 722-25

Kay, Dave. "Baptiste Morigeau," in *Cranbrook Courier* (B.C.), Sept. 23, 30, 1964

La Farge, Oliver. *A Pictorial History of the American Indian.* New York: Crown Pubs. Inc., 1956

Laubin, Reginald and Gladys. *The Indian Tipi.* Norman: Univ. of Okla. Press, 1957

Laut, Agnes. *The Conquest of the Great Northwest*. New York: Geo. H. Doran Co., 1908

Lavender, David. *Land of Giants*. New York: Doubleday and Co., 1956

Lewis, William S. "Archibald McDonald," in *WHQ,* IX, no. 2, April 1918, p. 93

———. "The Daughter of Angus McDonald," in *WHQ,* XIII, no. 2, Apr. 1922, p. 107

———, with Paul C. Phillips. *Journal of John Work*. Cleveland: Arthur H. Clark Co., 1923

Linderman, Frank B. *Kootenai Why Stories*. New York: Scribners, 1915

Lowie, Robert H. *Indians of the Plains*. New York: McGraw-Hill, 1954

Malouf, Dr. Carling I. "Montana's Original Inhabitants," as Chapter II, vol. I, of Burlingame and Toole, *History of Montana* *(q.v.)*

———. "The Montana Western Region," in *Research Studies,* WSU, XXIV, 1956

———. "Louis Pierre's Affair," in *Historical Essays on Montana,* J. W. Smurr and K. Ross Toole, eds. Helena: Western Press, 1957

———, with Thain White. "A Kutenai Calendar Record," in *Montana, a Magazine of Western History,* II, no. 20, Spring 1952, p. 5

———. "Early Kutenai History," in *Flathead Lake Lookout Museum, Bull. No. 10;* also in *Montana Magazine of History,* II, no. 2, April 1952

———. "Recollections of Lasso-Stasso," in *Western Anthropology Paper, no. 17,* 1954. MSU

McClintock, Walter. *The Old North Trail*. New York: Macmillan Co., 1910

McDonald, Angus, "A Few Items of the Old West," F. W. Howay, William S. Lewis and Jacob A. Meyers, eds; *WHQ* VIII, no. 3, July 1917, p. 188

———. Article about him, including extensive quotations from him; in *Whitefish Pilot* (Montana) (undated material in Sam Johns "Collection," *q.v.* herein under unpublished mss.)

McDonald, Duncan. Series of articles on the Indian side of the Nez Perce War, *New Northwest* (Deerlodge, Mont.) 1878, (discontinued; files at MHS)

McKenney, Thomas L., and James Hall. *The Indian Tribes of North America,* 3 vols. Edinburgh: John Grant, 1933-34

McLaughlin, David. "Son of a Pioneer." McLaughlin extensively quoted in this anonymous news feature, in *Spokesman-Review* (Spokane, Wash.) July 28, 1901

McWhorter, L. V. *Hear Me, My Chiefs!* Caldwell, Idaho: Caxton Printers, 1952

Merk, Frederick, ed. *Fur Trade and Empire* (from the journals of George Simpson) Cambridge: Harvard Univ. Press, 1931

Merriam, Alan and Barbara. "Ethnology of Flathead Indian Music," in *Western Anthropology Papers, no. 2.* MSU, 1955. (Also on file at *MSU* are the Merriams' recordings of songs and dances of the Flatheads)

Moberly, Walter. *Rocks and Rivers of British Columbia.* London: H. Blackelock and Co., 1885

Montana Almanac. Missoula: MSU Press, 1958

Mooney, James. "Tribes of the Columbia Region," in Bureau of Ethnology, *Fourteenth Annual Report, 1892-93, Part 2,* pp. 731 on. Wash., D.C., 1896

Morice, Rev. A.G. "The Denes," in *1905 Archaeological Report;* Minister of Education, Ontario, Canada

Mullan, Lt. John. *Report . . . Military Road from Fort Benton to Fort Walla Walla,* 36 Cong., 2 sess., H.R. Exec. Doc. 44. Wash., D.C., 1861

Meyers, Jacob. "Jacques Raphael Finlay," in *WHQ* x, no. 3, July 1919, p. 163.

Oakshott, Tom. "Koo-Koo-Sint, Red Hair and Jaco," in *Spokesman-Review* (Spokane, Wash.) June 30, 1957

Ogden, Peter Skene. *Snake Country Journal, 1824-25,* E. E. Rich, ed., 2 vols. London: Hudson's Bay Record Soc., 1950

OHS Scrap Book of Newspaper Clippings (indexed)

Palladino, L.C., s.j. *Indian and White in the Northwest.* Lancaster, Pa: Wickersham Pub. Co., 1922

———. "Historical Notes on the Flatheads," in *Indian Sentinel,* (Washington, D.c: Bureau of Catholic Indian Missions) Oct. 1919

Palliser, John. *Journals and Reports.* London, 1859, 1860, 1863 (under varying titles)

Partoll, Albert J. "Fort Connah," in *PNWQ* xxx, no. 1, Jan. 1939, p. 399

Peltier, Jerome. "The Council on the Spokane," in *Spokesman-Review* (Spokane, Wash.) Jan. 15, 1956

———. "Thompson Built Trading Post on Pend d'Oreille," in *Spokesman-Review* (Spokane, Wash.) July 11, 1954

———. "Neglected Spokane House," in *Pacific Northwesterner* (Spokane, Wash.) v, no. 3, Summer 1861

Ray, Verne. *Cultural Relations in the Plateau of Northwestern America.* Los Angeles: Southwest Museum, 1939

———, "The Plateau," *Culture Element Distributions,* xxii. Berkeley: Univ. of Calif. Press, 1942

Robertson, Colin. *Correspondence Book, 1817-1822.* Toronto: Champlain Society, 1939

Ronan, Peter. *Historical Sketch of the Flathead Indian Nation.* Helena: Journal Pub. Co., 1890

Ross, Alexander. *Fur Hunters of the Far West,* 2 vols. London: Smith, Elder, 1855

———. *Adventures of the First Settlers on the Columbia.* Chicago: R. R. Donnelley (Lakeside Press), 1924

Schaeffer, Claud E. "Molded Pottery among the Kutenai Indians," in *Western Anthropology Papers, no. 6.* MSU, 1952

Schoenberg, Wilfred P., s.j. *Jesuit Mission Presses.* Portland: Champoeg Press, 1957

Schultz, James Willard. *Signposts of Adventure.* New York: Houghton Mifflin, 1926

Simpson, Sir George. *Overland Journey Around the World,* 2 vol. London: Henry Colburn, 1847

Smythe, Fred J. *Tales of the Kootenays.* Cranbrook, b.c: Courier Press, 1938

Stevens, Isaac I. "The Flathead Indian Treaty Council of 1855," recorded by James Doty, Albert J. Partoll, ed. *PNWQ* xxix, no. 3, July 1938, p. 283

Stone, Arthur L. *Following Old Trails.* Missoula, Mont: Missoulian Pub. Co., 1913

Stuart, Granville. *Journals and Reminiscences,* Paul C. Phillips, ed., 2 vols. Cleveland: Arthur H. Clark Co., 1925

Teit, James A. *The Salishan Tribes of the Western Plateaus,* Franz Boaz, ed. Wash., d.c: Gov't Pntg. Off., 1930 (also in Bureau of American Ethnology, *45th Annual Report*)

Thiebodo, Augustus J. "Diary of Northwest Exploring Expedition, 1859," in *PNWQ* xxxi

Thompson, David. *Narrative,* J. B. Tyrell and T. C. Elliott, eds. Toronto: Champlain Soc., 1916

Thwaites, Reuben G. *Original Journals of the Lewis and Clark Expedition,* 8 vols. New York: Dodd, Mead and Co., 1904

Turney-High, Harry Holbert. *Ethnography of the Kutenai* (as Memoirs, Amer. Anthropological Assoc., no. 56) Menasha, Wisc: 1941

————. *The Flathead Indians of Montana* (as Memoirs, Amer. Anthropological Assoc., no. 48) Menasha, Wisc: 1937

Underhill, Ruth. *Red Man's America.* Univ. of Chicago Press, 1953

Weisel, George F. *Men and Trade on the Northwest Frontier,* from the Journals of Fort Owen. Missoula: MSU Press, 1955

————. "Ten Animal Myths of the Flathead Indians," in *Anthropology and Sociology Papers, no. 18.* MSU, undated

White, Catherine, ed. *David Thompson's Journals Relating to Montana and Adjacent Regions, 1808-1812.* Missoula: MSU Press, 1950

White, Thain. *Flathead Lake Lookout Museum Bulletins:* "Kutenai Place Names," in *no. 11;* "Kutenai Pipes," in *no. 9*

————, *Western Anthropology Papers, MSU:* "Battle Pits of the 'Koyokees,' " in *no. 10,* 1942; " 'Firsts' among the Kutenai," in *no. 8,* 1952; "Scarred Trees in Western Montana," in *no. 7,* 1954

Wissler, Clark. *Indians of the United States.* New York: Doubleday Co., 1946

————. "The Blackfoot Indians," in *1905 Archeological Report;* Minister of Education, Ontario, Canada

Woodstock Letters. Woodstock, Md: Woodstock College, 1872

UNPUBLISHED LETTERS, MANUSCRIPTS, ETC.

Biggar, Hugh J. "Development of the Lower Flathead Valley." Thesis, MSU, 1950

Campbell, John F. "Letters to C. N. Kessler," 1918, at Clark Library, Los Angeles; copies at MHS. "Letter to T. C. Elliott, Dec. 14, 1913," copy at Lincoln County Free Library, Libby, Mont.

Davis, Bert. "Kutenai-Blackfeet Campaign in Fisher River Country," "Legend of Lame Knee," and "Notes on Indian Trails." Copies at MSU, Dep't of Sociology and Anthropology. As told to Davis by two Flathead Lake Kutenais, William Gringas (Zhangra) and Kaye or *Ki-yi.* Gringas doubtless had some White blood; the name appears very early in the British fur annals. He was educated, served in World War I, was highly regarded by his associates. He died at Dixon in 1947, aged 60. Davis was a forest ranger in charge of the Indian huckleberrying camp on Fisher River for two summers, and here obtained the stories of Lame Knee and the Fisher River Campaign.

Fry, Martin. "Indians in the Kootenai Country," paper in *Women's Club History of Libby,* at Lincoln County Free Library, Libby, Mont.

Granjo, Eneas. Brief notes on the "Ways of the Flatheads," lent by his widow, born Helen Lumprey, later Mrs. John Paul, Missoula. Granjo was a tribal leader before his death in 1957.

Hollensteiner, James. "Letters to Ed Stahl" (James' uncle), including legends heard at Flathead Lake when Hollensteiner was a boy. Copies of legends now at MHS.

Iverson, Bayard O. "History of Wardner, B.C.," 1930. Copy in Provincial Archives, Victoria. Much of the included material on the regional Indians was obtained from Fred S. Ryckman, then Indian Agent stationed at Cranbrook. "Of the Kutenai Indians, perhaps few were more competent to speak on the subject than the late Fred S. Ryckman" (Smythe, *Tales of the Kootenays,* p. 46).

Johns, Sam. "Collection of Regional Historical Material," typed, bound and indexed, at Carnegie Public Library, Kalispell, Mont., through courtesy of Johns' son, S. Douglas Johns. This includes both original and published material. Authors and sources are not always indicated.

McDonald, Angus. "Letters to Judge Deady" (presumably Judge Matthew P. Deady, first Oregon territorial judge, later federal district judge), at OHS.

————. "Poems, Letters and Notes," MHS.

McDonald, Finan. "Original Journal at Fort Spokane, 1822-23." Entries written in part by McDonald's successor, James Birnie. At Spokane Public Library, Wash.

McLaughlin, David. "The Upper and Lower Kutenai," GUA.

McLeod, John. "Journal and Correspondence." Originals in Dominion Archives, Ottawa; paging where given is from bound typed copies at OHS; B.C. Archives, Victoria, also has copies.

U.S. Dept. of the Interior. "Federated Salish and Kootenai Tribes," Allotment Rolls.

INFORMANTS

A few were contacted by correspondence only, others in person.
Some are deceased since interviewed in the years around 1960.

ABRAHAM, ENEAS, chief of Bonners Ferry Kutenai in 1860. ANDER-
SON, W.A., Indian Agent, Cranbrook, B.C., in 1961. ASHLEY,
JOSEPHINE (Mrs. Antoine), St. Ignatius, Mont., wife of a grandson
of Francois Ermatinger. AWMACK, J.W., Cranbrook, B.C., Historical Association of East Kootenay. BURGESS, LORENA (Mrs.
Harry), Perma, Mont., Flathead-and-White; former member tribal
council. CAMPBELL, MAX, Libby, Mont., pioneer and Indian student. CORBEILL, HAZEL (Mrs. Vance), Kellog, Idaho, pioneer
parentage. DENNIS, JOE, Grassmere, B.C., oldest living Tobacco
Plains Kutenai at time of interview. ENEAS, JIM, Grassmere, B.C.,
among the oldest living of the Windermere Kutenais when interviewed. FLINN, PAUL, Bonners Ferry, Idaho, student of local history. FRANCIS, SIMON ("White Otter"), Bonners Ferry, educated
Kutenai tribal leader, and one of the most valued informants for Rose
Causton's history of the Bonners Ferry Kutenais. FRY, ALLEN E.,
Indian Agent, Cranbrook, B.C., 1960. GRAVELLE, AMBROSE, Grass-
mere, B.C., mixed Kutenai and White blood; wife a Tobacco Plains
Kutenai, sister of Joe Dennis (above). HEIDELMAN, ELIZABETH,
widow of a government doctor at Jocko Agency around 1900. IN-
CAS-HO-LA, PLAS (Polassie or Frank), St. Ignatius, Mont., Flat-
head Indian. JOSEPH, MR. AND MRS. C., St. Mary's Reserve,
Cranbrook, B.C., Kutenais. LESLIE, MRS. WILLIAM A., Bonners
Ferry, Idaho, pioneer settler. MARENGO, MRS. EMERENCE, Arlee,
Mont., daughter of Pial Finley. MALOUF, DR. CARLING I., De-
partment of Sociology and Anthropology, University of Montana,
Missoula. MATHIAS, MOSE, Elmo, Mont., Reservation Kutenai.
MATHIAS, BAPTISTE, father of last; Baptiste supplied much informa-
tion contained in some of the cited references by Dr. Malouf and
Thain White; he was a nephew of Chief Baptiste (see here page
297). MATT, BILL, Camas Hot Springs, Mont., mixed Indian and
White blood. MCELDERRY, MARY, St. Ignatius, Mont., born Fells-
man; great-granddaughter of Francois Finley. MICHEL, MOSE,
Windermere, B.C., Kutenai. MISHEL, ANDREW, St. Mary's Reserve,

Cranbrook, B.C., Kutenai. MORIAS, FRANCES (Mrs. Orville), Dixon, Mont., born Frances Newman; great-granddaughter of Francis Ermatinger. ODLE, HAROLD, last known at Wickenburg, Ariz., for many years had museum on west shore Flathead Lake. PEESO, FRED E., Libby, Mont., life-long Indian student; for many years had trading post at Camas Hot Springs, Mont. PIERRE, LOUIS, Camas Hot Springs, Mont., of Coeur d'Alene and Spokan blood; wife a descendant of Jocko Finlay. PIERRE, PETE, Arlee, Mont., mixed Indian and White blood; also MRS. PETE PIERRE. PRITCHARD, R., Invermere, B.C., Welshman who believes there are traces of Welsh in the Kutenai language. RAYMOND, AGNES (Mrs. James), Ronan, Mont., great-granddaughter of Francois Morigeau. ROGERSON, SARAH, Porthill, Idaho, daughter of David McLoughlin. ROULLIER, MRS. LUCILLE, Ronan, Mont., born Trosper; her daughter by blood of Lucille and her deceased husband, is a descendant of McLeods, Berlands, Morigeaus, Finleys. TRAAEN, MRS. ARNOLD, Edmonds, Wash., descendant of Jocko Finlay. VANDERBERG, JEROME, Arlee, Mont., Flathead. VINSON, SAM, Arlee, Mont., Flathead-and-White pioneer.

Index

Index

Note that items listed under the following group headings are not elsewhere indexed: Animals, native (buffalo indexed separately); Chiefs (admittedly a fragmentary list); Fur trading posts; Indian tribes (see this heading for tribes indexed separately); Missions (St. Ignatius indexed separately); Reservation agents.

Abbreviations used for names of fur companies: HBC, Hudson's Bay Company; NWC, North West Company.

Geographical features are located in Montana unless otherwise indicated.